Deadly Diet

Deadly Diet

Revised Edition of *Two Too Thin*

Camie Ford ❧ Sunny Hale

PARACLETE PRESS
Orleans, Massachusetts

1st Printing, April, 1995

Published by Paraclete Press
Orleans, Massachusetts

Cover Design: Tim Ladwig and Jim Hellman

ISBN 1-55725-137-1
Printed in the United States of America

This book is dedicated to
Cay Andersen and Judy Sorensen,
who have pointed the way to healing, and
to our husbands, who kept on loving us
through thick–and thin.

Table of Contents

Editor's Note

It may seem a bit strange to have the stories of two such totally different individuals as Camie Ford and Sunny Hale in the same book. On the surface, they could hardly be less alike–Camie, the glamorous socialite, whose life was unfolding like the happily-ever-after novels she loved to read; and Sunny, who by sheer grit overcame her rural background by setting seemingly impossible goals of academic excellence.

Yet for all their apparent dissimilarities, in one area they were startlingly alike: to compensate for vague, gnawing feelings of inferiority, they began to lose weight–and lose and lose. Camie, at 5'8", got down to 110 pounds; Sunny, 5'4", reached 88 pounds–years before this disorder became a nationwide epidemic. Today, according to the National Association of Anorexia Nervosa, more than a million Americans suffer from it, and 5% of the serious cases actually die of it. Yet because it is still relatively unknown, we have asked Jane Healy, an educational psychologist, for a professional assessment.

As you read, you will note Camie's and Sunny's symptoms beginning to overlap, and when their very lives begin to converge, you will see why we chose to present them in alternating chapters. For these are two classic cases, with distorted physical perception, suppressed feelings of hopeless inadequacy, a desire to control everything that impinges on one's world, and monumental self-deception–symptoms that are becoming frighteningly familiar to many apparently well-balanced American families.

For this reason, we urged the authors to tell it *exactly* as it was, and they have, although at times it was extremely painful for them to do so. But if their honesty jolts just one anorexic into reality, then it was worth it.

David Manuel

Foreword

The increasing incidence of anorexia nervosa is an alarming artifact of the socialization of young females in our culture. Medical science has yet to confirm effective treatment methods for this often irreversible disorder, in which avoidance of food and pursuit of thinness become obsessive quests. The anorexic's need to "measure up" reflects a product-oriented emphasis which appears, in many cases, to be both societal and familial. Thus, victims find themselves trapped–tragic products of their own obsessive needs.

This book, however, describes a process. It details an emotional and spiritual progression in two intriguingly candid first-person stories. Camie and Sunny, from dramatically different backgrounds, share striking commonalities in the anorexic life patterns characteristic of the disease. Their ingenuous accounts of adolescence and early years of marriage provide a view of the challenges of being female, as well as of the dynamics of anorexia. Most provocative, moreover, is their parallel progression in the faith through which they have been able to relinquish their compulsions by bending to a higher power.

The effects on husbands and children, first of the demands of living with an anorexic personality and then of the surrender to faith, are honestly and revealingly told.

Even though the hard-won answers detailed here may not be practicable in all cases, these stories suggest a new viewpoint in treatment of this disorder. The process through which pathology, despair, and anguish yield to peace and productive joy should be enlightening both for professionals and for other "fair ladies" enmeshed in the trap of anorexia.

Jane M. Healy, Ph.D.
Educational Psychologist
Vail, Colorado

1

My Fair Lady

The house lights dimmed, and the orchestra struck up the familiar strains from *My Fair Lady*. My heart was pounding, as I worked on my hair one last time. I took a deep breath to calm down, but it didn't help. Earlier I'd peeked out beyond the velvet curtains at row upon row of expectant faces, some known, others strangers, but all eagerly turned to watch the runway, as our annual Junior League Fashion Show was about to get under way.

Out front, the mood was hushed anticipation, but backstage it was frantic, as models, dressers, make-up people, hair stylists and fashion consultants flew back and forth between the dressing rooms. Months and months of planning, staging and rehearsing were, at last, about to come to fruition. The fashion show that every well-dressed woman in the city looked forward to as the herald of the fall season, was about to begin.

I was one of those models, putting the final touches on my hair and make-up. I had to look my very best before those hundreds of women waiting to see what the fashion designers were going to say this year. The outfit which I had on for my first turn had to have just the right shoes, hat, purse, gloves and jewelry to show it off to best advantage. Those details were well taken care of by others; what I had to do was walk gracefully and slowly down the long runway, while turning and opening a coat to reveal the dress beneath. After much training and practice, I was able to perform my turns with ease, yet I still did not dare look down from the elevated runway to the tables of spectators below. What had not come easily was the super-thin figure I had to maintain, in order to wear those fabulous designer clothes.

"Ten minutes till you're on, Camie."

"Okay, I'm ready."

Even though it was late afternoon on this crisp September day in 1968, I had yet to drink or eat anything but black coffee and some M & M's, my favorite candy. How else could I maintain 110 pounds? My height at 5'8" was perfect for stage or newspaper modeling, but my weight could go up three pounds with just one big dinner or a weekend of eating out. At this point in my life, I was determined to be a success at modeling, no matter what.

Up until now, I had been a nothing person. I had never achieved any form of acclaim in school or out, except in popularity with boys. I desperately wanted to be approved of, and now, at last, I had found my niche. I had countless opportunities to be photographed, admired, and fussed over, and I loved every minute of it—especially when salesladies made much over my size 6 figure, pictured in *Life* and *Town & Country,* and in color in the Sunday fashion section of the *Cleveland Plain Dealer.* Life was just starting; I was in my early twenties, with years ahead to enjoy the glamorous world of fashion. Of course, my budding modeling career was playing hob with my home life, but what did I care if I was never home? My husband was never home either. Dan was always so interested in his company, his work–not in me. And at that time, I was too tired to care much about our two daughters and our son. Besides, I had both a live-in housekeeper and a maid to look after the house. Tonight was worth everything to me, because tonight I was the star.

Preparations for this event had started early in the year. As the ladies of Shaker Heights were putting away their Christmas decorations, plans were already under way for the sixth annual Junior League Fashion Show to be held over three days in September at one of Cleveland's downtown hotels. Buyers from Halle's Department Store, sponsors for the show, would soon be out searching for new gowns and accessories.

What would the theme be for this year? How about "My Fair Cleveland?"

"Great!" said Pat, the Fashion Director. "Let's see if we can possibly borrow some of the authentic costumes from the movie, *My Fair Lady,* and duplicate some of the scenes!" The idea quickly took hold, and after many phone calls and letters back and forth to the West Coast, arrangements were made. Twenty-four of the costumes and hats designed by Cecil Beaton would be shipped to Cleveland a few days before the show. Nothing like this had ever been done before; the shows would be a sell-out!

As the last lazy days of summer drew to a close, my life picked up its fast pace again with rehearsals for the show, fittings and practice sessions. This year, the thirty-four models had a special problem to contend with: how to balance Cecil Beaton's hats which had brims as big as parasols. A few days before the show, massive wardrobe trunks arrived from Hollywood. Would the dresses really be the same as those in the movie? And who among us would be able to fit into Audrey Hepburn's clothes? I had thought about this off and on over the weeks, and hoped I might be one of the lucky girls. All the costumes were stunning, but Audrey Hepburn was the star, and hers were the most spectacular of all–even the torn and tattered ones she had worn in the opening scene in Covent Garden.

As these magnificent dresses were carefully unpacked and emerged from the trunks one by one, "oh's" and "ah's" could be heard throughout the room. Holding my breath, I slowly stepped into the most spectacular of all–the black and white dress from the Ascot Scene, and asked a friend to zip it up. As she did so, I felt the lace and velvet ribbons on the dress and wondered if it would go over my hips. . . . Oh, please let it fit, please, let me be able to wear it, I thought. It did! In this regal gown with its train out behind me, I felt like a queen, or at least a duchess about to be presented at court.

Every minute of starvation was worth it, to have the feelings of elation and triumph I experienced now! I put on the beribboned and feathered hat that completed the costume, and then turned to the show's producers for their approval. They nodded enthusiastically; the costume was mine! I had made it!

As it turned out, only two of us were able to fit into Audrey Hepburn's clothes. I scarcely noticed the envious stares of the other girls; nothing could stop me now! And I was going to enjoy every minute of my success. I had proved to myself and more important, to my husband, that I, too, could be the best, the top; that I, too, could achieve what I had set out to do. He was not the only shining star in the family.

I went home that evening, resolving not to eat one

bite of food that would cause me to risk not being able to wear that dress. I did nibble, as I prepared dinner for my family, but sat down to the table with my usual cup of black coffee and a cigarette.

"How did the rehearsal go today?" Dan asked. But I knew he was just making conversation; he wasn't really interested. I didn't want to talk to him, either; I just wanted to go to bed and sleep.

"Oh, fine," I finally answered. "Guess what? I'm going to wear one of Audrey Hepburn's dresses–the black and white one from the Ascot scene."

"Is that good, Mommy? Is that why you're not eating again? Are you excited?" asked Liza, our older daughter.

"Yes, I'm excited, but let's finish up these dishes and get your bath, so Mommy can put you to bed. I'm really tired out tonight, and I'm going to bed, too." I never looked at Dan, but I knew he had already opened *The Wall Street Journal,* and would be lost in the newspaper for an hour. That night, as I turned out the light, I calculated that I had eaten approximately 400 calories for the day, so I could look forward to another half-pound loss tomorrow. Great!

The remaining days before the show flew by, and then the magical night arrived. I could think of nothing else but that dress. And now, standing in the wings, I held my breath, as I listened to the hum of the crowd out front. Then silence fell, as the orchestra started to play, and one by one the models began their parade down the runway. The informal clothes would be shown first, to be followed by the more spectacular evening clothes.

"You're on, Camie." This is it, I thought, as I went out in the first of my dress and coat outfits–I took my turns and swirled open the coat–only three more outfits to wear before the Ascot number. The evening went on.

You could feel the tempo of the show quicken, as the evening clothes began to appear. Movie clips of *My Fair Lady* were shown to set the mood. The orchestra played the Ascot Gavotte, "Every duke on earth I'm sure is here; everyone who should be here is here."

"Now, Camie!" Slowly I walked out to the center of the stage, then moved carefully down the steps to the runway. The audience caught its breath and then burst into applause, as I smiled and turned first to the right and then the left, walking carefully in the very slim skirt. I floated back into the wings, two inches off the runway. Oh, I wanted that moment to last forever!

The show was a smashing success; everyone was thrilled with the new clothes, as well as with the costumes. The cocktail party afterwards was a victory celebration. All my friends were there, and every one of them told me how good I looked. I glanced over at Dan; he was talking business, of course, with his friends. We could as easily have been at the country club, for all the difference it made to him.

When we got back into the car to drive home, he said, "Well, you looked really nice." I waited, but that was the sum total of his comment. What did I expect, I thought later, as I lay in bed, waiting for sleep to come. I wondered if it all was really worth it. Yes, *it was!* I decided. It was. I had proved something!

Then why didn't I feel happier in my heart?

2

Mirror, Mirror

"Turn this way please." The fitter, on her knees with a pin cushion tied to the back of her wrist, reached up and took me by the waist. "Now, hold still just another minute. Let's take just a bit more out of the waist," and she expertly gathered and pinned the material. "There! That does it!" She got up from where she was kneeling on the thick cream carpet beneath the glittering chandelier, made some final adjustments to my gown, and then, gathering up pins and tape and chalk, quietly was gone.

"How fortunate that the dress fits your sister so well," Miss Phillips observed, pausing at the door. Tall, svelte, and impeccably dressed in black, the Hemphill Wells bridal consultant had been very gracious.

My sister Barbara nodded. "You'd never know that Sunny is taller than I; the dress looks as if it was made for her. We're so pleased that you could alter it for us."

Miss Phillips smiled. "We are always happy to alter any of our wedding gowns, and of course there will be no charge."

She, too, disappeared, and Barbara and I were alone in the quiet elegance of the salon.

"How do I look?" I beamed, concentrating on my reflection in the mirror, as I twirled round and round, the yards of white satin billowing out in all directions. Reluctantly I stopped and turned to my sister. "Thanks, Barb, so much for letting me wear this dress. I love it, and it helps with the wedding budget no end. My savings from my summer job will just about cover the flowers and the reception, and I couldn't ask the folks to pay for a dress, not after all they sacrificed to send me to school this last year." I twirled again, catching multiple reflections in the mirrors. "And can you believe they don't charge a cent for the alterations?"

"That's what happens when you shop at the best stores, dear; this is practically the Lord & Taylor's of West Texas." A frown crossed her pretty brow. "I can't believe it's been three whole years since I wore it—I wish I'd had a waistline like yours when I was a bride." With a sigh, she gathered up her purse and packages. "I'll get the car, while you change, and we'll have a nice lunch."

Lingering a moment, I turned for one last look in the floor-to-ceiling mirrors that encircled the room. And now, I tried to be as objectively critical as I could of the image looking back at me—front, side, and back. It was true: the dress was caught in snugly at the waist, and the tiny seed pearls accentuated the low neckline and close-fitting bodice. I did look thin, and as Barbara had admitted, I was thinner than she, and not only now, but when she had gotten married. That made the day perfect in every way! I was going to have the beautiful church wedding that I had always wanted, and in just a few weeks I would be walking down the aisle to begin the fairy tale life that I had planned for and looked forward to for so long. And best of all, I had kept the promise that I had made to myself. In my mind's eye, I could see the brides in the magazine ads–always slender. That was the kind of bride I was going to be, very slender, and for the first time in my life I had surpassed my sister.

"Lunch is my treat," Barbara said, glancing in my direction as she maneuvered the car into the downtown Lubbock traffic. "It's not every day that I take my little sister to have her wedding dress fitted. Where would you like to go?"

The choice was easy: "I love Luby's Cafeteria."

And today, walking past that display of culinary delight, it was easy to pass by the chicken-fried steak with cream gravy, the hot homemade rolls, the shimmering Jell-O salads, and the mouthwatering pies piled high with whipped cream. "I think I'll just have turnip greens, and um, maybe this cucumber salad. I love the vinegar dressing." After all, who needed food? Not when I could still savor the taste of triumph.

As we slid into the red upholstered booth, I caught a glimpse of our reflections in the mirror. "Do you think anyone would know we are sisters?" I wondered aloud. Barbara, barely five feet tall and petite, was the redhead in the family, and my father loved to tease her about the spray of freckles across her nose. "I think you take after the Davis side of the family," I told her. "You have Mother's little feet and tiny build, and I'm more like Daddy's sisters. I wear a size seven shoe!" Well, at least we were both thin!

For the first time Barbara noticed my sparse tray. "Is that all you're going to have for lunch? How can you shop all over town for a trousseau on a meal like that?"

"Oh, I'm much too excited to eat," I assured her. "I usually eat much more," I added with my fingers crossed.

"Sunny," she said frowning, "are you sure you're not overdoing this diet bit?"

I shook my head. "Oh, no, I never give it a thought," I lied. "It has sort of just happened."

I was glad that she had not seen me early that same morning, when I crept out of bed to go through my morning ritual, before the house began to stir. Even on such a special day, I kept to the familiar routine. Before putting on one stitch of clothing or having one bite to eat or one drop of coffee, I always stepped on the bathroom scale and held my breath until the needle stopped flickering at the lowest point. I would get off and get on again, and note the reading, and then repeat the procedure a third time, taking the lowest reading and carefully recording it in a small notebook, which was already filled with weights from the past two years.

Today I had weighed 94 pounds–my all-time low! Surely at 5'4" that would be a safe weight–a wide enough margin to relax and enjoy the day and forget about pounds and calories for a little while. For the truth was, little else had been on my mind during the past months. Getting thin and staying thin had become the most important thing in the world to me–more important than people, than relationships, more important even than the approaching wedding.

But right now I didn't want to think about that. Right now I just wanted to enjoy the lunch and visit with my sister, whom I really didn't see all that often, now that she was married. Soon she would be returning to Peru with her husband, to a satellite-tracking station high in the Andes, and we had a lot of catching-up to do. And the sooner we started, the sooner I could get off the subject of my weight. "Listen, Barb, do you remember . . ."

3

Your Daughter is a Pig

I lay on my back that night staring at the dark ceiling. Dan was softly snoring, as usual; he never had trouble sleeping. Instead of kicking him, I punched my pillow and sighed. I went back over the past evening, savoring each compliment, reviewing all the praises I had received. But that did not help to take away the hollow, empty taste in my mouth.

Was this all there was to enjoy after all the years of dieting? What about the rest of my life? Why didn't I feel more fulfilled? Inside, I felt brittle, hard and stretched taut to the breaking point, counting the minutes until I could relax. I had a very busy social schedule throughout the year, so I always had to have a bright smile on my face, even though my stomach was often in knots from hunger or nervousness. I was constantly trying to be like my mother, a social success. She was so competent, organized and involved in everything! I was exhausted from trying to keep up with her. I felt compelled to spend all my time making a name and a place for myself through "good works." Along with modeling, I was chairman of a day nursery board, program chairman of the Garden

Club, a volunteer worker at Babies and Children's Hospital, of which I was also on the Board of Trustees, a member of the Junior League of Cleveland and on the Vestry of our Episcopal church, as well as being actively involved in a number of other organizations. The more I did, the more impressed I hoped my family and friends would be. It seemed like everyone knew our parents and Dan, but who was Camie? What did she have to offer?

I tossed and turned, fluffing up my pillow, more wide awake than ever. I tried to recall my earliest childhood memories and found that they were often of food. With two large, active brothers in the house, our refrigerator was always full of all sorts of tempting goodies. My parents had a housekeeper who loved to cook special meals, snacks and desserts for all of us except Mother, who was forever on a diet.

They say that a tendency towards alcoholism may be hereditary. Well, that may be true of "Thinoholism" too, for my mother, who was a tall woman, was constantly battling to keep her weight down. I doubt that anyone ever thought of her as heavy—I certainly didn't—but she was always going to Weight Watchers, eating fish and salads and never desserts, not even on Sundays. But not I, back then. I loved to come home from school and eat a large piece of gooey, chocolate cake or a still-warm piece of apple pie. Then I felt good and happy; I was home, safe and sound in our cheery kitchen.

Dinner at our house was a ritual, the only family-time we had. In the elegant Georgian dining room, my father would sit at one end of the polished mahogany table, with Mother at the other end. I sat next to my father on his right side, Bill sat next to me, and David sat alone on the other side because he was left-handed. We ate together as a family with candlelight and flowers just about every Monday night through Thursday. On Fridays and Saturdays, my parents either went out or had guests in to dinner, and Sunday was informal. The evening meal was our one chance to talk with our parents about our day. My father arrived home each night at exactly the same time, 6:04 P.M., unless the Rapid Transit train from downtown was late, which it almost never was. He and Mother would sit together in our library, having a cocktail before dinner. We could be in the library too, but it was made clear that this was their time to talk.

At 6:45, the housekeeper would announce that dinner was ready, and we would take our places at the table, and the free-for-all conversation would begin. David, Bill and I would see who could tell the funniest story, report the highest grades, or receive the least correction. David always lost there; he was forever being spoken to about his elbows on the table or the way he forgot to shift his knife and fork, when he was cutting his meat. As for the story-telling and general conversation, it often moved so quickly it was like a fast game of doubles, with everyone rushing to the net for the volley, so that I felt hopelessly behind and left out.

My two brothers were successful athletes and students. David was on the swimming team at Deerfield and wrote for their literary magazine. Bill, my younger brother, graduated from his country day school as the top all-around student in the school, and proceeded to get good grades at Exeter. Both brothers were tall, well-built, handsome, and both graduated from Yale and went on to become officers in the Navy.

My parents were pleased and proud of their achievements, but there was nothing in my scholastic record to rejoice over; I was certainly never voted best of anything. My brothers were ahead of me, just because they went to

Yale, where almost every male member of Dan's and my families had gone for generations. Worst of all, they both had a quick sense of humor that left me several jokes behind, especially at the dinner table. And, because my parents were also quick, and my father put a premium on a well-told story, I felt like I could never catch up. And so, after a while, I gave up trying. But only at the table. . . .

All my childhood, and later teen years, I had thrived on competition with David and Bill. We were forever competing for our parents' approval, each of us struggling to be noticed and recognized. David was the first-born as well as the first son, and Bill was the darling baby with blond curls and a sweet disposition. So, I decided at an early age that the only way I could win this game was to be the most obedient–the perfect daughter. Unfortunately, I was frequently a disappointment–until it came to social occasions. Then I would shine. Over and over, my parents had encouraged us, when they introduced us to their friends, to give a firm handshake and look them in the eye. The boys were sloppy about it, but not I! I was a model of social decorum.

When the evening meal was finally over, we children retired to our rooms to do our homework–while my parents sat in the library and read books, magazines or the newspaper. We seldom spoke to them again except to say good-night. Mother usually came upstairs to give me a good-night kiss. As long as she came into my room and kissed me, I knew she loved me, especially on the nights when she went out.

I loved to snack. Every afternoon, while waiting to take the Rapid Transit home from school, I bought a cherry Tootsie Pop at the candy and magazine store at the Rapid stop. When I got home, I would head straight for the kitchen, and if there was no cake or pie, I would fix myself a thick peanut butter and jelly sandwich and have it along with a glass of milk. Then I would sit on the couch in the library with Patty, our springer spaniel, while I read a novel or the *Saturday Evening Post.* Better still, was to lie down on my bed, while I comforted myself with food. And as I had to work hard for average grades and didn't have a large circle of friends at school, I looked forward to getting home to my friendly house and something good to eat.

My family had always lived in Shaker Heights, which per capita was possibly the wealthiest suburb in the country.

My father had worked hard to make a success of his own company, which was an offshoot of one started by his father. My mother was a prominent New York debutante from the North Shore of Long Island. She fell in love with my father aboard the *Columbus* in 1933, when each was bound for a Mediterranean cruise, married him when she was 21, and then moved to Cleveland. After World War II ended, and my father returned from the Navy, we moved into the house I loved the most. It was very large, but comfortable, with six bedrooms and five bathrooms. Designed by John Sheldon Kelly, the house was made of stone and set well back from the street with many shade trees all around. There was a flagstone terrace the length of the back of the house, while the driveway was flanked by flower beds blooming in every color of the rainbow.

The living room and dining room were spacious, with French doors leading out to a sunporch with floor-to-ceiling windows overlooking an emerald green lawn. Mother loved flowers and filled every room with arrangements from her garden. Her rose garden was her pride and delight. I had a walk-in playhouse all my own, tucked away in a quiet corner of the backyard. It was painted white and had dark green shutters and window boxes filled with flowers. In our home, we each had our own room filled with our treasures. That room was our kingdom, and no one could enter without permission, as we would periodically remind one another with notes affixed to our doors. Mother let me choose my own wallpaper and carpeting, so that the room was truly my own sanctuary–my haven from the outside world.

I will never forget how frightened and homesick I was when I left home for the first time to go to summer camp at the age of 10. What a wonderful opportunity to meet all kinds of young people, my parents thought, to learn how to sail, canoe, play tennis, archery, swim and climb mountains. But in my own mind, going away to camp was like going off to prison.

Sports did not interest me in the least, and unlike my brothers, who loved camp, I was not good at making friends. My attitude never changed, and by the time I was fourteen, I was relieved to have finally outgrown camp.

In the meantime, food was the anesthetic, and I began eating as soon as the camp train pulled out of Cleveland terminal. Never happy, I went to three different camps in Michigan, Maine and Vermont in four summers, each of which featured strenuous activities from morning until bedtime. After "lights out" and the last trip to the outdoor bathroom, with my flashlight clutched tightly in my hand I would scurry under my covers, pull out my reading book, and nibble on whatever I had been able to tuck away from evening snack time.

My nonstop snacking became a real problem at the second camp. I was grateful for the uniform they required to be worn for supper and Sunday lunch. It consisted of shorts covered by a middy blouse top with a tie. The roomy blouse was worn over the shorts–a fact which saved me much embarrassment. For by the sixth or seventh week, I was having a hard time buttoning up my shorts, and by the eighth week it was simply impossible! That middy blouse saved the day!

The following summer at the same camp, was the worst. My counselor, I decided, did not like me. With my attitude about camp still rotten and expressing itself at every opportunity, I can well imagine why she might not have appreciated having my company in the cabin. The counselors wrote weekly reports on our behavior. As the weeks progressed and my shorts got tighter, she wrote to my parents that their daughter was a pig. Never had I been so humiliated, as when my parents had a few things to say to me after getting that progress report. To make matters worse, when I got home that summer, I was told by an older girl at the country club that I should no longer wear short shorts. I should wear Bermuda shorts to hide my thighs. I was shattered!

Each day at camp a mid-morning snack was served–the most favorite of which for me was doughnuts. Whenever the tray of doughnuts appeared, I would devour mine, then run ahead to meet the latecomers and ask each one if she wanted her doughnut. If I was really in luck, three or four campers might pass up their snack and give it to me. Then, I would find a nice, smooth rock warmed by the morning sun, and I would happily munch away on my special treat. Meals at all three camps were hearty, with plenty of biscuits, homemade breads and pies, warm cookies from the oven and always candy and gum from the camp store.

There was one peril–the possibility that I might get put at the diet table, if I gained too much. Only the real fatties sat there, and they ate only meat and vegetables. They didn't have any fun, and who wanted to sit with those poor creatures, where everyone noticed you and watched you eat?

Whenever a bike hike or walking trip was posted on the bulletin board, I immediately signed up. Not for the exercise–oh no! I wanted the ice cream treat at the end of the bike trip, and I loved the delicious snacks packed for the hikers. I would climb the highest mountains to get the Hershey bars, graham crackers and marshmallows awaiting me at the top.

All summer long, I missed being at home with only my parents and sleeping in my pretty bedroom. I hated sleeping in tents on small camp cots. When it rained, it seemed that we always got wet, and it was so cold every morning when we got up, especially in August. My idea of a good time was to lie on my cot and read my latest book in peace and quiet. I used to hope that I would get sick, so I could go to the infirmary and sleep inside a warm, heated building with indoor bathrooms. In fact, the only time I was ever really happy at camp was at mealtime.

But there was one time in my camp career that I was a success! Camp number three was divided up into several units with two leaders heading up each unit, who had been elected by the campers. The two leaders had to inspect the tents in their unit for neatness. A record was kept, points given, and a prize awarded to the neatest unit at the end of eight weeks. That summer I was *elected,* not appointed, co-unit leader! I was so proud, I couldn't wait to write my parents and tell them. Margo, the other girl who worked with me, became a dear friend; we went to boarding school together and to Europe after that, and she was a bridesmaid in my wedding. And all these years later, we still keep in touch.

The happiest day of camp was the day our suitcases and trunks got packed for the return trip home. Everyone else was crying because it was time to leave, and I was crying, too, because I was so glad to be going home!

Yet, despite all this, I never really thought much about my weight during those grade school and junior high years. I was tall, taller than most of the girls my age. At school, when we lined up according to height, I was always near the tall end of the line in my class. Whenever we had tumbling for gym and made a pyramid, I was always a base who held others on my back or knees. I dreaded those gym classes with apparatus equipment, because I could never climb the ropes, jump over the vaulting horse, or swing from the rings. I could not do a cartwheel, a headstand or a backwards somersault. I was mortified and embarrassed, and afraid I would fail gym class. By the eighth grade at age thirteen, I was almost 5'8" tall and weighed about 138 pounds.

I was bothered by my size when it came to dancing school, because the eighth grade boys, for the most part, came up to my chin. Happily the boys didn't care, and having been graced with good looks, I never lacked dancing partners. But that wasn't enough; I worked hard at being charming, talking as fast as I could about whatever I imagined might interest my partner. And no matter what the boys said, they had my fascinated attention for the duration of the dance. The girls all sat in a row on one side of the ballroom and waited for the white-gloved, navy blue-suited boys to come across the dance floor to choose them for the next dance. I always held my breath and smiled brightly, until I was chosen.

As a rule, I looked forward to dancing school, but one week almost finished me off. I usually washed my hair the night before dancing class, but this particular week I forgot. So when I got home from school, I quickly had a shampoo, but what to do about the curls? I grabbed some wave set lotion, squirted it all over my hair, and then rolled it up in curlers. It was not until I tried to comb out the stiffness, that I realized I had used spray cologne! I was in tears. I couldn't stand the smell myself—what would the others say? I hoped no one would notice the suffocatingly sweet odor, but when I got into the car that came for me, my best friend said, "Phew! What on earth happened to you?" That did it; I was so mortified I tried to hide in the ladies' room for the next hour.

I began to notice boys when I was twelve, in seventh grade. That was the year we began to go to parties, and dancing school became more interesting. By the time I was thirteen I had several boyfriends who would call me on the telephone every evening. I loved to talk on the phone and could talk for hours at a time, if Mother wasn't home. She usually had a fit and would make me hang up after five minutes. I had a small, close circle of girlfriends. We talked and giggled together a lot in school, while we compared notes about boys. There were four private schools in Cleveland in those days, Hathaway Brown and Laurel School for girls, University School and Hawken for boys. I went to HBS, as it was commonly called, and my brothers went to Hawken. Every afternoon, after I fixed my snack, I would call at least two or three of my girlfriends.

"Wait a minute, Susan, till I change ears," I said as I switched the phone around while trying to hold on to my pb & j sandwich. We talked so long that both ears got sore. Mother hated my tying up the phone so long. Every time she got angry, I'd ask her for my own phone.

"All my friends have their own phone; can't I have one, too?" I begged. "Please, Mom! It's the one thing I want more than anything else! I promise I'll be good, if you'll just let me have my own phone!"

"No, you can just hang up and stay off that phone!"

Stay off the phone? Impossible! I had to discuss my homework! First we did homework, and then we discussed boys and our plans for the weekend. We wanted to be sure to get to every football game, swimming meet, track meet and baseball game. We often went to slumber parties or spent the night over at a friend's house. And the main topic of conversation was invariably boys. Oh, it was such fun comparing notes! A steady boyfriend never lasted longer than a few months; we switched them around like trading cards in a cigar box.

There was one thing that I was good at, and that was keeping my room neat as a pin. My clothes were always picked up–nothing was ever left on the floor, behind the bed, or stuffed in the closet. I loved to get all dressed up to greet my parents' dinner guests and take their coats. Happily, my brothers were not interested; they stayed upstairs in their rooms, while everyone always made a fuss over me. The ladies looked so glamorous and smelled good, too, and after greeting them, I would go out to the kitchen to sample the tempting canapes and delicious desserts.

Having lots of people over for formal dinners was part of my dream of growing up and getting married. I loved to see my mother all dressed up in her evening dress, and I thought my father was the most handsome man alive. The house was filled with happy chatter and lots of laughter, whenever my parents entertained, and conversely, it was gloomy and depressing when they went out. On those nights, I liked to sit at the breakfast room table and have a cup of coffee with our housekeeper. She would pour a little coffee into my cup and then fill it with milk and lots of sugar. But the night seemed so long, as I lay in bed and tried to stay awake, until Mother came home to give me my good-night kiss.

My unceasing yearning for approval, first from my parents and then from my peers, had a lasting effect on my life. I did exactly as I was told, because I knew that obedience would bring the love and praise I so desperately craved. Outwardly, one might have thought I was the model child, but inwardly my rebellion was simply pushed down out of sight. To talk back or express any negative feelings was strongly discouraged by my parents. Sometimes, on rare occasions, I would have a temper tantrum–complete with slamming doors, and kicking my feet against the wall or door. I also packed my overnight bag and threatened to run away. Mother said good-bye and wished me well. One freezing winter afternoon, when I was around nine, Mother told me it was time to go outside and play–to get some fresh air. It was too cold, I exclaimed, and a battle of wills ensued. Out I went, only to *stand* fully bundled up in my snowsuit by the back door, from which I did not budge for an hour.

When I turned fifteen I left home for the last time, because once I went away to Miss Porter's School in Farmington, Connecticut, the same boarding school that Mother had gone to, I would return to our Shaker Heights home only for holidays and summer vacations. And sure enough, when it came time to leave for the drive to Farmington, I had the same sinking feeling I had when I left for camp. I had spent years building up friendships with my girlfriends. And even more important, I had a steady boyfriend; at least, he was steady until I left. I had a feeling he wouldn't be around by the time

I came home at Christmas, and I was right. My girlfriends and I were a very close group whose parents were also friends with each other. We not only went to school together; we took tennis and swimming lessons at the country club together every summer. I did not want to be separated from them, as I was sure they would forget all about me and exclude me from their holiday parties. Fortunately, my best friend, Susan, went away to school, too. We went to different schools, but we felt comfortable with the knowledge that we would always have each other. The girls had a surprise going-away party for us, and we all cried and promised to write every week.

Fortunately, that summer I had met a girl who had already been in Miss Porter's for ninth grade. She supplied me with a careful list of all the clothes I would need to fit in with those sophisticated Eastern girls. List in hand, Mother and I went on a shopping spree to New York City, to purchase all the proper outfits. I needed a camel's hair polo coat and brogue shoes from Abercrombie & Fitch, Shetland wool cardigans and button-down Brooks Brothers shirts. I would wear dresses for Saturday night supper and Sunday church and skirts and blouses with knee socks to match for school days.

Nevertheless, what I felt was low-level terror that first day of school as a sophomore. Out of some 200 in the school, I vaguely knew only two or three girls, and none would be in my house. One of my two roommates was a tall, slender girl from Long Island who knew how to play squash–squash? What was that, a game with a vegetable? It turned out to be a very fast racket sport, played in an enclosed, square room. My other roommate was a Congressman's daughter from Washington, D.C. She brought her own horse with her to keep in the school's stables, and she was studying Russian.

I spent the whole year frantically hoping that both girls would like me enough to want to room with me again. It didn't matter whether I was six years old in the first grade, or fifteen, I was that same little girl who desperately wanted a best friend that I could trust and cling to. Why? I don't know, except possibly my Mother had always been there, until I went to camp, and after that, things were never the same. Nevertheless, it would be years before I realized how totally dependent I was on Mother, and how lost I felt without her.

Once again, I thought about and ate food constantly. The pig in me was very much alive and well. Much to the distress of our housemother, we had caches of food in our closets and bureau drawers, and after lights out, we would have parties and stuff ourselves with any goodies we could find or save from treats sent from home. At meal times, there were certain specialities that we looked forward to—popovers with honey butter for breakfast, layer cake on Saturday nights, fried chicken on Sundays and the two best desserts: Chocolate Icebox and Lemon Angel.

The highlight of our weekends at school was our walk to the local bakery and snack shop, fondly called The Gundy. Rain or shine, we would make the Gundy loop, to savor our favorite toasted English muffins with peanut butter and jam. Sometimes I would have both muffins *and* a hot fudge sundae. Who cared? The only time we ever thought about our weight was about a month before spring vacation, when the entire student body, it seemed, went on a crash diet. We *had* to be slender and glamorous for that trip to Florida or Bermuda, where the boys were. Also, we always gave up sweets and seconds for Lent, but other than that, it was generally feeding time at the OK Corral. Besides, I had enough boyfriends who didn't seem to mind. No, the inner tension I felt most of the time came from my need to be accepted by the girls. This need for approval plagued me year after year, whether I was in grade school, camp, or now, boarding school. I never got elected to the good citizenship honor roll, never held any high honors, nor was chosen for the important clubs like Drama and Glee Club. I always dreaded that time each fall, when the elections took place, and my name never appeared on any of the lists of class officers or student council representatives that were posted on the school bulletin board. Let's face it: I was just an average girl who did average school work and played on the second-string teams.

Boarding school years continued to be one disappointment after another, and so my hand was always in the cookie jar.

The only thing that kept my weight in check was the strict rules and limited access we had to food. Somewhere along the way, I decided that the only way to get people to like me was to be nice to everyone–to be complimentary at all costs. I learned never to say what I really thought about something but to wait and watch and see which way the wind was blowing, and above all, always be pleasant and nice, no matter what. I was about as phony and two-faced as a three-dollar bill, but I was determined to win friends and hopefully influence people. I'd had difficulty making friends easily, because I held back, in case I might be rejected first. Other girls all seemed to know each other, have fun, and joke around, while I hung back on the fringe, clinging tightly to my own close group of "best friends." But slowly it was getting better.

Senior year was the happiest of the three years, because all my friends and I were together in the best Senior House. Thank heavens I was no longer one of those scared “new girls”! My marks in school had also gotten better with each year, so that by my Senior year, I was getting a B-to-B+ average. Having no telephones and no dates did help keep one’s concentration on studies. But, when it came time to apply for college, we ran into a bit of a problem. My father wanted me to go to Vassar; I wanted to go to a two-year college like Manhattanville or Briarcliffe, with my friends, because truthfully, I had had enough of school. I wasn’t looking for a career, just a husband. My college guidance counselor told my parents I didn’t have much chance of making it into Vassar, so I’d better have an alternative choice. We decided on Connecticut College for Women, and I applied there. I was not sad to be leaving Farmington. The school was excellent, as schools went, but I was tired of being shut away in a small town. I wanted to go places!

Graduation Day was warm and sunny, especially beautiful with all the fruit trees blossoming profusely, and flowers in bloom everywhere. My mother and father and brother Bill came for all the festivities, but David’s Naval Air squadron had just deployed to Newfoundland. Dressed in short white dresses and white shoes, we processed into the Congregational Church to the traditional strains of “Pomp and Circumstance.”

Afterwards, family and friends met with the graduates to offer congratulations with many hugs, kisses and tears, as we said our final good-byes. My parents presented me with a very delicate watch with a thin, black band and two little diamonds. I left Farmington that day, feeling very grown-up and hoping that college might be an answer to my problems. At college, I was sure I would find the right boy who would care for me, look after me and love me, just like it said in all the romantic novels I had read for years.

4

I Wish I May, I Wish I Might

It had been a real scorcher. This was the kind of August weather that made the cotton grow, but you couldn't walk barefoot in the yard without burning the soles of your feet. In the evening, as soon as the dishes were done, the whole family (Daddy, Mother, Barbara, and I) drifted one by one out to the front porch to enjoy the faintly stirring southerly breeze and to watch the pinks and purples of the sunset gradually pale across the flat expanse of the West Texas tableland. You could see clear to the horizon in every direction, with only a few houses and windmills and restless tumbleweeds breaking the endless stretch of row upon row of cotton.

Sometimes we would listen to the radio, but tonight we were content to sit lazily on the steps, leaning against the porch columns and occasionally swatting a persistent mosquito, watching the sky darken and come alive with millions of stars.

The grown-ups were talking farming, as usual. "Found a few boll worms today down at the Patterson place," Daddy murmured. He always told Mother all about the crops, for she was interested and almost as knowledgeable as he, but the whole subject bored me.

"Hey, Barb, why are you so dressed up?" I said to my sister in a teasing tone.

"I have a date, that's why, and I can see the car lights coming now. So don't be a brat, okay?"

"Don't tell me you're going out with that creep Horace again!" Why did sixteen-year-olds have to be so hateful to their ten-year-old sisters?

I pointedly ignored Barbara and her date, but out of the corner of my eye I watched them say a few words to my parents and then drive away. "I don't care if she does have dates," I said under my breath, picking up loose pebbles from the sand in the flower bed. "I don't care if she gets to go to fun places, and I'm always stuck at home. I don't care if she is older, and I'm always told that I'm too little. Someday it's going to be different!" I exclaimed, throwing the handful of rocks as high and hard as I could.

And then I saw it: a brilliant, blazing star falling slowly across the heavens directly over my head. It seemed to hang there suspended for a split second before disappearing, but in sight just long enough for me to breathe the magic words: "I wish I may, I wish I might, have the wish I wish tonight." And then, closing my eyes tight, I whispered the wish that I had repeated so often before. "I wish that someday I can grow up to have my own family with four children of my own and live in a beautiful house where we can always be happy, and where I can always do exactly what I want to do."

Later, lying in bed with my head near the open window where it was cooler, watching the sky and listening to the night sounds, I could see the Big Dipper and the Milky Way and thought again about my wish and how it would be when I grew up. My reverie was broken by the sound of a car door closing. Was that Barbara's voice? "Good night, Horace, I had a wonderful time! Thank you for the movie and the Coke."

I got up to peek out of the window, to see if he was going to give her a good-night kiss, but the front door squeaked open, and I jumped back into bed and pulled the sheet up over my head, pretending to be asleep.

My sister and I had grown up on the farm, living in the white frame house that my grandparents had built years before. In the summer, the fields stretched green and flat as a table in every direction; in fact, that was the name of our town–Lamesa, which means "the table" in Spanish. Both my parents loved the land, for they had helped to pioneer it. I had listened over and over again to my mother tell the stories of those early days. "When Grandpa Davis first came out here to settle in 1906, there really wasn't anything here but tumbleweeds and rattlesnakes. He cleared the land himself, and there wasn't time to build a real house until the crops were started, so the family lived in a half-dugout until the lumber could be shipped from East Texas. I was just a little girl when he brought the family out, but I can remember that it took all day to come thirty miles in the wagon from Tahoka, and we had to stop to water the horses at wells along the way."

They had all worked hard to settle this sparse country of sandstorms and mesquite, but by backbreaking labor and sacrifice, it had been transformed into fertile acres of rich sandy soil which, with the right kind of rain, could grow bale-to-the-acre cotton. There had been many hard times along the way, and some of the stories made me want to cry, as when Mother talked about her mother's death in a flu epidemic, and how after that, the older children in the family of eight had to care for the younger ones and especially for the little baby. It made me sad to think of my mother, just thirteen, without a mother of her own. But, there were exciting stories, too, about rattlesnake bites and running for the storm cellar when a tornado dipped out of black storm clouds overhead, with wind so strong that it almost ripped the cellar door right off its hinges.

My eyes had filled with tears when Mother had talked about her disappointment as a child when she had had to miss school to help harvest the crops, and what a struggle she had catching up when she did go back. But in those days a farm family all had to pitch in and do the work together; the girls put on bonnets and wore long sleeves to protect their complexions from the burning sun, as they hoed long rows of cotton beside their brothers, and in the fall everyone helped pick the cotton so that the crop would be harvested before bad weather came. I knew how much Mother had wanted to be a teacher, and what a crushing blow it must have been to her to have to give up college after one year when she was needed to care for her sisters at home. "The most important thing, Sunny, is to get a good education," she would tell me. "Then you can get a job teaching. Schoolteachers can always get a job."

Certainly I found life on the farm when I was growing up, to be very different. Times were better; the Dust Bowl of the 30s and the Depression years when cotton sold for 5¢ a pound, were just stories to me, not unlike the pioneer tales I grew up hearing. But those hard years were very real to my parents and always very much in their thoughts and fears. Their endurance of those difficult times had produced in them a fierce determination that their children would have the advantages that they themselves had been denied, and that things would be easier for my sister and me.

My father, almost six feet tall and soft-spoken, was generous to a fault. He could deny his children nothing, and tended to excuse and overlook our misdoings. That left Mother to be the disciplinarian of the family, and I soon learned to play one parent against the other, in order to do exactly what I wanted.

"Mart," my mother would call, "you tell those girls to come in here and help with the dishes."

"Now, Ollie, don't get excited. They've had a hard day at school. There's no reason to get so upset. Let them relax a little bit."

Often Mother ended up doing the dishes by herself.

Or perhaps I would approach my dad, as he sat in his big chair after dinner, feet up, reading the paper. "Listen, Daddy," I would say, kneeling on the floor and leaning on the arm of his chair. "I really do need a new sweater, and I've found the cutest one at Baldwin's for $9.95. It has batwing sleeves, and I'm just dying to have it." With a wink, he would slip me a ten-dollar bill.

Being the baby of the family had both advantages and disadvantages: I enjoyed being spoiled, but on the other hand, I could never catch up with my sister. With a six-year head start, she was definitely first, and I was second. I was especially envious of the easy relationship that she enjoyed with Mother. They just seemed to like each other's company, and I always felt like odd girl out. And not just with my mother–it seemed all the aunts and uncles and cousins who lived within visiting distance liked Barbara better. Weren't they always inviting her to go on trips? Vacations were a rare occurrence, but occasionally an aunt and uncle would plan a special trip.

"It's not fair," I told myself. "I've never been anywhere, and Barbara always gets to go. She went to

Colorado with Aunt Beth and Uncle Paul, and now she's been invited to go with Uncle Jim and Aunt Margaret to Tennessee, to see the Smoky Mountains. And I've never even been out of the state!" A length of pipe suspended from the cottonwood tree formed my trapeze, and I swung upside down, pigtails trailing, enjoying feeling sorry for myself. So what if she was sixteen, and I was ten. Life was unfair. Hadn't I spent hours looking at Viewmaster slides of the Royal Gorge, the Painted Desert, and Pike's Peak? I knew them all by heart. Someday I would travel more than Barbara. Someday I would see the world. I would show them all.

Barbara's senior year in high school was one success after another. Editor of the *Tornado Times,* best dramatic actress in the school district, and then the absolute pinnacle; she was elected Pioneer Queen. On the day of the parade, I stood in front of the courthouse on tiptoe, straining to see over heads and cars. Like most of the other spectators, I was in costume–long calico dress, apron, and bonnet. It was Pioneer Day, and I could hear the band coming in the distance. First came the American and Lone Star flags, carried by aging members of the American Legion and VFW, and then the sheriff's posse on big white horses. The IHS band, perspiring in black and gold wool uniforms, next turned the corner of the square, and right behind them in the place of honor came the Queen's float, pulled by a John Deere tractor. Four girls in strapless net formals waved at the crowd, and the Queen herself smiled in my direction. "Hi, Barb!" I yelled, jumping up and down. "That's my sister," I said to no one in particular. "My sister Barbara is the Queen." I was very proud, yet inside I felt an old familiar stomach ache begin.

Our home was an average farm home, plain and

unpretentious, but neat and comfortable, very much like many others scattered throughout Dawson County. Our farm was 320 acres, a half section of land, which was about the average size for that time. I dressed much like all my friends and lived a normal, everyday life. I knew that my parents loved each other, in spite of their differences, and I certainly knew that they loved me. In fact, there was a lot of love in our family, and it was warmly expressed. But somehow, I remember feeling very early that I was unacceptable. And sometimes I felt that my parents were unacceptable, too, which made me feel guilty and ashamed for thinking such a terrible thought about people that I loved so much.

"If Mother would just get out more and have friends," I thought, and I tried to get her to join the Home Demonstration Club and attend their weekly meetings, no matter that she had no real interest in watching Mrs. Moore show the latest method for pickling and canning peaches. "If Daddy would just go to church on Sundays, then his problems would be solved," and I would leave the *Baptist Bulletin* lying around, where he would be sure to see it. Always scheming to get my parents more involved in the social things that my friends' parents did, I would ask casually, "Didn't you and Daddy like to play forty-two when you were younger?"

It was very important to me that my parents look right and do the right things, and I was also very critical of my own appearance. Even in the first grade, I had cried all one afternoon because my father had gone into the hospital, and my mother had not had time to roll my hair the night before. When in the fourth grade I had my first permanent, I had rushed out of the shop in tears. "I hate to look so frizzy; why can't I have naturally curly hair like Mary Sue?" For years I almost never went swimming just because I didn't want to get my hair wet. This compulsion also extended to other areas–such as clothing. I learned very early to tie my shoelaces because I wanted them tied exactly the same way every time, even if it meant having to retie them over and over again, until they were absolutely perfect.

And when I felt lonely or sad or angry, I would have something comforting to eat–a mayonnaise sandwich on white bread, or something equally bland and soothing, while I read a book. I spent a lot of time by myself reading, and in the summer I made a weekly trip to Mrs. Townsend's rental library and stocked up on enough Cherry Ames books and all-day cherry suckers to last the week. At home I flopped down on the bed, engrossed in the story and imagining myself in a white starched nurse's uniform, oblivious to dinner preparations and housekeeping chores. I was in another world. . . .

Going to the movies was even more fun than reading movies. My friend Dee Ann and I loved to go every Saturday afternoon.

After the movie, we would come blinking back into the bright sunlight and walk halfway down the block to the Rexall Drug. "Let's sit here," Dee Ann suggested, pointing to the twirling stools as we went inside.

"No, I like the booths in the back better," and we walked back into the cool interior where the big ceiling fan lazily turned the air round and round. Pooling the remnants of our allowances, we had enough money for two cherry sodas, and we sipped contentedly and giggled about boys and school and other related topics. When the straw's loud slurp announced the end of the sodas, it was time to go. "Let's weigh, Dee Ann, do you have a penny left?"

"Just one. You weigh, and I'll get the fortune."

The big white scale stood over against the wall near the pharmacy counter. I loved the smell of the medicines and the interesting-looking bottles lined up so methodically. Stepping on the scale, I watched the hand settle. The numbers didn't really mean that much to me. "How much do you weigh, Dee Ann?" I asked her.

"I don't know; about the same." She was reading the fortune card.

"Well, anyway, when I grow up I want to be 5'2" and weigh 110 pounds. That's what my sister weighs and my mother too, and that's what I am going to weigh."

"That's nice," Dee Ann obviously wasn't listening. "Get this fortune: 'Your fondest dreams are going to come true.' I wonder what that could mean?"

One summer, when I was about ten, it looked as if all my dreams might come true, just as the card had said. I knew that something exciting was about to happen when my dad came in for lunch one Wednesday noon, for he was smiling broadly and whistling coming up the front walk. No matter what field Daddy might be plowing in, he always came to the house promptly at noon for lunch, for that was our big meal of the day. Sitting at the table as my mother served Wednesday's inevitable fried chicken and mashed potatoes, he teased us all with little hints. "This family is going to get something *very* nice."

"I know, I know!" I yelled, "a dog!"

"A new car?" ventured Barbara.

"Maybe, finally, a washing machine," Mother added hopefully.

But we were all wrong. With a flourish my father announced triumphantly, "We are going to have an oil well!"

An oil well! Maybe our luck was changing at last. I

knew that oil had been found on Uncle Jim's land, and now they were able to add a new bedroom onto their house and even take a trip to the Rocky Mountains. An oil well would be a wonderful thing to have. With great anticipation we all watched the big derrick go up, one mile straight across the field from our front door. At night the rig was brilliant with tiny white lights, and instead of watching for falling stars, I sat on the front steps and gazed at the beautiful sight, dreaming of what it could mean in my life. "If we strike oil, we can get a piano," I murmured. I'd always wanted to take piano lessons. "If we strike oil, then maybe we can move to town."

I hated living in the country. There were countless possibilities to consider, each one better than the last.

Every day we drove over to the big rig in our Jeep, listening to the roughnecks talk and watching the drilling. Sometimes I was allowed to go up on the platform with my dad.

"How many feet today?" he would ask the driller.

The answer came: 2,000 feet, then 5,000, then 8,000. At every level it was the same. "No sign of oil yet, but maybe just a little deeper and we'll hit it."

"Sure we will," Daddy would agree. "It can't be much farther down to pay dirt." The drilling went on all summer, and I could see the disappointment grow in my dad's face as the same answer continued to come.

"9,500 today. Sorry, Mr. Barrow, nothing yet. Maybe another couple of hundred feet or so."

With the fall came 11,000 feet and reality. The lights went out, the tall derrick was dismantled and loaded onto long trucks, and soon there was just a bare spot in the cotton field where all my dreams had once been. "How could it have been a dry hole?" I wanted to know.

"Just bad luck, honey. There was a little oil, but not really enough to make it pay." He turned away, and I knew he didn't want to talk about it anymore.

"It never works to get your hopes up about anything," I told myself. If you didn't get excited about anything, then you didn't get disappointed.

We never did get the piano, but my disappointment was lessened in the fall, because it turned out to be one of those unforgettable cotton years. A real bumper crop happened about once every decade, when all the conditions were right. There had to be lots of rain at the right time, no hail, few insects, plenty of sun but not too hot in August, a late frost, and most important of all, a good price. Bumper crops happened all too infrequently, but when they did, farmers remembered the date and spoke of it lovingly for years to come. And so, this was a year to remember. Now things would be better. My father would not be so worried about paying the bank and the payment still due on the tractor; my mother would not be so fearful about the future, and surely we would all be happier. And best of all, we really were going to move to town!

For as long as I could remember, I had wanted to live in town. It was lonely on the farm, and I hated sharing a room with my sister. To me, the country was depressing. My mother loved to get out and walk through the cotton fields, but I thought the terrain all too flat. I wanted trees and flower beds, and lots of neighbors with plenty of kids to play with.

We picked out the house just as it was being built and watched it go up. A red brick ranch style with a picture window in the living room—the most beautiful house that I had ever seen! Mother and Barbara spent a lot of time choosing wallpaper for the kitchen, but I got to pick out everything for my room. My own room—I was going to have a room all to myself! I knew exactly what I wanted. It had pink walls, white ruffled curtains, and polished hardwood floors with fluffy pink throw rugs. It was beautiful! My parents took me down to Gaither Furniture to look for a brand new bedroom set. "Oh, Mother, look at this one! It's just what I want." It was blonde oak, very small and dainty, and it had a tiny desk to match. Now would it be fun to have friends over to spend the night!

Junior High started out to be a lot of fun. I lived just a block away from Carol Ann Smith, and we spent a lot of time together, roller skating on the long sidewalk that ran all the way down the block between our houses. We had good times together, but gradually I was becoming aware that there was an "in" clique in school, which I wanted very much to be part of. It took some painful lessons, however, to learn how to be accepted.

One of the lessons had to do with clothes. Autumn days in Texas often averaged temperatures of 80 degrees or more, and I arrived at Sunday School one very hot September Sunday, dressed in my new red corduroy vest and skirt. I knew that it was a little hot, but I was eager to wear my new outfit. The opening hymn was sung, and the lesson had just begun, when I heard snickering from the back row. Without turning my head, I knew that Linda and Mary Frances were laughing at me in my hot corduroy. Slowly my face blushed as red as the suit I wore, and I fought back the tears. "Never," I vowed silently, "Never in my life will I wear the wrong clothes again and let myself be made fun of this way. I will never be humiliated again."

I worked hard to make the right friends and to wear the right clothes, and by the seventh grade I had arrived.

I wore green jeans on Fridays like the rest of the "in" girls, and we all went to the movies on Friday nights and looked to see who was sitting with whom. There were slumber parties almost every weekend, and soon I was getting an invitation to them all. When it was my turn to entertain, I was especially glad that we had the nice new house in town. It was fun to be part of such an exclusive group, and even more fun when we excluded girls who wanted to be in. "Look at JoAnn Franklin. Can you believe she is wearing that tacky sweater? Quick, look the other way. Pretend that you don't see her when she walks by." How secure and pleased with myself I felt, to be in, and I enjoyed feeling sorry for JoAnn–poor thing, she was just never going to make it.

And then, suddenly, I found myself back with JoAnn on the outside of the group, looking in. I was never quite sure how it happened. One day I was part of everything, even a ringleader, and then abruptly I wasn't called on the phone as often by the girls, and there were too many Friday nights, when I found myself at home with nothing to do. I certainly couldn't go to the Palace by myself, when all the rest of the girls were going together.

One bleak Friday night I sat forlornly on my sister's bed, watching her try on her new clothes. She had been shopping for college, and I felt very lonely as I looked around the room at her open suitcases. In spite of all my jealousy of her, I was going to miss her badly. Tomorrow we would be driving her to Abilene, and I felt as if I was being deserted. Where had all my friends gone? Why had they dumped me? Surely Patsy hadn't really gotten mad at me for flirting with her boyfriend at the football game? It was a bad beginning for my eighth grade year. And now my stomach hurt almost all the time.

I had been so wrapped up in my own problems that

I had scarcely noticed that my parents were having problems of their own. My father's health had been failing as his emphysema grew progressively worse, and then in addition he went into the hospital for gall bladder surgery. They were also under a great deal of financial pressure. What was worse, there was not enough rain the following spring to get up a good stand of cotton, and the farmers had to borrow more and more from the bank to meet the crop expenses. I closed my eyes to what was happening; I was interested only in having nice clothes to wear and winning my friends back again.

But by graduation from Junior High, I could no longer avoid the reality. It should have been a happy occasion; I was graduating second in my class. My mother had had a special dress made for me, yet as I stood in front of the mirror, admiring the pale blue organdy with puffed sleeves, the scooped neck, and full, gathered skirt over three stiff petticoats, I could hear my parents in their room across the hall. At first I paid no attention, but then I caught a word or two that made me strain to hear the rest of the conversation. What were they saying about our house?

"It's really the only thing we can do, Mart," I heard my mother's low voice. "If we do sell this house, we can pay the bank note, and we can move into the house out on the Evans place. It's a nice location, very close in, and the house will be fine if we fix it up a little. Besides, you know that we've never really felt at home in town anyway."

I could tell that my dad was asking a question, but I couldn't make out the words.

"Of course, Sunny will be disappointed," Mother went on in reply, "but I know that she will understand that we have to do it. There's just no other way."

I had heard enough. I pulled my door shut quickly, then leaned against it in disbelief. Sell this house? They couldn't mean it! How could they do this to me? But I knew that they were serious, and that the situation must be desperate. I threw myself across the bed, not caring anymore if the new dress wrinkled. What was I going to do? How could I ever give up my beautiful room? It was too much to ask of me; I just couldn't do it. I turned on the radio, so they couldn't hear me crying. I would have to pretend that I didn't care. But I did care; the Evans house was a real dump. Now I could never ask anyone home with me again! Maybe it was just as well, that I didn't have any friends anymore, anyway.

"Sunny, it's time to go. Let's don't be late to your graduation."

Sighing, I stood up and smoothed my skirt. Maybe a little powder on my nose would help cover its redness, but the self-pity would be more difficult to hide. My gloom was more than obvious at the graduation ceremony, and for weeks afterward I felt angry and depressed.

I was glad that Junior High was over and behind me; the quicker I could grow up and get in charge of my own life, the better. And I would see to it that things never turned out this badly for me again.

5

I Could Have Danced All Night

September–the end of summer, and the beginning of college–came all too soon, as far as I was concerned. I was having too good a time visiting all my friends and roommates from boarding school. I had spent my seventeenth summer happily traveling all over the Eastern seaboard and then out to Lake Forest, Illinois for one gala weekend after another. It was such a carefree time–meeting new boys, going to one stunning debut party after another, and dancing into the wee hours of the morning. The June following graduation was the traditional time of elegant debutante balls given under garden tents at home or a country club.

My party was in June, with three other girls from my group of friends. It was a dinner dance at the Chagrin Valley Hunt Club, a setting so beautiful that if you saw it in a movie, you wouldn't believe it. The club was near Hunting Valley, in Gates Mills, a tiny community which was so quaint and picturesque it looked as if it had been forgotten for half a century. At the heart of the little village was the spacious Hunt Club with endless, close-cropped green fields that used to be used for polo, and now were used for occasional horse shows, if at all. Many of the villagers were members of the club, and most of them rode and kept their horses there. There were also four excellent *en-tout-cas* tennis courts, but they were really a grudging concession to the march of time. The focus of the club remained what it had always been: horses. And there were still one or two hunts every year, complete with red coats, black hats, and hounds. The clubhouse itself was low and rambling, with flagstone terraces and wide awninged verandahs from which, across sweeping manicured lawns, you could see towering willows by the banks of a little creek that meandered through the grounds.

On this June evening–my evening–the setting sun made everything green seem greener, and what wasn't green was limned in a golden haze by the last rays of the sun. It was so beautiful, it made me want to cry, and I gave my father's arm a special hug. This was our turn to invite all our friends from boarding school to Cleveland for this special occasion. Every bedroom in the club was filled with chattering girls getting ready for the party. The night was warm and starry, just right for dancing outside on the polished wood porch of the club. I had a beautiful sapphire blue dress of silk organza with thin straps, and a skirt that was all layered like the petals of a rose. I felt terribly elegant and grown-up, because Mother had given me her diamond-and-sapphire pendant to wear. A photographer came and took pictures of us four girls with our fathers and then with our escorts, families and friends.

Promptly at ten minutes to eight, twenty fashionable minutes late, big town cars and snappy convertibles began to pull in to the club's gravel parking lot, disgorging gaily dressed girls and white-jacketed escorts, and older couples who were friends of my parents. The band was Cleveland's best, doing its best to imitate the New York sound. My feet were tapping, and everyone who arrived seemed as excited and enthusiastic as I was. I knew everyone, but still it all seemed fresh and special.

There were cocktails, canapes and conversation, and pretty soon it was time for dinner–a magnificent buffet of roast beef, lobster thermidor with shrimp cocktail first, lyonnaise potatoes, spinach salad and, for dessert, ice cream pie on an Oreo cookie base mounded with whipped cream and hot fudge sauce. Throughout the dinner, champagne was served for the toasts, and my father, who had never looked more handsome, gave the most moving toast of all. And I couldn't keep the tears from coming. He was so sweet and loving that night.

And then the dancing began with the daughters and their fathers taking a turn around the floor. After that, I hardly ever sat down again. One o'clock finally came, and "Good Night, Ladies." I couldn't believe it! I could have gone on dancing all night! Everyone thinks her own coming out party is the nicest, and maybe there were others that were more elaborate, but for me, mine was absolutely the best. I went to bed that night humming Broadway show tunes and thinking about all the boys who had asked me to dance. Oh, it was all so much fun, I couldn't wait for tomorrow.

The next evening, another friend had her party, and so, once again, we were dancing until early into the morning hours. The whole weekend was filled with lunches, tennis games, cocktail parties and dances. I had invited a boy from New York to be my date for one party and another boy from Pittsburgh for the next night. I would show those Cleveland boys that they were not the only fish in the sea!

During the summer weeks, between trips out of town, I decided to take a speed reading course at Case Western Reserve University to prepare for all the college reading that I knew was coming up. Monday, Wednesday and Friday, I drove down to the University to improve my reading skills. In addition to my course, I volunteered weekly at University Hospital. I had been a hospital volunteer in the summer for several years, either in the snack shop, gift shop, reception desk or blood bank. My father was on the Board of Trustees of the hospital, and it was expected that since I didn't have to earn money during the summer months for school, I would volunteer.

My eighteenth birthday was September 1st, 1957, just as that fairy tale summer came to an end. Soon after, my parents and I set off for New London and Connecticut College for Women.

Conn College, as it was nicknamed, loomed gray and foreboding, high on a hill overlooking the Thames River. These buildings were large, massive stone structures totally opposite from the charming, ivy-covered brick and frame houses of Miss Porter's School. As we drove up to my freshman dorm, East House, my feelings were definitely mixed–I was excited about the new life of freedom I was going to have after three years of restrictions at boarding school. But it also brought back memories of that September, three years before, when I had left home for boarding school, scared and apprehensive. Once again, I looked forward to meeting new friends, but I felt somewhat alone, in that I only knew a few other girls in the entire student body of 950 women.

Of course, that didn't really matter; my real purpose in going to college was not to have more girlfriends, but to meet more boys! On that score, the college was ideally situated between Harvard and MIT in Boston, Brown in Providence, and my favorite, Yale in New Haven. Another hour and a half would take me to Princeton, another popular choice. And just in case there were any dull evenings in the middle of the week, right across the street was the United States Coast Guard Academy, and across the river was the U.S. Navy's Submarine School for graduates of Annapolis. They had an officers' club full of lonely young men who liked Conn College girls.

My room in East House was a single at the end of a long hall on the third floor. It was very small with one window, a bed, desk, chair and bureau. We had to bring curtains, bedspread, sheets, lamp, rug and bookcase in an attempt to make the room cozy. Looking at that sparse room, and at my cheerful parents waving good-bye, a large lump formed in my throat. How ridiculous! Here I was, eighteen years old and feeling homesick again.

I am *not* going to stay in this room by myself, I thought, so I'll just have to see who's around. I set out to meet the other girls who were also unpacking trunks, hanging curtains and filling bookcases. The first girl I met was my next door neighbor, Edie. She was a tall, attractive blonde from Summit, New Jersey. We hit it off immediately, when we found out we had both been to a private school and enjoyed playing tennis. Edie reminded me of the girls I'd grown up with. Across the hall was Alice, whose father was a doctor in central Connecticut, and then Janet, who had never been away from home before and was feeling very homesick. Well, at least this was not my first time away–I knew some of the ropes. We all went off to the coffee shop to get better acquainted over cigarettes and coffee. Smoking was still new for me. I had snuck my first cigarette in the ladies' room of the country club when I was fifteen, and had smoked in Florida on spring vacations and at dances when the chaperones weren't looking. But I never smoked at boarding school, because in those days one got expelled for smoking on campus. Edie, Janet and I became very close friends, spending many hours together that year talking about everything–school, parents, boys, and the future, though not necessarily in that order.

That coffee shop where we met became my home away from my room–a source of faithful comfort whenever I got bored or restless, or afraid of some big exam that was looming, and for which I was desperately cramming. My favorite treat was a cup of coffee and a doughnut–no, make that two doughnuts, or even three, or . . . I was horrified to discover that I could eat half a dozen doughnuts at a single sitting, if I didn't watch myself! Oh, my heavens, a doughnut-oholic and still a teenager! Sheer vanity was the only thing that kept a check on my snacks, and even that wouldn't have worked, if I hadn't been dating all the time. I knew girls who would pig out and let their weight climb up fifteen or twenty pounds, and then start frantically crash dieting to get in shape for the big parties at Thanksgiving and Christmas. Some would eat nothing but liquids for two or three weeks straight, popping diet pills or swilling down coffee to keep going. But, in my case, never knowing when I would be invited out, and usually busy every weekend, I had to stay in shape. Even so, come January, I had to get out my fullest skirts–no more A-lines until spring vacation!

Once I was at college, I decided I was going to enjoy the next four years, and hopefully, find a husband in the process. I had no intention of becoming a successful businesswoman with a 9 to 5 job in New York City, as most of my college friends wanted. I intended to *marry* a successful businessman and then have lovely children, do all kinds of interesting charitable work, and live happily ever after. That was what my mother had done, and it had worked for her. At eighteen, life was golden. As long as I kept my grades up, I had nothing to worry about, except which date to accept for the next weekend. My home life was secure with no financial problems; no marital difficulties for my parents, no health problems for anyone in my family. There were no clouds at all on my horizon, just bright sunny skies.

Over Thanksgiving, my parents took a suite at the Westbury, in New York, so that we could all be together, while I went to the Junior League Assembly Ball on Friday night and the Grovesnor on Saturday night. Both took place at the Plaza, where long black limousines pulled up to the brightly lit entrance and beautifully dressed girls in ball gowns swept up the red-carpeted stairway to the ballroom. The young men in white tie and tails surrounded the dance floor, watching the girls. I couldn't bear to have the music stop.

Mother had bought me two new ball gowns, one peach taffeta, one red satin just for these parties. I hated to take them off, when I returned to the hotel room. That meant the party was over–but not for long. There was always another dance coming up.

The first time I ever got along with David was when I met and dated his long-time friend and roommate, George. David had to be nice to me, whenever I came down to Yale to see George. Up until then, he could do without my presence, and I could certainly do without his. Bill we saw only briefly over the holidays. He was very quiet and kept to himself. I never knew what was going on with Bill, who had an exceptional mechanical aptitude and liked to tinker with things, taking lamps apart, fixing broken toys, or building model engines in his room late at night. He was gentle, but had a quick and keen sense of humor.

The summer after my freshman year, I went on a trip to Europe, a two-month grand tour with friends from boarding school days. I loved the luxury of traveling to Europe on an ocean liner. We spent a lot of time by the pool, or sunning in our deck chairs, or in the dining room eating sumptuous meals. I gained a pound a day in the week it took to reach Algeciras, Spain, our first port. I loved every minute of that whole trip, because there was nothing I liked better than to travel, see new places, and eat new kinds of food in all the restaurants of the various countries we visited. We went to bullfights in Madrid, to Buckingham Palace in London, climbed the Eiffel Tower in Paris, fed the pigeons in St. Mark's Square in Venice, took a boat trip down the Rhine and went to the World's Fair in Brussels. And we visited all the famous museums and cathedrals which we had studied in History of Art. All the pictures and all the postcards now became my own memories, and too soon, we were back on our liner, sailing for home.

Edie and I roomed together sophomore year. Fall was filled with football games and fraternity parties, and I made a great deal of effort to be fun to be with, by being attentive and laughing at my dates' jokes and stories. I never allowed any angry, negative or otherwise unpleasant feelings to show–and afterwards was emotionally exhausted from the effort.

We had a fathers' weekend at Connecticut, and Edie and I invited our dads. We planned tennis games, dinners out, and many other activities to help pass the time. I was more nervous about my father's coming to visit than I had been about any date I'd ever had. What on earth would we talk about? Never in my nineteen years had I spent this much time alone with my father. It was very hard for him to share his feelings, good or bad, so one really didn't know where one stood with him. And as he had never expressed much approval of my performance, I was doubly nervous. The fact that Edie had her father visiting, too, saved the day. How stupid to feel awkward, dumb and clumsy around your own father, I told myself, but it didn't help.

And then when he came, I could tell he was nervous, too; he tried so hard to be appreciative, that I didn't know what to do, to help him relax. If only I could have said, "Hey, Dad, look at the two of us–so uptight with each other, we squeak!" We might have laughed then, about how silly we were, and really talked and started a whole new relationship. But I couldn't, and we didn't, and we both went on trying so hard that it was painful. I'm sure he was relieved as I was, when the weekend was finally over. But I was sad, too, because I sensed that there might never be another chance to just be real together.

Before I ever got home for Christmas, I was dated up for almost the whole vacation. It never occurred to me to wonder how my parents liked having me go out so much. I came home for the holidays but never spent any time with them at all. I slept late every morning, went out shopping or visiting during the day, and partied at night. I was always eager to go, because I never knew whom I might meet next. A new boy was always a challenge–how long would it be before he asked me for a date?

The Christmas dinner-dance at our country club was one of the highlights of the holiday season. My date and I were just one couple in a large group that had gathered together in the bar for cocktails before dinner. Quickly I scanned the room to see if there were any new faces in the crowd. No, no—but wait! Yes, definitely yes! Over there, by the fireplace—there was a young man I did not recognize. Was he from out of town? Someone's cousin? Another girl's imported date? Affecting disinterest, I asked my date who this stranger was, and we were soon introduced. He was from Cleveland, but "older," compared to the college boys I was used to dating. His name—Dan Ford. He was 25 years old, a graduate of Yale, ex-artillery officer, and now working for an industrial real estate company in Cleveland. Most important of all, he was awfully good-looking, much more mature than the boys I was used to, and he was not going with anyone in particular.

Dan and I spent as much of the rest of the evening together as we politely could, without being rude to our dates. It was two A.M. when I got home, but I was too excited to sleep and had to wake up Mother and tell her all about this most marvelous man I had met! Suddenly I wished mightily that my holiday evenings weren't all booked. But there were still daytime lunches, skating, drives—every minute that he could spare away from work. We spent as much of the next ten days together as our schedules would allow. I would drive downtown to meet Dan for lunch, then rush back to dress for the next evening's party. All I could think of was, how was I ever going to go back to college and say good-bye to this answer to my dreams?

It was true: Absence did make the heart grow fonder. Ours was a long-distance, whirlwind courtship. One weekend, I went into New York to see Dan, and we did all the things tourists did. We went to the top of the RCA building and rode around Manhattan on a ferry boat in the freezing cold. We met friends of Dan's for drinks at Trader Vic's and went dancing at the Waldorf. Where did the night disappear to? One minute I was sipping an exotic pineapple drink to South Sea island music and the next I was saying good-night at the apartment door. I was still very much in awe of this older man, afraid that I would appear young and unsophisticated. Somehow, this date seemed more important than all the others. I didn't want to blow my chances with Dan. Sunday we found a cafe in a hotel near Central Park, where we lingered over brunch and listened to our favorite music played on the piano. We bought a recording for me to take back to college, as a reminder of this weekend. I couldn't wait to tell Edie and Janet all about it. It was very hard to say good-bye, because I knew it would be weeks before we could see each other again. For I would be spending spring vacation in Delray Beach, Florida, with my family, as I did every year, so I counted the days until Dan could come to New York again in April. As soon as my final exams were over, June 1st, I flew home, and we spent every single evening together in June.

One warm, summer evening, we sat out on our porch, having played tennis and had dinner. I had had several "steady beaux" before Dan, but never anyone as serious as Dan. Yet for all the time we had spent together, I could hardly believe my ears, when I heard, "Will you marry me?"

I was flustered and stunned: Wait a minute, help! What do I do now?

"Oh, yes!" I exclaimed.

Here I was, imagining myself to be so worldly, and all of a sudden I felt very much out of control and unsure of myself. I had just said I would marry this man who was still something of a stranger to me. Well, it was done, and I just let myself get caught up in the romance of it all and tried not to think about what I had just commited myself to—a marriage partner for the rest of my life!

My parents were quite surprised, when I woke them up after Dan went home. I heard my father ask my mother if I had been drinking! I should say not! We had nothing more than a Coke. But, as soon as it really sank in, they were great! They put on their robes and got up, and Mother wanted to know everything—What had Dan said? What had I said? What were our plans? My mind was still spinning with the excitement of the evening. One minute, I was just their daughter home for the summer, and the next I was engaged to be married in the fall!

Mother went into action the next morning. Dan and I had decided that it would be fun to be married at Thanksgiving time, when my friends would be home from college for the holiday.

"Well," said Mother, "that's a very popular time for a wedding. We'd better get busy right away." She called the church to reserve it for Saturday, November 28th, and likewise the florist, and the photographer and the country club, where our dinner reception would take place. Mother was extremely organized, and knew exactly how things should be done. She engaged a secretary to help with all the details, and together we proceeded to plan the wedding. We did not officially announce our engagement until August, but no one was surprised, when I finally put on the emerald-cut diamond engagement ring I had previously worn only in my bedroom.

Every day, from June 22nd to November 28th, was spent in preparation for the most important day in my life. About weddings, my mother had strong opinions, and I knew nothing, so it was easier just to follow her lead. The next weeks were a whirlwind of shopping for silver, china, furniture, linens, trousseau; having my picture taken for the papers; attending showers, luncheons, dinner parties and dances in our honor, and most exciting of all, going to fittings for my wedding gown. Fortunately, I didn't have to worry about putting on weight—the pace was too frantic. Any extra calories, I worried off before the next meal, and sometimes I was too busy or nervous to eat at all. In fact, it was the first time in my life that I lost weight without trying. The pounds just seemed to melt away in the summer sun. By the time of my last fitting, I had lost ten pounds. The fitter at the bridal salon assured me this was quite usual for brides, but she cautioned me to try to eat enough so that my dress would fit perfectly.

The Manuel and Ford families had lived in Cleveland since before the turn of the century. Both families had a large circle of friends, many of whom wanted to entertain the bride-and-groom-to-be. The month of November was filled with one exciting day after another, as the biggest day of all approached. The secretary and I wrote down the gifts as they arrived at the house—each one beautifully wrapped with a white, satin bow. My parents turned our recreation room into a wedding display room with tables set up along all four walls. Before long, the tables were covered with silver, crystal, and china of every description; in fact, the room reminded me of a gift shop ready for the Christmas holiday season. I was overwhelmed and a little frightened by it all.

Between going to parties and opening gifts, Mother and I went to New York one more time to buy clothes for my trousseau and for her to find her Mother-of-the-bride dress. And Dan and I spent many hours looking for our first home and the right furniture to put in it. At last we found a small three bedroom house, which we painted and papered together with friends, to get ready for our return from our honeymoon in Jamaica.

In the midst of all the whirl of preparations, every so often, I would stop and ask myself—what am I doing? Is this what I really want? Do I want to spend the rest of my life with this man I was just beginning to really know? But the train was moving full speed ahead, and it was too late to jump off now. Anyway, I was too caught up in all the attention I was receiving. I *loved* being the bride-to-be, the guest of honor; for once in my life, I was the center of my family's attention. I was also the first of my group of girlfriends to get married, a fact which helped me to feel more secure and successful. This highly approved-of marriage put me, temporarily, way ahead of my brothers in mv longstanding competition with them. David was single and in the Naval Air Force, and Bill was still in boarding school. They would have a hard time to match my feat of snaring one of Cleveland's most eligible bachelors, and someone that our father obviously thought the world of. Yes, I was Cinderella who had captured her Prince Charming.

Wednesday, November 25th, began the final countdown. My ten bridesmaids, from colleges all over the country, met for dinner at the home of my maid of honor. There were several parties on the following days and then came the rehearsal dinner. Friday evening, while we danced away the hours of the last night we would have different surnames, a snowstorm swirled into Cleveland with blizzard-like winds that covered everything in layers of white, fluffy snow. It made the whole world look like a winter fairyland, but my mother was frantic with worry. We had trouble getting the car through the ice and snowy drifts, so I was very late arriving home. And this time, Mother was sitting up in the living room, smoking, and waiting for the phone to ring with bad news.

Our wedding took place at Christ Episcopal Church, where I had attended Sunday School and been confirmed. The church, which was very large, was filled to capacity with family and friends. I can remember Mother and Mrs. Ford spending hours going over the guest list, to be sure no one was forgotten.

There were five hundred at the reception and probably almost that many in the church.

I loved my dress and veil. The dress was ivory satin with a fitted bodice, sweetheart neckline and three-quarter-length sleeves. Tiny, unpressed folds of satin started at the side waistline and extended into a full chapel train. The bouffant skirt made my waist looked tiny—and it really was, compared to my usual size. My veil was of handmade, imported Belgium lace, worn mantilla style, its fragile, delicate design fell all the way to the floor.

We gathered together in the narthex waiting for the signal to begin the march. Everything was ready and in order—the church glowed with candlelight in the winter twilight. My bridesmaids wore dark red velvet dresses with matching red velvet ribbons in their hair, and carried beautiful colonial bouquets of white roses and ivy. As the organ began the familiar strains of Lohengrin's wedding march, my heart pounded. My father turned and gave me a big smile, as I took his arm and began the long, slow walk down the aisle to the sanctuary. Dan stood there with his brother, George, as his best man, surrounded by college friends, roommates, and my brothers for his ushers. I could hardly believe it was actually happening; it was like the ultimate dream come true.

Our minister stood before us with the Episcopal wedding service in his hand. How short the actual service was! A dozen minutes that brought a man and woman together for a lifetime—the vows were simple: "to love, honor and obey, in sickness and in health, for richer or poorer, until death do us part." I firmly believed in every word of those vows and fully intended to love and cherish Dan forever. Our marriage was made in heaven, or so it seemed, as we stood side by side at the altar rail.

The faces of our guests were all a smiley, weepy blur, as we turned and walked quickly back down the aisle, while the organist triumphantly played Mendelssohn's wedding march for our recessional. Laughing and chattering away, we climbed into the waiting, black limousine for the long drive out to the club where our dinner reception would be held.

Once we arrived at the club, we had to pose for endless pictures of the wedding party, as well as formal pictures of both sides of the family, after which we stood in the receiving line for what seemed like hours. Just when I felt like I would collapse, we sat down for dinner.

We had fun cutting the cake and eating the first piece. Then, we moved out to the ballroom to waltz to the music of Strauss waltzes, and soon everyone joined us, as we spun round and round the dance floor. I remembered scenes of the Embassy Ball in *My Fair Lady,* and truly felt I could have danced all night.

But, all too soon, I threw my bouquet to the waiting bridesmaids, and we were off on our own. It was done! I was Mrs. Daniel Ford, Jr. for the rest of my life.

Only I wasn't, and that was the problem. The wedding announcement may have said my name was Ford, but inside I was still Camie Manuel, still unbelievably dependent upon my mother and father for my identity. I thought marriage was going to be a start of a new independent life of my own—and perhaps it would have been, had we suddenly moved to a far-distant city. But, instead, I talked to my mother every single day, and I did the calling, not the other way around, and I stopped by their house at least twice a week and often more. I was no more mature or independent than a fifteen-year-old schoolgirl—less, in fact; at boarding school we called home only when necessary.

6

Addicted to Approval

I squinted into the sun and could just make out the name carved in stone over the entrance: *Lamesa High School.* For years I had passed it almost daily as I drove by on North 14th Street, the widest and busiest thoroughfare in the small town of Lamesa. I had always admired the school's white brick facade and thought that the complex with its auditorium, library, and large football stadium was most impressive. Typical to West Texas, there were no trees or flower beds, just a neat square of sometimes green lawn; but to me it was wonderful, and I had long looked forward to the day when I would be a student there.

Now at last I was fourteen, and that day had finally come. Mother stopped the car, and I jumped out. "See you later," I called back over my shoulder, as I scanned the front steps to see if I knew any of the kids who were already gathering there. Dodging past a school bus, I was glad that I didn't have to ride one of those anymore. A bus had come right by our front door, but I always managed to miss it, so that I could be driven to school. Now I walked quickly past the long row of sharp and not so sharp-looking cars, where the boys sat waiting for the last bell and calling out remarks to the girls as they walked by. Larry Phillips rolled down his window as I passed in front of his car. "Hey, Toothpicks, where you going in such a hurry?" I was too excited to bother even giving him a drop-dead look. It was the first day of school, and I was a freshman at last!

It was easy to spot the other freshmen. There seemed to be safety in numbers, so we huddled close together as we milled around on the front lawn, clutching brand-new zipper notebooks, and waiting nervously for the 8:20 bell to ring. Finally, it did. "There it goes!" someone yelled, as the front doors swung open, and I was part of the laughing, pushing crowd surging into the building. I wondered where my homeroom was. The building seemed huge and totally unfamiliar, and I didn't see a single face I knew, but instead of feeling scared, I felt tremendously excited. There must have been 600 students or more!

"This is going to be great!" I told myself. It was a chance for a fresh start, and I couldn't wait to get involved. From that very first day, I was determined to succeed, which to me meant doing everything my sister had done five years before. She had been a good student, a class officer, was elected Pioneer Queen, and had been well liked and respected by both students and teachers. I looked up to Barbara and wanted to be like her–no, it was more than that; I wanted to surpass her.

"Answer the roll, please," Mrs. Thompson, the English teacher, began the second period. "Atkins?"

"Here."

"Bailey?"

"Barrow?"

"Here."

Mrs. Thompson looked up and smiled. "Oh, yes, you must be Barbara's little sister. Well, I hope you're as good a student as she was."

I smiled back and said to myself: Anything she could do, I can do better. "Oh, yes, Mrs. Thompson," I said sweetly out loud, "I certainly do hope so."

The first place for me to get established would be in the student publications. In her senior year, Barbara had become editor of the school newspaper, the *Tornado Times,* but I had already decided to compete as a part of its rival–the yearbook staff. Only two freshmen were needed on the annual, and I had worked hard all summer to make sure that I would be one of the two selected. "Listen, Maureen," I had told an upperclassman friend, "I will just *die* if I don't make the annual staff. I've always wanted to be on it; it's so much better than that dinky newspaper! I know that they select the new members by vote. Anything you can do, I will *always* appreciate!" Maureen had been a big help, and I was pleased when I learned that my good friend Susan and I were the new freshman editors. I liked Susan, and besides, I thought it should not be too difficult to beat her for editor-in-chief four years hence.

I had also been thinking about the class officer elections for weeks, but I didn't want anyone to know it. I didn't really think I had much chance of being elected a freshman class officer, but that didn't stop me from desperately wanting to be. On Friday, at activity period I stopped at my locker on the way to the class meeting in the gym. My hands felt cold and clammy, and I had a nervous feeling in the pit of my stomach. "Save me a seat," I called to Martha. "I'll be there in a minute." Putting my books away would give me a few extra moments to pull myself together, for modesty demanded that I appear to be unconcerned about the election.

"What if I'm not even nominated?" I whispered to myself. My past experience was not too good; after all, being secretary of the Good Citizenship Club in my eighth grade homeroom was hardly in the same league with a real class office. But if I *could* make it, I would know that I really was acceptable—acceptable to the other kids and acceptable to myself. It would mean far more to me than just a nice honor; it would prove that I really was who I wanted so badly to be. As I headed for the bleachers, I tried to look cool and casual, hoping that no one guessed that my life practically depended on this stupid election.

Squeezing into the seat next to Martha, I bit my nails as Mr. Ingram, the class sponsor, called the meeting to order and asked for nominations from the floor for the office of president. A hand waved from the back row, "I nominate David Wilson."

"Who would nominate that birdbrain for president?" I wondered.

The next nomination came quickly. "Jimmy Cox." Unfortunately Jimmy was smart—*and* popular.

"We've got to get some girls in there," Martha whispered, and suddenly her hand went up. "I nominate Sunny Barrow," I heard her saying beside me.

"Oh, no, now she's done it," I wished that she had waited. Maybe I could have had a chance for secretary or treasurer, but girls were never elected president of anything. One more nomination, and they were over; and then came the agony of waiting for the show of hands to determine the two with the most votes for the run-off. Keeping my head down, I tried not to look to the right or to the left, wishing somehow that the whole ordeal would pass quickly. Mr. Ingram was saying something, and then Martha poked me in the ribs.

"Get up," she said, "you're in the run-off!" Somehow I was on my feet, walking out of the room with Jimmy Cox, to wait in the hall while the next ballot was taken.

Smiling and trying to chat pleasantly with Jimmy was difficult, for we had been rivals for years. "It *would* have to be Jimmy," I groaned to myself. "Anybody but him; he's impossible to beat!" Our competition had begun with simple arithmetic board races in the third grade and continued on through to class standing in the eighth grade, where he'd had a 95.5 average to my 94.0.

We walked back inside just in time to hear Mr. Ingram announce, "Our new class president, Jimmy Cox!" Forcing a smile, I swallowed hard and blinked back tears. As I joined in the applause, I tried to look happy, but inside I was devastated. Maybe it was true, and I really was a nobody and could never measure up. I felt very sorry for myself and hated that smug Jimmy Cox.

Amazingly enough, it was possible to be on the bottom one minute and then in an instant forget the pain and humiliation of defeat and rise to the top again. All it took was another nomination, another run-off, and this time victory over Larry Phillips in the contest for class vice-president. Miraculously I felt good about myself again; I was someone after all! Walking down the hall later, I smiled at everyone and felt just a little superior. After all, there were only four class officers in a class of 225! That had to make me just a little special. And that evening, I could hardly wait to share the news with my mother. She smiled, and I could tell that she was very pleased. "Of course you'll make a good vice-president," she said, "but you'd have made a good president, too. And there's always next year."

For days I was soaring, but eventually I had to come

back down to earth again. Funny thing about approval—the fix wore off all too quickly. Once again I had to prove to myself that I was the much-better-than-average person that I knew myself to be. I was addicted to approval, and like a hard-core user, I could never get enough. My demand to be liked, looked up to, respected, and praised was insatiable; the more I got, the more I seemed to need. I *knew* that I was special, but I had to reassure myself over and over again that others knew it, too.

About six weeks later, Mrs. Thompson was handing out the term themes in Freshman English. I took mine and eagerly turned to the last page, where she always wrote special comments. Sure enough, the grade was what I had hoped for, A + over A. Then I read her handwritten note, and read it again and again: "Sunny, keep up the excellent work. This paper is beautifully done." There it was, in black and white: I do beautiful work; it says so right there on the paper.

But I already believed all the good things about myself, choosing to see myself as the mirrored reflection of what my peers, my teachers, and my circumstances said that I was. If people liked me, I was happy. If they voted for me, I was important. If they said I was smart, then I must be superior to other people. This helped me feel better for a while, but it was a shallow life, with short-lived benefits, and it always seemed in danger of collapsing around me at any moment. What if people didn't like me? What if I made an average grade on a test? What would become of me then?

During all this time, my sister Barbara was a ubiquitous presence all through high school. "Sunny, are you going to try out for the one-act play?" Susan asked me.

"Oh, no, I don't think I really want to. I was in a play once when I was in Junior High, and I didn't like it very much." The truth was that my sister had won the Best Actress award two years in a row at the area inter-scholastic contest, while I had played a very mediocre Mrs. Gundersen in my seventh grade acting debut and had never tried again.

When Mrs. O'Brien announced the oratorical contest and poetry reading try-outs, she asked me to stay a moment after class. "Sunny, I remember that your sister was so talented in speech; I hope you are going to try out."

"No, thanks, Mrs. O'Brien, my voice doesn't carry very well at all, and besides I'm really not very interested in that sort of thing." To me, it was no fun participating in anything if I could not excel. To be a part of things was not enough; I had to be the best. But in areas where I thought I could win, I went all out. It was especially gratifying to be selected by the faculty as the outstanding student in English and in Spanish, and listed in the school's "Who's Who" for two subjects in the same year; Barbara had never managed that. And because I knew that Barbara was highly skilled in shorthand, I worked hard to take faster and faster dictation, until I was one of the fastest in the class, and, I was quite sure, also faster than she.

Even with the pressure to succeed scholastically, high school was a lot of fun. I felt much more secure in my circle of friends than I had in years past. I felt that I had a place, and that I was important enough to keep that place in the group. Somehow it seemed that the open spitefulness and petty feuds of the preteen years had changed, and about ten of us girls remained close friends all during the four years at Lamesa High. There were slumber parties and long, involved telephone conversations, rehashing all the exciting events of the school day. "Sunny, will you *please* hang up that phone? You've been talking more than half an hour!"

"Just one more minute, Mother; this is really important. Okay, Linda, are you listening? And then he said. . . ."

Actually, there was just as much jealousy in our group as there had been in junior high school, only now we had learned more subtle and sophisticated ways of handling it. I was especially jealous of my best friend Peggy. Peggy was just one of those naturally sweet girls who never had an unkind word to say to or about anyone, and everyone just adored her. Try as I might, I was not naturally sweet; I often said unkind things, and thought them even more, and lots of people couldn't stand me at all. Sometimes it seemed that Peggy was just too good to be true. It was especially hard to be Peggy's best friend in November, around Homecoming time. Each year one of the home football games was chosen to be the Homecoming game. Theoretically it was the time for all LHS alumni to return to visit their alma mater; there was a big bonfire and a postgame reception, but those were all secondary motives. The real reason to have Homecoming, as any high school girl knew, was to elect a Homecoming Queen. Each class selected a girl as its nominee, and after an all-school vote, the senior candidate always won. Each year the selection for our class nominee was monotonously the same. Freshman queen candidate: Peggy Taylor. Next year, sophomore candidate, Peggy Taylor. And so on, until finally in her senior year, Peggy was duly crowned Homecoming Queen.

"Oh, Peggy, I'm so glad you've won!" I said publicly. But in private I was more real: "Susan, I just can't understand who keeps voting for Peggy anyway. I certainly never have!" Well, at least if I couldn't be the most popular girl in the school, it was nice to be her best friend.

With my future hopes of becoming Homecoming Queen obviously thwarted, I looked around for other possibilities. Pioneer Queen, Barbara's unforgettable moment as royalty, was no more, and there did not seem to be that many other opportunities. But the problem was solved when I was elected Sweetheart of the Lamesa chapter of the Future Farmers of America. Since Lamesa was chiefly an agricultural town, in the high school a large and active club of boys interested in all aspects of farming made up the FFA Chapter. As Sweetheart, I would represent the club at various functions and contests during the year. After checking back to see who had been FFA Sweetheart in past years, I was very pleased to find that they had all been popular girls, and although it might have been more prestigious to be Football or Basketball Sweetheart, this would do very nicely. It was fun to wear the special white corduroy jacket and the pretty locket with the FFA emblem, but taking part in the different contests during the year proved to be more difficult.

For months I had been dreading the FFA Queen Contest at the South Plains Fair in Lubbock, the really big town of 120,000 some sixty miles to the north. This fair was well known throughout the state, and thousands of people attended it every year. One girl would be chosen from the FFA groups in the area, and one from the 4H groups. There had been pictures in the paper of the contestants, and each one looked more poised and beautiful than the last. "Oh, this is going to be terrible," I worried. "I am definitely not beauty contest material." I considered coming down with a cold or spraining my ankle, but there was no escaping my responsibility to the Lamesa group. I would have to appear and hope that I would not disgrace myself by looking like a complete fool.

On the afternoon of the contest, about thirty of us

waited nervously behind the stage in the big drafty auditorium for our moment to walk slowly across the stage in front of the assembled judges. My mouth felt very dry as I took one last peek in the mirror and smoothed my bangs. I was glad that I had insisted that Mrs. McMullen take in the blue linen princess-style dress as tight as possible. It was a snug fit over my "waist cincher," a beauty aid which was designed to give everyone a 22" waist regardless of build or weight, and although it was a little hard to take a deep breath, it was well worth a few minutes of discomfort. Standing just behind the curtain, I watched the girl ahead of me as she walked smoothly to center stage, pivoted, and turned to smile graciously at the audience. "How can she do it so easily?" I marveled. I just hoped that I could remember my name. There! That was my signal to begin. A bit unsteady in the higher than usual heels, I felt my three petticoats, starched stiff with sugar, swing scratchily against my legs as I started across the stage. My heart was pounding so hard that I thought I might actually faint, but I seemed to be moving along fairly naturally. I looked out at the sea of faces, but they were all just a blur, and the lights were very bright. My gosh, that's a TV camera!

The master-of-ceremonies was handing me the mike, and I heard myself answering his questions. "Yes, my name is Sunny Barrow. . . . That's right, I'm from Lamesa. . . . Yes, it's very nice to be here, and I think it's a wonderful fair." The voice was mine, even though a trifle shrill. Hold on for a few more seconds, and it will all be over. When I reached backstage, my knees were shaking so badly that I had to sit down in the nearest chair to wait for the results to be announced. I didn't care who won now, as long as I hadn't fallen down or forgotten my own name.

But wait! What was the loudspeaker saying? "Third place: Sunny Barrow from Lamesa." Someone was motioning me forward. Third place! That's not too bad; at least it was in the running. And that evening I watched my brief moment of glory on the 6:00 news with my parents, and the more I thought about it, the more I was actually relieved. I didn't really want to pin ribbons on all the winners at the Fat Stock Show, and I certainly didn't want to wear the required costume of tight riding breeches, cowboy boots, and ten gallon hat–hardly my style or my shape. No, third place was just right.

Perhaps the reason that I got along so much better with my set of girlfriends in high school was that so much more of our attention was now being spent on boys. In junior high, I had been much aware of the opposite sex and who would be sitting by whom at the Palace Theater on Friday nights. But with high school came dating, and this presented a whole new set of problems. Some girls had started dating earlier, but my parents had insisted that I wait until the end of the ninth grade. Although I complained that they were too strict, secretly I was glad, because I didn't think nice girls should go out much earlier. And when permission was finally granted, I had a few dates with boys that I had known since the first grade, and who, newly licensed at fifteen, were barely tall enough to see over the steering wheels of their family cars. There was something definitely lacking; this couldn't be romance. Perhaps an "older man" would be different. And then one winter afternoon in the school library, I saw him. I had gone down during study hall to sit at the big round table and use the reference books to complete my term paper on Robert E. Lee. I always spent a lot of time on term themes; they were my specialty. "I think I'll call it 'The Gray Knight,' " I mused.

And then all thoughts of General Lee vanished, as I glanced across at a group of upperclassmen at the next table. He was with them–very tall and lanky, and he was wearing a black and gold letter jacket. Hm, probably basketball, I decided. Someone at the table said something funny, and he looked up and smiled. It was the nicest smile that I had ever seen, and I put down my pencil and observed him as long as I dared. I was almost fifteen, and he must have been at least seventeen, probably either a junior or a senior. I wondered what he was studying. He certainly was taking lots of notes–h'm, right-handed. As I watched, I could see that there was a gentleness about him that was different from most of the boys I knew, and I wondered who he was, and why I had never seen him before, and how I would ever get him to notice me.

My devotion to library work increased dramatically over the next few days, and I was in the same spot every afternoon, flipping through thick volumes and keeping one eye surreptitiously on the door. On the fourth day my vigilance was rewarded, when the same group of boys returned to the library, but unfortunately he never seemed to notice me at all. Undaunted, I continued in my campaign to find out all about him. "Listen, Susan, I have met–well, not actually met–anyway, I've seen this boy. From last year's yearbook, I found out his name is Bud, and he plays basketball. Also, he was the Junior Favorite, and Maureen told me that he is sure to run for Student Body officer in the spring. And listen to the best part: he doesn't have a steady girl! Maureen says he is very shy! What? Well, no, he doesn't actually know me–*yet!*" The possibility of an upperclassman was definitely intriguing, but first I would have to get his attention.

My luck held–a perfect, tailor-made opportunity

soon presented itself in the form of the May end-of-school picnic. Plans were already being made by the yearbook staff for this annual event. The rugged setting of Mullens Ranch was the site each year for a wiener roast, and each of the staff members would be inviting a friend.

"Susan, what do you think? It's the perfect chance, but do you think I should ask him to go with me, even if I've never had a date with him? What if he says no? Or what if he thinks I'm forward?" There were a million pros and cons to consider, and my work on the yearbook suffered, as I wavered back and forth for days and held endless discussions with my friends in the yearbook office.

One day Miss Speck, our faculty advisor, stopped by my desk in the middle of my dialogue and listened for a moment. "Sunny, by all means ask him and please get it over with, so that we can get some work done around here! Don't forget, we have deadlines to meet!" With this unofficial blessing, my mind was made up to issue the invitation. But when and where should I do it?

It seemed best to proceed as quickly as possible, and I decided to encounter him on neutral ground, the library, of course. By now, I knew his schedule as well as my own, and Thursday afternoons he always came promptly at 2:30 to spend an hour doing reference work. I was in my usual spot fifteen minutes early, and I had brought Susan along to lend moral support. I had rehearsed my speech some dozen or more times, and Susan was tiring. "Just relax, Sunny, and ask him naturally." Naturally! Fine for her to say; she didn't have to do it! The big clock on the wall showed 2:30, and sure enough I could see Bud coming in the door with Billy, his best friend and inseparable companion. Leaving

Susan, who was grinning broadly, I strolled casually toward the check-out desk, just happening to pass by Bud's table en route.

"Oh, hi," I said, feigning surprise at seeing him there, "Excuse me, but do you happen to have Volume XI of the *Readers' Guide to Periodical Literature?* No? Well, thanks very much anyway. Listen, I'm not sure we've met. I'm Sunny Barrow; I'm a freshman. Oh, you knew that? Really? Listen, my friend Susan," and I nodded in her direction; I might as well get her involved, too, I thought, "and I were wondering if you and Billy would like to go to the Annual Staff Picnic on the 14th? You would? Really? That's great!" Mrs. Hudson, the librarian, cleared her throat and frowned pointedly in our direction. "I've got to go now! See you around."

Susan followed me to the hall, where we dissolved in laughter as soon as we were out of sight. "Well, what did he say?" she demanded.

"I can't believe it; he actually knew my name! And he said yes, he'd like to go to the picnic! I just can't get over it! Oh, and by the way, I hope you won't mind going with Billy!"

"What? You want me to go with Billy? What if he turns out to be a creep? Oh, well, anything for a friend, I suppose, but you owe me one."

After weeks of anticipation, May 14 arrived, a perfect mild spring day. And there we were, driving along in Billy's family's sedan, on our way to Mullens Ranch. "Well, Maureen was right about one thing," I thought. "Bud certainly isn't the talkative type." But Susan and I talked enough for all four of us, and whenever the conversation lagged, we filled the silence with giggles.

For about an hour we drove south down U.S. 80, then turned off on a dirt road for another twenty mintues or so. And then suddenly the canyon was before us, and no matter how many times I had seen it, I was always surprised and moved. The flat fields dropped away, and almost like magic, the canyon appeared out of nowhere, snaking its way across the level plain. Bud got out to open a gate marked "Mullens R. No Trespassing," and we drove on into the breaks, as the rough pastureland on the edge of the Caprock was called. This was where the high plains of West Texas (the Llano Estacado, as Coronado had called it) drop sharply to the east, forming a rough terrain with jagged rocks and ledges where scruffy little bushes cling perilously to the steep-sided hills. The winding road down into the canyon was bumpy, but Billy was driving slowly and wasn't showing off or anything, so we could relax and have a really good time. The radio was playing a ballad and the late afternoon sun was low enough to be warm, but not hot. We had the windows down a little, not so far that it would blow Susan's and my hair. Bud leaned back in his corner of the seat and looked out the window, and whenever someone made a joke or said something funny, he would smile that beautiful smile.

"There they are, just ahead," Susan said, and as we pulled up alongside the other cars, we could hear the shouts and laughter of a fast game of softball.

"Come on, we need a third baseman," someone called to Bud, and he was soon in the thick of the game, while I (the non-athletic type) preferred to sit on the sidelines and watch. After the boys had won a resounding victory over the girls, there was time for a little exploring before the campfire was ready, and we strolled hand in hand down one of the smaller canyons.

"Just look at those steep walls," I pointed ahead, "and do you see that cave over there in the shadows?"

"Better watch out for rattlesnakes and coyotes," Bud said with a straight face, and I shivered and stopped in my tracks.

"It's getting late; we'd better get back now." Maybe Bud was teasing, and maybe he wasn't; but I didn't intend to see any kind of wildlife whatsoever.

But any fears had vanished later when, long after the sun had set, we gathered around the glowing fire, toasting marshmallows, enjoying the softness of the May evening, and watching the moon rise. And later, after I had been dropped home, I lay wide awake in bed, thinking about how special it had been and hoping that I had not giggled too much and that Bud would call me again.

He did; that summer was a marvelous summer of American Legion baseball games, watermelon feasts, and games at our kitchen table. By July we were going steady, and in spite of my parents' protests that I was much too young to go with just one boy, I was proudly wearing his class ring on a chain around my neck. I knew what I wanted, and Bud was *exactly* that. In the fall, I loved going to the football games wearing a big golden mum decorated with his number 85 and black and gold streamers. He was a senior, and I was a sophomore, and it was fun to be included in so many of the upper-class activities.

On Sunday afternoons we usually went for a drive around Lamesa in his slightly battered pick-up. My favorite part of town was Park Terrace, where the nicest houses were. "Oh, look at that house, Bud! Someday I'm going to have a house just like that one. Do you like the green shutters?"

Often we talked about the future. "Of course, you know that I am going to go to college. I would never get married, until I had my college degree. My mother would have a fit, and besides I want to finish school first. It's really important to me."

Bud wanted to be a farmer, like his father and mine. "Oh, Bud, why would anybody want to farm? I hate farming!" Oh, well, there was still time to change his mind about that.

All too soon, it was time for Bud to graduate. "Of course I want to keep going steady, Bud. Who wants to go out with any of those silly high school boys anyway? And besides you'll still be around to go to almost everything." The question of Bud and college had caused plenty of arguments between us.

"Sunny, I just can't see why I need to go to college. How will that help my farming? And you know how I feel about writing term papers and all that kind of thing. The whole idea is ridiculous. I want to start farming now!" Bud was determined, but I was adamant.

"Listen, Bud, even if you do plan to farm, you still need to get a college degree. I can't imagine not getting one, and I should think you would want to be there too. Besides I just couldn't marry someone who didn't have a college degree!"

Finally we agreed on some sort of compromise. Bud would farm for two years while I finished high school, and then we would both enroll in Texas Tech the same year. It seemed like the perfect solution. It meant that we could still go steady, and I would have a date to almost everything in Lamesa, and he could get started in the farming that he loved. Besides, I reminded myself, if he went on to college this year, and I wasn't there, he might meet someone there that he liked better than me! No, I wanted him to stay around, for in many ways he had become my security, and he seemed to be the answer to all my dreams. Nice looking, respectable background, stable and dependable temperament–who could want more? We were beginning to make plans for the future, even though the future would be many years away.

For all my parents' protests that I was too young to be so serious about one boy, I knew that they liked Bud very much. This meant a great deal to me, because most of the time I tried to do the things that they approved of, at least outwardly. But even as much as I wanted their approval, there were times when my very willful nature showed through, often in the area of food and meals. "Hey, Mother, what's for supper? I'm starving!" I threw my books down on the living room sofa and headed straight for the kitchen, where Mother was standing at the sink peeling potatoes.

"Black-eyed peas, mashed potatoes, and cornbread," she answered, wiping her hands on her apron and smiling.

"Oh, no, not again! You know how I hate black-eyed peas, and we had them just the other day! I think I'll take the car and go into town and have a sandwich at the drive-in."

"But, Sunny, your father's going to be home in an hour, and we–"

I cut her off. "You can't expect me to eat black-eyed peas again!" Starting for the door, I checked my purse and found just 25 cents "Oh, do you have any change?"

With a sigh of resignation, Mother turned back to the stove. "Look on my bureau," she said quietly, "and don't be gone too long."

The culmination of four years of proving that I could make it came in May of my senior year. For weeks we had been waiting for the arrival of the yearbooks, and as editor-in-chief, I was especially eager to see them. To be honest, I knew that there had been better yearbooks, but we did have some exciting additions. This edition was special because it was "mine." I had pushed for the first color photograph ever, and the senior ring on the cover had been beautifully engraved. The yearbooks were going to be given to the school on Presentation Day, and we had worked hard decorating the gym and setting the stage for the big event. It was really the highlight of the year for me, and I felt a sense of accomplishment and pride as I opened the yearbook and turned to the senior class achievements listed beside our pictures. The picture of me wasn't too good, but I looked over the list of activities and awards with satisfaction. Freshman Class Vice-President, Student Council, National Honor Society. . . it was a list I could be proud of, and comparing it with some of the others, I felt good about myself. I had met the goals I had set; in my eyes I was a success. Who cares if I never was a cheerleader? Surely someone who had been elected Secretary of the Senior Class must be important. And when the favorites were announced (winners of the all-school popularity contest), and I had been voted Most Valuable Senior Girl, I was on top of the world. I am valuable; that proves it! In fact, I am the *most* valuable. I am special, someone who matters! But if I *really* was, why did I so often doubt it and have to reprove it?

After the high of Presentation Day, graduation was almost anticlimactic. Solemn in our black robes and mortarboards, we lined up waiting for the signal to march inside. It was hard to believe that I was really graduating at last. So, why didn't I feel more excited? Maybe when I got this speech over with, I'd enjoy it more. My delight at coming in first in our class (ahead of Jimmy Cox!) was slightly diminished by the fact that I would be making the valedictory address, and try as hard as I might, I had not been able to write a speech that I felt would be good enough. Even my topic, "gratitude to our Parents," sounded ordinary and mediocre. I had spent days crying over it, but now it was just going to have to do. Oh, well, I was not going to let this moment of triumph be spoiled. And I walked firmly to the lectern, which I held onto with both hands so that no one could see them shaking. I remembered to speak slowly and distinctly as I tried to spot my parents and Bud in the back of the large auditorium, and when it was over, I thought I got perhaps five or ten seconds more applause than politeness dictated. All in all, it was a night to remember; I was first in the class! First–exactly where I had always wanted to be. First–Jimmy Cox was second, for once, and even my sister Barbara had only been third in her class. First, ahead of them all! Well, I was going to enjoy this night, the last night of a part of my life that had seemed to be everything that I had wanted it to be.

7

And Baby Makes Three

Tradition holds that a girl is a bride for a year, and I loved every minute of 1960. I enjoyed keeping house in our beautiful home with handsome wedding presents adorning every room. I loved cooking for two in our cozy, little kitchen and entertaining our friends and family. It was such a treat to serve dinner on elegant china, to drink from sparkling crystal, at a candlelit table set with fine linen and sterling silver. I looked forward to every opportunity to show off what a good homemaker I was. All the years of playing house as a little girl and watching my mother were now becoming real-life experiences. We had enough money to do what we wanted, so there were no clouds at all on my horizon. For company we had a pair of parakeets, and then we went to the pound and found an adorable taffy-colored spaniel puppy who became my constant companion.

The only question I had to decide each day was how to fill the hours from 8:00 in the morning when Dan left for work, till 6:00, when he returned. What did I *want* to do? I really didn't know. Cleaning our house took no time at all; besides my mother-in-law's cleaning lady came in one day a week to help so I was quite free to pursue any path I chose. I couldn't stand being bored and so immediately began looking around in several different directions. Here again, Mother had some suggestions about the proper path for a young married girl in Cleveland, and just as with the wedding, I depended heavily on her guidance.

There was the garden club, for instance: my mother and mother-in-law were both involved in gardening and were extremely knowledgeable and gifted with flower arranging, and encouraged me to join them–though they belonged to rival clubs. But I really didn't want to; garden club meetings were mostly for ladies over sixty, who loved to talk about their roses. Nevertheless, Mother kept saying things like, "If you don't join now, you'll never learn anything," or "Now's the time to join, when you aren't so busy with children." I started to weaken; in my heart, I knew that anyone who was anybody belongs. So I finally succumbed and joined. Not knowing a daisy from an aster, I signed up for every course available. I did not want to embarrass my mother, and found, much to my surprise, that I learned a lot and had a delightful time, too.

Then came the next step: the Junior League. Once more, Mother took charge. One of her best friends proposed me for membership, and five or so others wrote letters of recommendation. After being carefully considered by the admissions committee, I was invited to become a provisional member of the Cleveland Junior League. The League was a highly esteemed organization, and I was very honored. Its members worked hard in areas all over Cleveland, in every kind of volunteer job available, at hospitals, as tutors in city schools, as tour guides in museums, as caring friends and teachers to visiting foreign doctors and their wives, and so on. There were also tremendous fund-raising projects, like the Fall Fashion Show, and the city benefited greatly from all the time given to so many organizations. Being a member of the League was an excellent way to meet many girls my age or a little older, and to make new friends beyond the group I had gone to school with. I would remain active for many years and gladly served on many League Committees, including the all-important admissions committee.

In addition to my involvement in the garden club and the Junior League, I also became an active member of the Women's Board of Rainbow Children's Hospital that Dan's mother and sister, Amanda, were deeply committed to. There was no doubt in my mind that I would follow in their footsteps, and I was proud to be a part of one of the finest hospitals in the country. Then, too, my own mother cared very much about the Day Nursery Association of Cleveland, and one day-care center in particular—the Wade Day Nursery, located in one of our inner-city neighborhoods. Well, I would certainly want to be part of this worthwhile organization, so I joined Mother in the activities of the day-care center.

Each one of these committees, boards or clubs met at least once a month, and in an effort to have some variety, I met weekly for lunch and bridge with a group of girls who were also newly married. We had a wonderful time fixing yummy lunches with delicious desserts, gossiping away the afternoon. We started with four girls and increased to eight, and met without fail on Thursday afternoons for many years. My college alumnae also met once a month, as did my young adults' church group. Then, too, as a provisional member of the League, I had a training course to take, along with a weekly volunteer job at the hospital. Before I realized what had happened, I had something scheduled for every single day of the month, a schedule which would remain unbroken for the next fifteen years, and which, instead of fulfilling me, made me more than ever obsessed with becoming a success.

It was more important to have people's approval than to have them like me, but I very much wanted them to like me, too. Some did; others didn't, because I was an awful snob and know-it-all. That was a laugh; I really didn't know much of anything and felt insecure most of the time. But I tried to cover up that weak side, to hide my insecurity by clinging to my group of girlfriends. So I said "yes" to every invitation to join a club, whether I wanted to or not. To say "no" might bring disapproval, which I could not bear.

There were a couple of areas where I finally did put my foot down and said a shaky "no." Mother belonged to a women's club downtown called The Intown Club. As a child, I could remember Mother and me dressing up, complete with hat and gloves, to go downtown to lunch. A gourmet lunch was served buffet style, but the elegant dining room was filled with well-dressed, carefully coiffed, older ladies. The club sponsored interesting speakers every Monday afternoon after lunch, and while I enjoyed being a guest occasionally, I did not want to join the club.

There were also Thursday evenings at the symphony. Everybody who counted had season subscriptions to Cleveland's famous symphony orchestra, under the baton of George Szell. Dan's parents often went, and we would join them or be given tickets of our own. No sooner would the house lights lower at 8:30, than my eyelids would lower with them. I would awaken with a start, and embarrassed, would sneak a peek at Dan, only to find him fast asleep, too. We were just not meant to be patrons of the orchestra.

In between all these social engagements and meetings, I needed to learn how to cook. I had never cooked a meal before we were married, because our family always had a cook, and I just hadn't wanted to be bothered. But, now, I felt very inadequate and realized how much I had to learn. A few months before our marriage, my friend Susan and I had enrolled in a night-school cooking class to learn the basics, so that we wouldn't starve to death. We drove down to a high school near the innercity to learn how to make biscuits, pie crust, gravy and other necessities. I will never forget our first meal in our new home. We postponed it as long as we could, by going out to eat—at my parents' house, at Dan's parents' house, at his sister's house, at his brother's house. Then in the nick of time, a friend got married, which meant a whole round of wedding parties as well as holiday parties to attend during the Christmas season.

Finally, however, the night arrived when we had no invitation out, and I was forced to cook our supper. I had decided on a very uncomplicated menu: broiled lamb chops, baked potatoes, brown-and-serve rolls and Stouffer's spinach souffle. Everything went fine, until I burned myself taking the souffle out of the oven and with a cry of pain, dropped the dish inside, so that spinach spilled everywhere, sticking and burning all over the inside of the oven! I burst into tears.

Things did not improve much, at first. The first night my in-laws came to dinner was a disaster. After carefully setting the table with our best china and silver, I had spent anxious hours deciding what to eat, based on what I was able to cook. Lamb roast was safe, because I couldn't overcook it. All the preparations went smoothly, and I forgot only one thing: to turn on the oven. It wasn't until I went out to the kitchen to replenish the hors d'oeuvres, that I discovered my hideous mistake. We had a very long cocktail hour that evening. The Fords were very gracious and chatted away, but inside I was a wreck. I had ruined the evening, just when I was determined to show them what a good cook I was, especially after learning that Dan's sister was a gourmet cook.

But gradually I did learn, and food could now be important to me as a means of earning praise, not for comfort, as it had been in the past. At boarding school, we had lived to eat; at college, we ate to live–and usually on the run. I was no longer eating primarily to feel better. My weight settled down to around 135 pounds, and I really didn't pay that much attention to the scales or bother to weigh myself. I had been quite happy in college and had actually felt more secure there than before. And marriage made me even more relaxed and at ease about weight. As time went by, I found I enjoyed my own cooking and gained back a few of the pounds I had lost over the wedding. But I wasn't the least concerned–at that point.

What did concern me, however, was our first Christmas. We had been married a month, and I wanted to begin our own traditions, to celebrate Christmas our way. But what was supposed to be a joy, turned out to be an unbroken trauma. It is amazing how deeply people are committed to the Christmas traditions which they were brought up with. I wanted the biggest, bushiest, fattest tree we could find, and Dan said that was ridiculous, and before the day was over, I was in tears on the phone to my mother. My idea of a happy Christmas was to spend most of the day with my family, as we opened lots of gifts, ate a huge turkey dinner and relaxed in front of the fire. I had totally forgotten that there was now another set of parents, Dan's, plus his brother and sister who wanted to see us, too.

And so, we began a tradition of alternating going to his parents' house and mine for the holiday dinner. It seems impossible now, that we could have maintained that hectic schedule, year in and year out, and kept it up with three children, but we did. After a while, I felt very torn about the situation. Part of me wanted to stay home and celebrate our own Christmas quietly, but the child in me did not want to miss one moment of time with my parents and many aunts, uncles, and cousins. Christmas to me meant visiting *all* your close relatives. And Sundays were often like miniature Christmases, with visits to both sets of grandparents.

Dan and I really did not know each other very well when we married. Our engagement had lasted five months, during which time we saw each other constantly, but it was always for lunch, dinner or a party—never for just a quiet evening, sitting at home. I didn't know what to do, and began to fill the time with watching TV every evening, or if the television selections were dull, I would read the latest best-selling novel. Dan never liked television and always brought a lot of work home at night, poring over it at his large desk in the den. The evening would pass with our scarcely speaking to each other, each of us going our separate way.

Having children was a part of the successful wife scenario, so having a baby was exactly what I wanted to do next. I became pregnant in September, 1960, and enjoyed every minute of the nine months. I couldn't wait to start wearing maternity clothes. I was so happy to be pregnant that I gained twenty-five pounds during the nine months. At that time, it seemed normal and natural to gain—all part of having a baby. Elise Meyer Ford—Liza—arrived almost on schedule, June 8, 1961. We were thrilled to have our little girl born healthy and beautiful, but oh my goodness, what on earth was I going to do with this squirming, crying baby? I had never done any baby-sitting for little children and had not the first idea of how to be a mother. I was terrified that I would drop her, or that she would spit up or mess her diapers—I had never changed a diaper.

Fortunately, we had a baby nurse waiting for us, when I returned home from the hospital carrying this pink-and-white bundle. We had fixed up the nursery in colors of aqua and cream, with a new crib, bureau, changing table and an old rocking chair that had been in my family for generations. I had a lot to learn about schedules, no sleep at night, baths and diapers. The nurse was very patient with me, but the day came when it was time for her to leave, and I was faced with taking care of Liza alone.

Dan was just as inexperienced at child care as I was, but he was a real help in the evenings, when he came home from work, doing dishes and tidying up. I was so exhausted that I usually slept in the morning after the 5 or 6 A.M. feeding, so we had even less time together, but I was too tired to care. Thank heavens the weather was warm and sunny that June and July! I could put Liza outside for her nap in her carriage with Toffee, our dog, to guard her, and that way I could lie down and take an afternoon nap, too. I think, as I look back, I was more exhausted emotionally than physically, with this new pressure of having to be the perfect mother, as well as the perfect wife.

Liza had her fussy time of day between 6:00 P.M. and

10:00 P.M. just when her daddy came home from work. In our neighborhood, the houses were small and close together, and I worried that her crying would disturb our neighbors, so we would put Liza in her Port-a-crib in the back seat of the car with the dog, and off we would go to drive around, until she went to sleep. One evening she cried for almost an hour without stopping, while we tried to entertain guests for dinner and bridge. Our foot-loose and fancy-free life-style was drastically curtailed by the arrival of a baby.

Liza was six months old at the time of our third Christmas. She had just begun sitting up alone, and she loved to watch the sparkling ornaments and twinkling lights of the tree (which was a little taller and a little bushier this year). I took her everywhere, to show her off to family and friends. The grandparents were always happy to have us visit. I went over to my parents' house all the time now, just for a change of scene and to have someone to talk to. I always felt at home and relaxed there, and I discussed everything with my mother–in fact, I used my parents for companionship, instead of my husband. I would talk to Mother for so long that, by the time Dan came home, I was talked out, and all I wanted to do was read or watch TV.

It was about this period that I began to be jealous of the amount of time Dan spent on business and office work, instead of on me. Of course, I myself was all wrapped up in our child, but now she was on a good schedule, and my evenings were free. But we had both gotten into such a rut of each doing our own thing, that we had forgotten how to communicate with each other–if we ever really knew. Then, too, we both had such strong feelings of pride that we would easily get hurt and take out our anger on each other. Dan would retreat to the den and his work, and I to bed. We never talked at all anymore, and certainly not about what was going on inside of us–we didn't even know how.

During that summer that Liza turned one and began walking, we were asked by my aunt and uncle if we would like to house-sit for them, while they took a long vacation. We were delighted at the prospect of spending a month in their beautiful house in Gates Mills to see what semi-country living would be like. Their house was a rambling, charming old home, nestled in the woods and surrounded by fields of wild flowers. It was so quiet and peaceful away from the noise of cars, neighbors, and other city sounds, that I had taken a leave of absence from most of my many activities. The long, lazy days of August were twice as restful in a country atmosphere.

We entertained a great deal, spending delightful evenings on the patio, watching the sun set behind the woods. It was the last truly restful time that I would have for many, many years.

It was during that month in the country that I first noticed that I seemed to be a few pounds lighter. My skirts and summer shorts seemed to be a little bit loose in the waist, and then one evening, my bridge group remarked that I looked thinner, and that it was becoming to me. Well, isn't that nice to hear, especially after having a baby! Maybe it wouldn't hurt to lose a few more pounds. The change in scenery helped to keep life from being boring, and I wasn't paying so much attention to food, because I was so busy enjoying our new life-style. I liked living in Gates Mills, just minutes away from the club, and I liked the house with its long, winding drive through the trees. With all these lovely surroundings, food was not so important.

When we returned to Shaker Heights, it was

September, 1962, and all the fall activities picked up again. My weight continued to drop slowly, as I once again became involved in my endless round of social duties. I definitely liked being a few pounds thinner, especially with all the compliments that came my way. I was an active member of the Junior League now, and eligible to model in their annual fashion show. I began to have my picture taken for different organizations for newspaper or program publicity, I loved to wear the beautiful designer clothes.

It was just about Christmastime that I discovered that I was pregnant again, and would have our second child in August. We had certainly wanted more children, so we were delighted with the new baby on the way–except that now I definitely did not want to gain twenty-five pounds. I watched what I ate at every meal and was especially careful the week I was due to see the doctor and step on that big, gray balance scale. In fact, I usually ate nothing for two days before my appointment. The doctor never said anything about my being too thin, and actually in those days, doctors were much stricter about limiting the number of pounds that could be gained during pregnancy.

As soon as the weather turned warm in the Spring, I was out on the golf course, ready for exercise. I was a terrible golfer and much too embarrassed to have a caddie, so I always pulled my clubs around on one of those handcarts. I'm sure all the walking was good exercise, but what I was primarily concerned with was keeping my weight down. I did, all right–I gained only 7 1/2 pounds during the entire nine months. I was quite proud of that, never thinking that my nutrition, or lack of it, could affect the baby's nutrition, and that if I didn't eat properly, then the baby would be deprived of the nourishment it needed while growing. All I cared about was staying thin.

Alexandra Corlett Ford arrived Saturday, August 17, 1963. We were not the least disappointed to have another girl, quite the contrary; I loved girls and thought the two would have such fun together growing up. I felt much better physically after Lexa was born, even though she and Liza had weighed almost the same–a little over seven pounds. Subtracting Lexa's weight, I had actually lost a pound during pregnancy.

After Liza was born, I had eaten everything in sight. But now, after Lexa, I drank lots of liquids, because I was nursing, but I did not indulge in anything rich or gooey, chocolate or otherwise. My new, thinner figure had become far more important than eating goodies. I liked the way I looked and felt, and just because I had a new baby, did not mean I was going to stay home and stuff myself. I had better things to do and think about.

We had engaged a baby nurse for a month, and then I had lined up baby-sitters to help, so I could get out and go to all my meetings and luncheons. To be really on top, I thought, a woman should come back quickly from pregnancy, and look even better than before, and that meant–thin!

During this last pregnancy, I'd had trouble with phlebitis in my right leg, an inflamation that often occurs in women who have varicose veins, as I did. My doctor suggested it would be best to have my leg stripped of the veins giving me all the trouble, but I decided to wait until summertime, because we had exciting things happening in our family that winter.

My older brother, David, announced his engagement to a beautiful girl from New York City. He had met her at West Chop on Martha's Vineyard, visiting Cleveland friends, and then taken her out in New York, while working as an editor for Doubleday. I liked Barbara immediately upon meeting her, when we went to New York for their engagement party. She was one year older, had gone to boarding school in Connecticut, graduated from Smith College, and was acting director of admissions at Finch College. I hoped we would become good friends, and we did. Barbara and David asked Dan and me to be in their wedding. We were thrilled to accept and looked forward to the April date.

What a happy and exciting time that was–going to New York City for all the festivities. There were luncheons, a rehearsal dinner-dance that my parents gave at the River Club, and then the wedding at St. James Episcopal Church and reception at the Colony Club. For those events, I had gotten my weight down to 114 and thought I looked smashing, although my mother made sure I heard that my Long Island uncles were shocked at how thin I was. In fact, so strong was their reaction that for a while I did let up. Eating out in New York was such a treat, I decided not to diet and splurge. I could starve myself when I got home again, but not while we lunched at the 21 Club! The morning of the wedding, I had my hair done at Elizabeth Arden's. I watched all the elegant New York women eating yogurt while they sat under the dryer. I didn't like yogurt, and didn't know how to tip the waitress who brought the pink tray and napkin. But, I did love my hairdo and thought it worth every penny just spending a few hours in such a glamorous place.

The wedding took place in the hushed splendor of St. James. We bridesmaids all looked stunning, I thought, but Barbara was positively regal, coming down the aisle. I was so happy for David, but jealous, too, of all the attention he was receiving. I had been well ahead, but now my number one competitor was gaining on me fast, by marrying such an outstanding girl. Well, I was still in the lead; I had produced the first grandchildren!

That June of 1964, I checked into the hospital to have my leg operated on. I was nervous and fearful, because I really did not know what to expect and how much pain there would be, even though the doctor had explained the procedure. My mother spent the day with me after surgery, for which I was awfully grateful, as I was feeling very sick. Before the operation, I weighed in at 112 pounds. Again, no one said a word to me about being too thin, but I made sure I weighed each morning, before I would allow myself to nibble on the brownies and cookies my friends brought to me.

It was about this time that my diet became a full-blown obsession. Up until now, I thought I was just being cautious; with a pregnancy, a wedding in the family, more modeling to do–I was just taking care of myself and being sensible. But now things had gotten out of control. I had reached the stage where I felt guilty if I overate or overindulged myself. I became more and more disgusted with my lack of self-control and self-discipline. I would never have termed it an obsession, of course; I just saw myself as needing to be more disciplined, not so lax. But I had already crossed over that thin line between dieting severely and self-induced starvation. My thinking became disoriented, and I continued to see myself with bulges and places where I needed to slim down. At 112 pounds on a 5'8" frame, I was literally skin and bones. Other physical changes began to show up. My periods became irregular and finally stopped. My hands and feet were always cold, regardless of the temperature outside. My blood pressure dropped abnormally low, and I no longer had any energy–by evening I was invariably exhausted. But I was much too busy to notice.

Sunny

8

The Price of Perfection

The campus certainly didn't look very friendly, I thought, as my father turned off College Boulevard, and we passed through the stone gates marked Texas Technological College. As we drove toward the red-tiled buildings, which sprawled on 160 acres of flat, treeless grounds, I wondered again if I had made the right choice of a college. There had never been any real discussion about it. Mother and Barbara had both gone to Texas Tech, and I had always assumed that I would go there too. Besides, it was close to Lamesa–only sixty miles away, close enough to go home on weekends.

Daddy carefully parked in front of the three-storied brick dorm, and we sat for a moment, watching the steady stream of freshman girls, assisted by parents and boyfriends, carrying in all the paraphernalia needed for nine months of higher education. The back seat of the car was overflowing with dresses and blouses on hangers, new luggage that I had received for graduation, giant wastebasket, and portable hair dryer, while I was squeezed between my parents in the front. I took a deep breath. "Well, here we are at Drane Hall," I announced brightly. "I guess I might as well get settled in."

We got out, Mother and Daddy both grabbed an armful, and before long all my appropriate earthly possessions were stacked in the middle of Room 206. I was its first occupant, and the room looked very empty. Testing first one bare mattress and then the other, I made my selection. "I think I'll sleep here, and I like this closet best," I said, mainly to myself, as I looked into the musty space. "I can't wait to see who my roommate is. Maybe she'll be here before too long." Remembering my parents, I smiled at them. Now that I was in, I was eager for them to leave.

Still, it was going to be hard to see them go, and waiting just made it harder not to cry. "Thanks for everything! Mother, be sure to write, and I'll be home next weekend." And I waved them out the door quickly, hoping they had not detected the quaver in my voice. Standing at the window, I watched the car drive away and wondered what to do next.

Suddenly I felt very much alone. Oh, well, I thought, busying myself putting away clothes in the bureau nearest my bed, I would feel better when I got acquainted; the only question was how to do it. I could hear squeals and laughter in the hall as girls greeted one another; they all seemed to know each other already. Had they *all* come up for Rush Week?

The subject of Rush had first arisen during the summer, when the college had mailed out information forms to incoming freshmen: "Women who wish to join one of the college's fifteen sororities are invited to arrive August 27, for a week of Rush activities, and bids will be given on September 5. Complete this form and return it to the Registrar's office."

Reading this letter had brought to mind a movie that

I had seen years before and had never forgotten. Sorority parties and teas, chitchat, lots of clothes–it was a world totally foreign to me and one that I would never feel comfortable in. I always felt awkward at big parties and usually ended up standing in a corner by myself feeling conspicuous. No, there was absolutely no way that I was going to let myself in for anything like that! And besides, I could still remember how the actress looked when she was blackballed by the group that she had wanted so much to join. "Sororities are barbaric and undemocratic," I had announced self-righteously. "I certainly don't want to be in one. Barbara never bothered to pledge, and besides it's much too expensive." Even though Tech was a state school, and I had a scholarship and a part-time job, it was going to be difficult enough to pay for everything, without putting an extra burden on my parents.

All these reasons sounded good, but the real reason that I didn't want to go to Rush Week was my fear of not being accepted. I wouldn't want to be in anything but the best, and I knew that I would never be asked to join one of the top groups, and maybe I wouldn't get any bids at all. It would be far better to appear completely disinterested. I tore the notice about Rush Week into little pieces and very deliberately pitched them into the wastepaper basket.

Now I reminded myself of this wise decision, as I sat on my bed with the door ajar, watching the girls visiting back and forth between rooms and showing off their new pledge pins. It was a long, lonely afternoon and my roommate didn't appear until hours after dinner. Even then, her long-anticipated arrival proved to be a total disaster. Shelley breezed in around 9:00 and had scarcely dropped her suitcase in the room and given me a little wave, before she disappeared down the hall to visit with some of her Tri Delt buddies. I looked at the monogrammed bag and the Burberry raincoat casually tossed on the other bed. Obviously we were not the same type at all! I sighed. Maybe it was time for a snack, and I opened the big box that my mother had so carefully packed. "Since you'll be away on your birthday, Sunny," she had said, "I'm sending your birthday cake along with you." My birthday was still a few days away, but it was definitely time for a piece of vanilla wafer cake with thick caramel icing. I cut myself a large piece and sat right down in the musty closet and ate it, wiping away a few tears, as I thought of my mother who really appreciated me. Eight hours at college and already homesick! The cake helped a little, and I put it away carefully, dipping into the closet frequently during the next few days, whenever I felt especially in need of comfort. Every crumb was gone long before my birthday arrived, though I thanked my mother profusely over the phone that day, as if I had just tasted it.

Gradually I was beginning to get the feel of the place. I met a nice girl named Sandra who had not come for Rush Week either, although she was certainly cute and popular enough to have done very well. We decided to room together, and I happily said good-bye to Shelley and was not too sorry to learn later in the semester that she had flunked out. So far, the best thing about college was Bud, who met me in the Student Union every Tuesday and Thursday morning for doughnuts. On Friday nights, we went to the movies, even though I did have to spend a lot of time studying. Going steady with Bud was safe and secure, and I was so pleased that he was going out for the freshman basketball team. Almost every afternoon he dropped by the dorm after practice, but I didn't always have time to stand around and talk.

"Listen, I've got to go now. I have a paper due tomorrow, and a quiz in Math. If I don't keep my grades up, I won't be able to keep getting scholarships, and then what will I do?"

The first day in the freshman honors English class had been a bit unnerving. Dr. Stroudt, a hunched-over professor in an old-fashioned suit and neatly-trimmed goatee, was well known for bringing egotistical freshmen into reality. "Any paper with more than one grammatical error will be returned with an F," he growled to the class; and with that, he began to delve into the mysteries of *The Iliad* and *The Odyssey*.

Heart pounding, I was challenged. "I'll show him I can do it!"

I especially wanted to do well in English, my favorite subject, but of course my major was going to be Education. My mother had wanted to be a teacher, and my sister had gotten a lot of approval from her and others, by teaching school. After all, Mother had told me many, many times: "No matter what happens to the crops, or to the rest of the country, you can always get a good job if you can teach school." The course of study was not that difficult, and it certainly looked like a secure future.

History class presented another shock to my system. As the class assembled on the third floor of the administration building, rumors were flying about the new professor. "Have you seen him yet? I heard that he taught at Harvard last year," the girl behind me whispered loudly. All eyes were on the door as the crew-cut, fiftyish Mr. Manning entered—wearing a polo shirt and Bermuda shorts! Our smiles at his appearance faded as he began to lecture in clipped, no-nonsense tones. Well, this was certainly not going to be a snap course; I was going to have to study like crazy!

I was learning there was a lot to learn in college, and most of it was not in books. An interesting girl named Sherry lived with Bette, right across the hall from Sandra and me. Sherry knew all about everything, and I was eager to learn. "Oh, Sunny, that's a nice scarf–is it a Vera? No? Well, of course you know that Vera scarves are the best."

Of course I did *not* know it; in fact, I had never heard of a Vera scarf before, but from that time on, I checked labels to make sure to buy only Vera scarves. Sherry helped form my opinions on Old Maine Trotters, Izod shirts, and cashmere sweaters. Sometimes we teased Sherry about being a first-class snob, but secretly I envied her poise and her confidence that she knew the best way to do everything. I wanted to be a snob, too, but I needed a little more information to be able to pull it off successfully.

Living in the freshmen dorm was fun, but I was always conscious of the difference between the sorority girls and the "independents" as we were called. It was very much a "them" and "us" situation. One day, just about the time when I had finally gotten to the point where I could stop reassuring myself constantly that I had made the right decision about not coming up for Rush, I met Bud in the coffee shop at the Student Union. He smiled as quickly as ever, but I knew him pretty well by now, and there definitely was something on his mind. Should I ask him right out what it was? No, better wait and let him tell me in his own time.

"Uh, Sunny? Guess what? Some of the Fiji fellows want me to join." He looked at me, waiting for a positive response, since Phi Gamma Delta was just about the top fraternity on campus. It was a tremendous honor–the more so, because he hadn't even rushed!

He stood there, his head cocked, waiting for me to say something. But I couldn't; I was too stunned. How could he do this to me? He knew how I felt about fraternities and sororities–the traitor! But I couldn't tell him *that.* "Why that's wonderful, Bud," I managed, in a lack-lustre tone.

He seemed disappointed that I obviously wasn't very enthusiastic. But why should I be? Here, he doesn't even bother coming up to Rush Week, because he knew I had decided not to, and then he's so popular that his basketball buddies invite him to join the top fraternity anyway! The Tri Delts and the Thetas and the Pi Phis don't even know I'm alive; why, not even the bottom sorority had asked me to join, out of the blue like that. But, I told myself, taking a deep breath, that was undoubtedly because I had let everyone know exactly how I felt about the whole sorority system. Why, I'd out-snobbed the snobs!

Soon we began to fight about going to Fiji parties and functions. I was determined to go to as few as possible. "A pledge party Friday night? Do we have to go? You know how I hate parties!"

"But Sunny, it's just a few of the guys and their dates getting together and playing records. It sounds like fun."

"Fun? You know I'm not a social person. I don't fit in well with those people; they don't like me anyway, and I always feel awkward and uncomfortable. And I'm a terrible dancer. It doesn't sound like fun to me, but I will go, if you absolutely insist." True to my word, if I did end up going, I made the party absolutely deadly for both of us.

It was impossible to avoid the Fiji Homecoming reception after the Tech-Texas U. game; even I knew that we would have to make an appearance at that one. The Fiji lodge was right across the street from the stadium, and it was late afternoon, as we cut across the street through the heavy post-game traffic. "Remember, I don't want to stay long," I reminded Bud for the third time. Walking through the door into the hubbub of music, smoke, and laughter, I felt uptight and self-conscious. I looked around for someone that I knew to talk to, but there was a jumble of people everywhere. A helpful pledge appeared, "Would you like something to drink?"

"No, thank you; I don't drink."

"Well, can I get you a sandwich then?"

"No, thank you, I'm not hungry." For a while I tried half-heartedly to chat with a girl I had seen once or twice in the Science Building, but we soon ran out of small talk. Where was Bud? Didn't he know that I was ready to go? He was tall enough, so that he was pretty easy to find. There he was, laughing and talking with a group of Fijis, who were also laughing as they looked up at him. How could he be having a good time, when I was so miserable! I glared at him, until he looked my way. Giving him a look that said, "Let's get out of here now," I nodded toward the door, and we left.

Perhaps it would be more fun to go to parties if I danced better, I thought, so I signed up for two semesters of ballroom dancing. But the rhumba, the foxtrot, and the waltz did little to increase my self-confidence, and more than ever it seemed to me that I was just not the social type. I couldn't understand why Bud didn't feel the same way that I did. He wasn't a very good dancer either, but it didn't seem to bother him. And he was no great conversationalist; in fact, he was the strong, silent type. Why didn't he feel awkward and out of place, too? But he liked people, and they liked him back, while I felt that they simply tolerated me.

We were going to try one more time. “Wouldn’t you like to go to a picnic at the Swift Ranch in Post?” Bud asked hopefully. “I don’t think there will be any dancing.”

“Well, it’s not exactly the way that I would choose to spend my Sunday afternoon, but I guess we ought to go, and it might be fun to see a real live Texas ranch in action.”

The November day was crisp and clear, as we drove the fifty miles across the plains to Post, passing through acres and acres of green blanketed fields—this time of year polka-dotted with fluffy white. “It looks like they’re just waiting for a killing frost to be ready to strip the cotton around here,” Bud remarked, ever the observant farmer.

Some time later we turned off the road and, opening a wooden gate, rattled across some horizontal bars over a trap built into the road. “What’s that?”

“Cattle guard; the livestock won’t walk on it, and it keeps them from getting out.”

The neat squares of crop land lay far behind us now, and we were deep in grazing country, where the gentle roll of the golden autumn grass was broken only by an occasional windmill and water tank. “We’ve been driving for miles, and I’ve only seen one cow. Some ranch this is!” The weather-beaten old ranch house came into view, looking like something right off a movie set of Giant, with its shady verandahs on three sides of the house—a perfect setting for a picnic.

Once inside, Bud took me around introducing me to some of the members and their dates. I knew a few of the girls from the dorm, but soon they were gathering in little groups and talking about things that I didn't know anything about. It seemed to me that the Pi Phis stuck together, and the Thetas had their own private jokes. It was hard to think of anything to talk to them about, so for a while I trailed around behind Bud, but I felt more and more in the way. It's no use, I told myself; I was willing to make an effort today, but it just doesn't work out. What has happened to me since high school? I used to fit in, but I don't anymore. Giving in to my self-pity, I went into the ladies' room and stayed as long as I dared, hoping when I came out that no one could tell that my nose was red. It had been fun to be a big fish in the little pond of Lamesa, but I was finding it difficult to accept that I was a small fish indeed in this big pond of college. Bud could have his fraternity! But there was another way I intended to make my mark—quite literally.

Now more than ever, it was apparent that I would have to make top grades, if I wanted to succeed or be recognized in any way. If there was to be a place for me in this large impersonal university, numbering more than 5,000, perhaps I could find it by excelling scholastically. By the end of my first semester, long hours of study had paid dividends; and in spite of my fears about Dr. Stroudt and Mr. Manning, I had made an almost unheard of 4.0 average out of a possible 4. Merely excellent grades were no longer enough; I wanted to make *perfect* grades. And when the Lubbock *Avalanche Journal* had written an article about the three freshmen with perfect grade-point averages, I loved the attention, and my ego was somewhat salved. Being elected president of the honor society, Alpha Lambda Delta, helped to make up for the embarrassment that I felt about not being in a sorority, even if I suspected that the 4.0 average was the real reason that I had been chosen. And later on, I wanted to be a dorm legislator and be on the Junior Council–honors that would be dependent on my demonstrating somehow that I was special. Grades were the only thing I had, so the pressure was unrelenting.

It is hard to pinpoint exactly when I began to think of myself as chubby. Certainly it had not been during the first part of my freshman year, when my room was next door to the dorm's refreshment room, and the only bright spot in a hard evening of study was the 10 P.M. break, when I visited the candy and Coke machines. And on mornings when I slept too late to make it into the dining room before they closed the doors, I could always pick up a Dr. Pepper and a Baby Ruth to tide me over until lunch. The Spudnut Shop, located near the campus, made the best doughnuts in the world, and I was a steady customer when I could afford it. Often, after the movies, Bud and I stopped off at the Toddle House for hamburgers and then ordered the house specialty, butterscotch icebox pie, for dessert. Even though dormitory food was not exactly home cooking, eating three regular starch meals a day was beginning to show, and finally I began to wonder if the "freshmen fifteen" that everyone joked about gaining, was going to be true for me, too.

Perhaps I began to think seriously about my weight on a warm May day, late in my second year, when several of the girls and I were spending a relaxed Saturday, picnicking in the State Park across town. I loved it there. There were trails you could stroll along, that took you by little ponds that had fish in them, and benches where you could sit and look at the water or the sky reflected in it. But best of all were the trees–tall, narrow-leafed pecan trees, with their lacy boughs intertwining overhead and making sun-dappled tunnels to walk through. What a relief, after endless miles of flat, treeless Texas terrain! We would walk slowly, sometimes talking, but sometimes just sharing a comfortable silence. I liked those times best, not talking, not even thinking, just drifting, feeling the breeze on my face and listening, as it gently moved the leaves overhead.

We all had a touch of spring fever, as we frolicked like children, climbing to the top of the jungle bars, pushing each other higher and higher on the swings, and squealing as we flew down the slide, until finally, we collapsed on the grass for our picnic lunch. "You know, we really ought to do this more often," I said to no one in particular when we'd finished.

"Yes, if we could ever get you out of those books!" Sandra laughed .

I picked up a clod of dirt and threw it at her, "Race you to the car!" As we tore out across the grass, the sight inspired someone behind us to call out, "Hey, Pudge! Wait for us!" Pudge! I stopped and laughed, but the nickname had stung. I never forgot it, and I never wore that outfit again.

When I got home, the mirror confirmed the bad news. Dressing that evening to go to the movies with Bud, I got a good look at my side view in the floor-length mirror on the closet door. Good grief! How long had I looked like this? No wonder the zipper on my straight gray flannel skirt felt a little snug! It's a good thing my chemise dresses aren't fitted! I leaned closer for a look at my face. Ye gads, where had my cheekbones gone? The "freshmen fifteen" looked alarmingly like twenty pounds to me. Out of the corner of my eye, I compared myself to Sandra, who was dressing for her date with the quarterback of the football team. She was so trim, and it wasn't fair that she had naturally curly hair. No wonder she was chosen as ROTC drill team sweetheart. Of course, who wanted to do all that marching, but it would be nice to be noticed. Anyway, something was definitely going to have to be done about the way I looked.

For the time being, however, it was just too hard to think about a diet with exams coming up, and then I had to register for summer school on the first of June. One of the girls had protested, "But why are you going to summer school this year? It's so hot in Lubbock, I'd go crazy!"

I was surprised at the question; the whole thing seemed perfectly obvious to me. "Listen, ever since I was in high school, Bud and I have been planning to get married just as soon as I could finish college. We'll have been dating six years by next May, and that's long enough to wait. So I'm going to finish school in three years instead of four. And besides, I'm going to drive back and forth this summer to school; that won't be quite as bad as staying in the dorm."

Bette still looked puzzled. "But Bud will still be in school won't he?"

"That's different! The most important thing is that I graduate, before I get married. My mother would be terribly disappointed if I got married first; I just couldn't do that to her. She'd be crushed, and besides I feel the same way myself. I have to have that college degree first! Then I can get a job teaching school, and Bud can finish his senior year."

Bette shook her head. "Well, okay, but the whole thing sounds weird to me."

I was furious. Why was she having so much trouble understanding something that was so clear? Anybody should know that six years was a long enough time to wait to get married; what if Bud got tired of waiting around for me and found someone else? And I couldn't disappoint my mother. Besides, I was so sick of studying and classes that the sooner I could get the whole thing over with, the better! (I had conveniently forgotten that I had talked Bud into going to college in the first place, when he had wanted to start farming.) And underlying all of this was a certain pride, never even acknowledged to myself, that not everyone would be able to finish four years of college in just three *and* maintain a straight A average. Barbara hadn't done it, and I didn't know anyone else who had, either. If I could keep my grades up, I would be graduating summa cum laude in just three years. That ought to prove something!

More and more, I was enduring the present and living for a rosy future–a future that Bud and I would have together when we finally got married, a future which I had carefully planned out every step of the way. In high school I had been very proud as a sophomore to wear his senior ring on a chain around my neck to show that we were going steady, and then at college we were "dropped"–that is, I wore a necklace with a small Fiji charm. We decided to skip the traditional next step of being "pinned"–or, rather, I insisted that we skip it. "I just don't want to be pinned, Bud, and that's all there is to it. I think it's dumb."

He was obviously hurt. "I don't think it's dumb, and it means a lot to me. I just don't see why you don't want to do it."

"Bud, you know how I feel about fraternities; and besides in the pinning ceremony when all the Fijis come over and serenade, who is going to sing back? It's one thing if you have a sorority there to take part, but without one, I'd feel like a fool."

The subject was dropped–and I went around secretly jealous of everyone I knew that had been pinned. Only my pride kept me from giving in; how could I draw attention to the fact that the president of the women's honor society did not belong to a sorority? The whole thing was too painful to even think about. It would be much better to wait and get an engagement ring next Christmas; then we could start planning our wedding. But first I had to get out of school. That was the way it was to be done. And to relieve a little of the pressure that summer, there was always peanut butter and crackers.

Summer school classes started at 7:00, which meant that I had been up since 5:00, for the hour's drive to Lubbock from Lamesa. One warm, summer morning I sat yawning in my government class, hoping that I could keep my eyelids open until the bell rang. "When I get home this afternoon, I'm going to take a long nap," I promised myself.

I was startled wide awake when Mr. Williams turned from the board: "Miss Barrow, will you please stay for a few minutes after class?"

Had he seen me half asleep? But he was smiling when I went up to his desk. "I want to congratulate you on your work in this class," he began, and I relaxed. "In fact, I would like to suggest that you consider applying for a Rhodes scholarship. I am on the committee here; have you ever considered anything like that?"

I was floored. I had just barely heard of the program, and knew that it was the crowning achievement of a serious student's scholastic career, but I was not at all sure if it was something that I would be able to excel in. "Thank you, Mr. Williams, but I really couldn't do anything like that." I was flattered at the suggestion, but the truth was, I was not studying for the joy of learning; I was racking up grades for recognition. Anyway, I already had the rest of my life and Bud's mapped out—and two years at

Oxford, in the company of real scholars, was not in the schedule. Besides, what if I applied for the program and was not accepted? Or what if I got in and couldn't do it? No, it would be much better to stay right here and get my degree in elementary education and not rock any boats. This way, I could always remember that I had been considered.

For me, the most important event of my last year in college was the "tapping" of new members for Mortarboard–*the* prestigious group of senior girls. Selection was based on scholarship, service, and character, and for three years I had looked forward to the time that I would be eligible. I had gone over and over my chances, for this would be the ultimate test of my worth. Once more, I went over my qualifications: I did make dorm legislator, and I had been asked to be in Junior Council, which should be a big plus. And my grades were certainly high enough. . . . I didn't talk about it to my roommate or even to Bud; it was far too important to risk admitting how much it meant to me.

When "tap day" finally arrived, I sat in my English Poetry class, trying to pay attention, as Mr. Thomlinson droned on about the peculiar idiosyncrasies of the Lake Poets, and the interrelationship of Shelley, Byron, and Keats with the economic conditions of nineteenth-century England. But it was no use; I'd have to borrow someone else's notes for that day's class. All I could think of was the sound of distant, muted singing, as the Mortarboard society wound solemnly from classroom to classroom, tapping the shoulders of those who were deemed worthy of joining its ranks. The singing was beautiful, haunting–and coming nearer. Would they turn into my class? Yes! Thank heavens, they were stopping! I held my breath and did not even dare to look up.

They were stopping–but not at my seat. Three seats ahead of me, Jean Murphy, a Pi Phi and president-elect of the Panhellenic Council, was rising to follow the group out of the room, and around her shoulders was draped the black stole of membership. And then they were gone.

Tears sprang to my eyes, and my hands were shaking as I grabbed my chair until my knuckles turned white. "I'll bet I know why I didn't get in," I thought frantically. "It must be because this is really just my third year, and it's too confusing to be a junior and a senior all at the same time. I wish now that I'd done the full four years. I'll bet if I had, it would have been different." But I knew that that wasn't it, and I bit my lip to keep from crying out loud, hoping that the bell would ring quickly, so that I could get out of the room before I fell apart.

As the weeks wore on, I felt increasingly unhappy about myself and more and more unacceptable. Well, at least I could do something about the way I looked. The time for the diet had arrived! I had never done very well on diets in the past, but this time I had an incentive. I wanted to be a thin bride, and so I set the wedding date as my goal. Surely I would be happier and feel better about myself if I lost some weight. And then I remembered that my sister had lost a lot of weight a few years before, when she had married and moved to California, bringing compliments from friends and favorable comments from my mother. Well, if Barbara could lose weight, so could I. And I set my will to do it.

In the beginning, it was very, very hard. I loved to eat, especially snacks. Reluctantly I said good-bye to giant-sized Butterfingers and Dr. Peppers. When Bette brought over a box of homemade Toll House cookies sent to her by her mother, it was almost impossible to say no. But not quite. "No, thanks anyway, I'm just not hungry," I lied. Or when the girls on the wing were sending out for pizzas during Dead Week, while we were studying frantically for final exams, I declined, "No pizza for me. I'll just eat an apple."

At first, I felt hungry–and angry–all the time. But as soon as the scales showed that I had indeed lost three whole pounds, my determination became even greater. I was going to prove that I could do this! I hated the way I looked–I hated myself, and I was going to change Pudge Barrow. It was almost an endurance contest against myself, as my whole world narrowed down to studying and dieting. I thought more and more about grades and food, and less and less about anything else.

And I was strict, working out a daily routine which I followed religiously. Sleeping as late as possible before my 8:00 class, I would get up just in time to make it into the dining room, where I would push my tray past the tempting display of buttered pancakes, golden brown French toast, and crunchy English muffins. I would take a small glass of orange juice and place a special order: "May I please have one piece of whole wheat toast, unbuttered?" A cup of hot tea completed my breakfast, while I sat and watched Sandra and Bette polish off the rest of their pancakes and maple syrup. It just wasn't fair that Bette ate all the time and was skinny as a rail!

After a busy morning of classes and an hour or two at my secretarial job in the Electrical Engineering Department, it was time for lunch. That didn't take long–lettuce and tomato salad–and then it was back for afternoon classes and geology lab. At 5:00, I rushed to the dorm for the high point of my day. Not only was it time for dinner, but it was also time for my daily moment of truth. I was ravenously hungry, but before joining the dinner line that stretched all the way down the front hall of Doak, I would dash to my room, throw my books on the bed, and calling to my roommate to be sure to save me a place in line, I would disappear in the direction of the Home Ec Building next door. There, looking quickly down the hall to see if anyone was coming, I kicked off my shoes and removed extra sweaters before stepping on the big iron-gray doctor's scale in the Nutrition classroom.

At first, I had not even wanted to look at the numbers, they were so high. 126 pounds! I had never thought I would weigh that much at 5'4". But slowly, surely, the numbers began to drop, and slowly, surely, I grew to enjoy this challenge. What would my weight be today? How much would I have lost? 123–121–118. It was exciting to watch the numbers change. Every so often, it would seem as if I had hit a plateau. I just couldn't get below 118. I'd be there for three or four days, and always dieting, I would give up at that point, and just resign myself that it was impossible to go any lower. But not now. Now, it had become a contest between my body and my will. And this time my body was not going to win. I didn't care if my weight stayed at 118 for a whole week; I *was* going to win! And I did: the 118 barrier fell, and 117 and 116 were pushovers. But 115 turned out to be surprisingly hard, simply because my new goal was 114. Nor was I going to settle for 114 ½ or 114 ¼; I was not going to compromise.

Finally, I made it! 114 on the dot, without leaning backwards on the scale, or rounding off the nearest eighth of a pound. In my mind I could hear the stands cheering. But the cheering died away, after a while. Now what? I'd won. But I missed the contest–and the sense of power that came with winning. I needed a new goal, an even safer weight. . . . "You know, I would look even better at 110, and then I wouldn't have to worry if I should eat a little. It would be much harder, of course, because I've already taken off all the easy pounds. But if I really set my mind to it, I think I could do it." And I grinned; the contest was on again. It would be tough, the toughest yet. But I was a winner, and I was going to prove it. I was in control of my life, and I loved it. If I could just lose enough weight, all my problems would be solved! I could almost hear the shouts of encouragement from the sidelines.

But not everyone was cheering. Standing in the phone cubicle outside my room, I tried to figure out why Bud sounded so angry.

"What do you mean you don't want to go anywhere Friday night? I *never* see you anymore! All you ever do is study, study, study! And whenever I do see you, you're a real grouch. What's gotten into you, Sunny? You just aren't any fun anymore."

Now I was getting angry. "Well, if that's the way you feel about it, that's just fine with me! You think I *like* studying all weekend for this geology test? You think I *enjoy* memorizing 54 different kinds of rocks? If you don't care any more about me than that, good night!" Slamming down the receiver, I finished the conversation to myself, "And besides it's not much fun going anywhere, if I can't eat."

When Friday night arrived, and the dorm was soon deserted, I wished that I had not been so adamant. Propping myself up on my plaid bedspread with piles of pillows, I prepared to spend the evening making lists of all the key points to memorize from my class notes. How could I ever remember all those stupid igneous and sedimentary rocks? Well, let's see: the sedimentaries all start with S: sandstone, shale, soapstone. That's not too hard. Now igneous look a little harder: granite and rhyolite, and how can I remember those from the metamorphic gneiss and schist?

Chain-chewing one stick of gum after another to curb my hunger, I tried to forget the hurt that had been in Bud's voice. "After all, I really don't have any choice," I assured myself out loud. Bud should understand how hard this is for me; besides, I'm really doing it all for him, anyway. Haven't I crammed four years of college work into three, not to mention working part-time, so that we can get married sooner? He's not being reasonable. And after all, this won't last forever." And confident that reason was 100% on my side, I returned to my memorizing.

The lonely evenings and the constant hunger seemed all worth it, when I began to get compliments from girls in the dorm. "Gee, Sunny, tell me your secret; haven't you lost a lot of weight?"

"I almost didn't recognize you, Sunny! Whatever have you done to yourself?"

I also felt good when people noticed how little I ate. "You mean, that's all you are having for dinner? Just one tiny piece of chicken and a few green beans?" Consumed with the contest myself, I now noticed everyone else's size and shape, and felt quietly superior to those who seemed to have a definite weight problem and continued to overeat. When I entered a room, I compared myself to everyone present.

Was I the thinnest? Whenever I passed a mirror, or even a storefront glass, I quickly checked my appearance. How did I look? I liked my senior pictures much better than any that had been made of me in years, and looking back at previous yearbooks, I was appalled by my round face. I should have done this years ago! I will never, never let myself be plump again! And maybe–just maybe–I could get all the way down to 100 pounds! Now *that* would really be a safe weight!

On weekends that I didn't have to study for a quiz or work on a paper, Bud and I would go home to Lamesa. Promptly at noon, he would pick me up at the Electrical Engineering Building and we would drive along the arrow-straight highway toward Lamesa. I could feel myself begin to relax. Tahoka. . . O'Donnell. . . as we sped through each small hamlet, I seemed to be leaving the pressures and demands of school far behind me. The closer we got to Lamesa, the better I felt. Then we would pass the Adair field, just five miles more to go. Now I could see the water tower in the distance. My spirits rose with each familiar landmark, and finally, turning in the drive, I admired again the remodeling that my parents had just completed. The house was small, but it was comfortable and neat. They had done a really good job. Oh, it was great to be home! Nothing was expected of me; I sat around, watched TV, slept late, unwound. Sometimes I would take books home to study, but I always took my laundry home, and my mother worked hard all weekend to wash and iron all my clothes, so that they would be ready for the next week.

"Sunny, you are not eating enough!" I heard my mother's words and smiled to myself. When she said, "too thin," I translated that to mean "look good." In fact, if she ever said that I was looking a little better, I began to worry that I might be getting fat. When other people expressed concern that I might be getting awfully thin, I discounted their comments as jealousy. I knew best, and I knew that I looked better than I ever had before. The only concern that I had now was not to gain it all back.

But the weekends were short, and just as I began to really unwind and enjoy life, all too soon it was 6:00 on Sunday afternoon, and time to go back to school. No matter how often it happened, I always felt the same lump in my throat when I hugged Mother and Daddy good-bye. Sometimes I had to make a quick dash to the car to keep the tears from showing. This was crazy! I was almost twenty years old. Why should I be crying, when I left home and parents behind? There was no reason to cry. I was doing well in college. I would soon be graduating with a 3.92 average, with high honors. What was the matter with me anyway?

I knew Bud felt uncomfortable when I acted like such a baby. "Maybe I don't act happy now," I tried to explain to him later, when we were well on our way back and the lights of Lubbock illuminated the horizon twenty miles ahead. But it was hard to communicate the indescribably sad feelings I had inside, when I really didn't understand them myself.

"This won't last forever," I promised. "When I graduate and can stop studying, and when I've lost enough weight and can stop dieting, then I'll be happy. Then we will get married, and live happily ever after. I promise."

9

How Much Do I Weigh Today?

I had the same dream year in and year out, well into my teens—to meet a handsome young man who would love me more than anything or anyone else, and would sweep me off my feet into a marriage that would be happy-ever-after. It was the age-old *Cinderella* story, complete with Prince Charming on his white horse. It was a fantasy, of course, but a fantasy I wanted to happen so badly that I really believed in it. Ever since I could remember, I had loved to read novels about romance, from illustrated fairy tales, to *Cherry Ames, Nurse,* when I was twelve, to *Love is Eternal,* the love story of Abraham Lincoln and Mary Todd. It seemed that no matter what the problems were, everything would turn out all right when the right man came along.

And for me, the right man *had* come along, almost as good-looking as the prince, and a lot better looking than young Abe Lincoln. But after five years of marriage and two children, things had definitely not turned out happily-ever-after. Dan was doing extremely well in his business. He was on his way to becoming president of an industrial real estate firm that was on its way to becoming one of the largest in the Middle West. Looking back, I can see that my jealousy and competition with my two brothers was now transferred to my husband, who was so well-liked and increasingly prominent in his field.

I accompanied Dan on business trips two or three times a year and visited over the years every major city in the United States, from Honolulu, to San Francisco, Houston, Chicago, New York and Miami. But, even though we stayed in glamorous hotels and ate in the finest restaurants, I hated those conventions. Eating out was no treat, because I always had to be so careful about how many calories I consumed. In fact, my brain was on automatic pilot now, where calories were concerned. It had gotten to the point, where I no longer had to consciously calculate; it happened automatically. I would go up to the gorgeous gourmet buffet, and as I walked along, looking at those delectable dishes, my mind would be tabulating the calorie-bill, as if it were the cash register at the end of a cafeteria line–one half deviled egg, 125; two shrimps, 50; cocktail sauce, 15; spoonful of salmon mousse, 110; and so on.

But, it was like the sorcerer's apprentice, who couldn't shut off the magic, bucket-carrying broom: Every time I saw food, even in an ad in a magazine or on someone else's plate, the calorie counter clicked away, and I could not stop it! Moreover, on these trips we were constantly going out for breakfast, lunch and dinner. Trying to keep my weight under control, not eat too much and still look normal under those circumstances, I was frantic. The exotic foods were so tempting, but then I would remember how angry I would be with myself, if I gave in to the temptations. Day after day, I would be in terrible conflict, and then angry, when faced with quantities of delicious dishes that I would not allow myself to eat.

I disliked the large crowds of people I didn't know, and the endless receptions with their long hours of drinking. For one thing, I had never enjoyed drinking, and did it only to be sociable. Most drinks didn't taste very good, and those sweet ones that did, went down much too quickly, and there I'd be, standing there with an empty glass. I would light up another cigarette and take a scotch and soda from the waitress passing drinks, if it was winter, or a gin and soda if it was summer, and just hold it with an occasional sip. If it was a really long cocktail hour, and they often were, I would have a second and leave it half empty, while our friends would have three or four. But even so, one and a half drinks with no-cal mixes still came to around 400 calories–one third of my total allowance quota for the day! And they were trash calories of the worst kind.

Each time we went away, I was faced with the usual concerns–who will we eat with tonight? Who will sit at our table at this luncheon or that breakfast? Who will sit with me on the bus, when the wives go out on tour? Will I be dressed properly for the climate and season? Do my clothes look dowdy and Mid West? Will I stick out like a sore thumb? For days preceding the trip I was a bundle of anxieties and angry at Dan that I had to accompany him. In truth, Dan never insisted that I go with him. But I knew I should go, for his sake, and I also knew I would be madder still and jealous, if I ever did wind up sitting at home and wondering what fun things he was doing. Nevertheless, I punished him, by letting him know just how resentful I was. I would make up my mind to have a miserable time, despite the wonderful shopping and terrific sightseeing. Fortunately, over the years, I changed my mind on that score and managed to make friends with several of the other wives, and always looked for them at each convention.

Other than business trips, we took long vacations south to get away from dreary Cleveland winters. We came to love the Bahamas and the Caribbean, and visited several of the islands during the winters in the sixties. But once again, the calorie counter was clicking; I carefully watched every morsel that went into my mouth. On these trips at least, our meals were not preplanned, so I had much more control over when and what I ate. If I wanted to skip breakfast or lunch, I could, and did, because we were not dining with potential customers.

When the girls were six and four we started going to the Key Biscayne Hotel in Florida for spring vacation. As usual, I was very, very careful about my figure and took great pride in being able to wear a two-piece bathing suit. That awkward, pudgy teen at the country club pool no longer existed, and would never be seen again. *Never* would someone have to suggest that I wear longer shorts or a skirted bathing suit. At the hotel, we had a villa which had a kitchen, where I could keep in complete control of what I ate each day. We ate breakfast and lunch in the villa, but we went out to dinner each night. So, in order to eat dinner, at breakfast I would have one egg and a slice of diet toast, and no lunch, except iced tea or coffee, and even then I would eat only a small amount of supper.

Basically, that was the way I ate all year around, except that when I was home, I never allowed myself to eat dinner at all, except when we went out or entertained. Because I had so many luncheon invitations, I usually had my one meal a day at lunch, with coffee and a cigarette for breakfast and dinner. Thus our children were never taught the importance of eating well-rounded meals and never had their mother for an example to look to. I did watch their table manners, but not what they ate. I usually picked and snacked a little on what I fixed the family for dinner, so that I would not go to bed with a growling stomach. Licking spoons didn't count when counting calories.

The effect of my not eating was devastating on the family. I never connected the fact that I was perpetually angry and tense with the fact that my body was reacting in desperation to being quite literally starved to death. In fact, the only time I was not short-tempered and irritable, was when I had just eaten something. But since I wouldn't eat with my family, those intervals did not coincide with our rare moments of shared time at the dinner table.

I would sip a cup of coffee while they ate, just waiting till the meal would be done (and they seldom took more than fifteen minutes), so I could clean up and then go off and do my own thing. In short, we were not exactly a happy family, sharing the day's activities as they ate the mashed potatoes and meat loaf I'd hurriedly put together for them. Many evenings when Dan had to work late, the children ate grilled cheese sandwiches and tomato soup while we watched the evening news on TV.

If someone had suggested to me then, how incredibly unloving my attitude was toward my children, I would have quickly explained all the pressures that were on my own life, and why at the end of such a day, I just didn't have the stamina. If someone had suggested that I was selfish, I might have nodded thinking, yes, aren't we all? I even doubt I would have felt convicted then, had they used another definition of selfish: ungiving. By ungiving, I don't mean ungenerous; a person can give lavish gifts (and I did) and still be ungiving. Giving means giving of yourself–caring enough to listen, to take a real interest, to share, to communicate–to care. Giving means giving up some things that you wanted to do, in order to be with someone else or do what they want to do. Giving means getting out of yourself to the point where you don't even think about yourself, but can be moved to joy or tears by another person's problems or situation. Giving means doing for others spontaneously, and loving doing it. Giving means preparing a delicious dinner for your family, and then eating it with them, and in the course of it, finding out how their day went, not because you should, but because you really want to. I'm beginning to learn a bit about giving now, but back then, if you had said all that to me, you might as well have been talking about the dark side of the moon.

Our annual vacations in Florida were happy times for all of us, because I was the most relaxed when I could just lie in the sun by the pool, or take a long, leisurely walk on the beach to the Key Biscayne Lighthouse. The reason, of course, is that when the body is being starved to death, it goes into "survival mode," so to speak. The metabolic rate of consumption drops way down, and it endeavors to maintain itself on half the calories it would normally need. So to keep losing, you cut down even further, and the body panics, because it can lower the metabolic rate only so far—hence the heightened level of anxiety and the overreactions, and the fact that all you can think about all day long is food. All these symptoms have long been observed in prisoner-of-war and concentration camps, but it has been only recently that medical science has connected this with the sort of thing anorexics have been experiencing. The point is, when I was alternating between lying on the beach and reading, my caloric expenditure had dropped way down, and my body had stopped panicking. It began to relax, and so did I.

I easily convinced myself that the children loved the special activities planned by the hotel staff, and only learned years later that they had hated being sent off with the playroom supervisor. They wanted *me* to take them to Sea World or the Planetarium, but I was too busy looking after me. For two weeks in March, I could do exactly as I pleased, and I deserved this time for myself.

The truth was that for fifty-two weeks of the year, I did exactly what I wanted to. Some days were busier than others, but I had chosen the clubs and organizations I belonged to, I had chosen to serve on all those boards, and I liked playing bridge with my friends. Not only were my mornings and noontimes filled, but also my afternoons, as I drove the children to piano, ballet, sewing, and skating lessons. Here again, I found out only years later that the girls did not really want to take all those lessons. I had pushed them into it, thinking that of course every little girl would want to learn how to dance or sew or ski or skate.

Somewhere I realized that if I kept busy enough, I wouldn't have to face that Dan and I no longer felt about each other at all the way heroes and heroines from the novels felt. What had happened to us so soon? Why had the warm feelings disappeared?

Well, if I could not control the disintegration of our marriage, I could at least control what I did or did not put into my mouth. The less I ate, the thinner I became, and the more superior I felt, especially around my friends who seemed to lack my self-discipline. Every morning I would begin my day by stepping on my bathroom scale before getting into my robe to go downstairs for breakfast. Whatever the scale said would dictate my mood for the day, as I marked my weight in a little notebook. I always hated Monday mornings, because I would inevitably have gained over the weekend and would have to starve all week, getting by on black coffee and cigarettes, with an occasional secret treat–a doughnut, some jelly beans, or M & M's–to get back down again, so I could eat out on Friday and Saturday nights. And now it was getting to the point where I began weighing more than once a day. At first, it was just one extra time, in the late afternoon before dinner, but after a while I began to check before lunch, too. And then I would also check *after* meals, and finally I was even weighing just before I went to sleep. I smiled to myself at the similarity between an alcoholic's craving and my own–smiled because mine was harmless. I was a scale junkie! I laughed at that–and went on weighing.

There were several physical changes that took place in my body due to lack of food. Later, I would learn that these changes were common among European women during World War II. Women, at that time, were often deprived of food and in a state of semistarvation. Their diet was very unbalanced, causing their bodies to be severely undernourished. When this happened, many functions shut down. With me, my menstrual periods ceased after the birth of our second daughter. At first, it did not bother me at all, and I was relieved to have one less thing to worry about. But later, as two years went by, I became very concerned, because Dan and I were talking about having a third child. I went first to my obstetrician, who tried to treat me with medication but to no avail. None of the pills he gave me worked. We began to think that maybe I was going through early menopause–at 26 years of age! My doctor then sent me to the head of Gyn-Ob at the University Hospital. The doctor examined me and said the only thing for me to do was to take very strong fertility drugs. But this medication was so powerful that I had to sign papers saying that I would not hold the hospital responsible for any multiple births resulting from taking these pills. At this point, I was willing to try anything. Nothing was ever said about my low weight by these doctors and, of course, I never told them that I was subsisting on less than a third of the caloric intake that was normal for a person of my height, age and activity level.

At the same time, I noticed that my hair had lost all its shininess and bounce and was falling out. My hands and feet were always cold, and for several years, I had suffered acute pain and discomfort during the freezing temperatures of the winter months. My blood pressure, body temperature, and metabolic rate were all abnormally low. I didn't care about those things; what I did care about and recorded in my notebook was that my hips measured 33 inches, my waist was 24 inches and I wore a size 6!

So there I was, striving for self-perfection via starvation, and trying to get pregnant in the process. Finally with the aid of the miracle drug I was taking, I did manage to conceive. I was thrilled and relieved at this happy news. Yet, even knowing about the importance of eating properly while pregnant, I still refused to allow myself to gain any weight. Once again, I was determined to go through the nine months in complete control over my ever-present hunger pangs.

But I really looked forward to having this baby. The girls were in school now, Liza in first grade and Lexa in nursery, and I wanted someone to love me. I hoped to find love again through this baby, since Dan and I were now in the middle of an unbroken cold war.

Dan Ford III arrived right on schedule. There was

much rejoicing among the Fords and Manuels; and my hospital room was filled to overflowing with bouquets of flowers, telegrams and cards. I was considerably cheered up because this pregnancy had been particularly difficult with my swollen legs. My varicose veins were so bad that during the last three months, I had to wear Ace bandages around both legs, from the top of my thighs down to my feet. At the very end, I was unable to wear shoes at all, my ankles were so swollen. But, through it all I had managed to hold my weight down, so that when I came out of the hospital with the baby, I weighed *less* then I had when I started the pregnancy nine months before. I had weighed 116 pounds, when I went to the doctor for my first check-up. When I got home, I weighed 115.

Shortly after the baby was born, when he was about five weeks old, Dan and I took a trip, just the two of us, to the Coral Beach Club in Bermuda. Dan had planned this trip as a surprise to me, to have a rest and change of scene. It should have been a second honeymoon, but it turned out to be a nightmare of a vacation. Nothing went right from start to finish, and my complaining attitude and nasty frame of mind had a lot to do with spoiling everything. To begin with, our room happened to be very close to an area of construction, so that the workmen began hammering and sawing at 8 A.M. every morning. Then it rained almost every day making trips to town on a motorbike dangerous, if not impossible. That meant we were confined to that dreary room to read or sleep. Even that would have been okay, except that I was anxious to get my figure even thinner after the baby's birth, and was as compulsive about exercise as I was about eating. I looked forward every day to playing tennis, but my disposition on the court, however, was never the best, and playing singles with my husband did not help.

Looking at him over there on the other side of the net, I saw him as an enemy, a traitor. He didn't care about me; all he cared about was his stupid business. It came to me, then, that I really could not bear to be with him. He made me so angry, because he would not give me his undivided attention. The rain didn't bother him: he didn't care if he played tennis or not. He did not like to shop, so reading in the room was fine with him, and he loved to take long naps. It didn't matter to him that I felt like I would jump out of my skin, if I had to spend fifteen more minutes sitting in that room. There we were, in this elegant resort night after night with absolutely nothing to say to each other. Our second honeymoon–I hated every minute of it, and hated Dan for having done such a loving, thoughtful thing.

Back home in Cleveland, I was so busy and distracted that I did not have to look at the fact that I felt hopeless. We had not even been married ten years, and I had blown it; I was a failure again. What on earth was I going to do with my life? With my two daughters and baby son? I didn't have any answers–just anger and depression. We had no life together, no communication, no enjoyment together as a couple. And I was super-critical of everything, and everyone, starting first with myself, and with Dan and the children, second through fifth, and our parents next. In constantly trying to be perfect, I was never satisfied with anything I did and had no belief in my abilities or that the future was going to get any better.

My life was controlled by fears, the most dominant one being my fear that if I ever did start to eat, I would be unable to stop!

"Camie, why *won't* you eat?" Dan asked over and over. "Don't you know that it's crazy to think you'll get fat, if you eat one decent meal?"

"You don't understand!" I shouted back. "If I eat too much, I'll gain weight. In fact, every weekend I gain weight. All I have to do is eat one sandwhich, and I've had it!" I was frantic now, because even though I had gotten my weight down to 110 pounds at 5'8", to me I still looked fat. My legs were still too heavy, my thighs were too large, and no matter what I did, my stomach was never flat enough, especially after three babies. Nothing would help except less food and more exercise–as much as I could get. All I had to do was pick up the phone and find friends to play tennis or golf with.

As a young child, I began tennis lessons almost as soon as I could hold onto the racket. My parents belonged to two country clubs, where I took private lessons, as well as being in the tennis clinics. Both my parents played tennis at least three times a week, year round, and tennis was the most socially acceptable sport; everyone in our group played. But I had a hard time going to the tennis clinic each summer, taking lessons, and practicing by the hour. Coordination was not a gift I possessed; year after year, I would struggle out to the court and be relieved when summer was over. At first, I was lazy and just didn't care, but then after marriage, I realized it was socially important to know how to play and play well. Many of our weekends were spent on the tennis court and then having drinks and dinner at the club. As I began to diet and get serious about losing weight, I realized that the more exercise I got, the more I would lose. Suddenly my interest in sports perked up, and my stamina improved so that I, too, was playing every day possible during the summer months and especially on the hottest days when I would literally sweat off pounds.

At some point in my early twenties, I took up golf as

an alternative to tennis which I was simply not good at, no matter how hard I tried. I took lesson after lesson to learn how to hit that little, white ball down the fairway. Dan was a good tennis player, but he preferred golf; that had been the sport that *his* family played together. They were so pleased to see me trying to play that they encouraged me and supported my feeble efforts. And golf was a form of exercise I could use to help hold my weight down, unless the weather was too stormy. Then I did my exercise indoors, running, doing the Royal Canadian Air Force exercises–anything to get rid of those hateful calories.

As if tennis and golf were not enough, I also took up skiing. Once again, I forced myself to get out and exercise, and once again I had to hide my misery. I nearly froze to death and suffered excruciating pain from frostbitten fingers and toes when they began to thaw. There was not one extra ounce of fat on me to insulate me from the cold.

"Hey, Camie, wasn't that great this afternoon?"

"Terrific!" I smiled brightly, trying to remember if it was on the second or third run that I had lost all feeling below the knees.

"What did you think of Giant's Despair?"

"Well, to tell the truth, I didn't take that run this afternoon." That's it; smile brightly. Don't tell anyone that the reason I didn't take it was because I'd tried this morning and fallen off the T-bar half way up the mountain. I'd known that would happen–I hated the T-bar and was always afraid my ski would catch on the ice, and down I would go–and sure enough, down I went and then had to scramble on hands and knees out of the way of the next skier. I was so angry I cried, and the tears froze on my cheeks. I just sat there trying to decide what to do–take my skiis off and walk down to the lodge or walk up to the top and ski down. I looked up at the ridges of snow above and opted for the trip down.

Nonetheless, my ski pants fitted perfectly and snugly, as was the fashion. Needless to say, with all this exercise on top of my regular routine, I was usually exhausted. But even more than from malnutrition, this exhaustion came from living in a state of constant stress.

Having three children did not hamper my social schedule one bit; we hired nursemaids and cleaning women. I was hardly a joy to work for, but if one left, I simply put an ad in the newspaper and found a replacement. Yet God had his hand on our lives even then, though I didn't know it, or Him. Frances worked for Dan's parents as well as for us, and was the kindest, most patient and loving lady. Lily and Lula cleaned for us for years, showing great love towards the children and really caring for them, more than I did. And we had one very kind, Christian woman named Gladys who lived in with us right after Dan was born. She came to us through an ad in the paper when the baby nurse left, and stayed for three years. We all loved Gladys and considered her a part of our family. She was a widowed grandmother with five children of her own, but she had a special place in her heart for little Dan.

She got very upset with me on several occasions, when I would be abrupt, angry or annoyed with my husband or one of the children. When she got nothing but more anger from me, in desperation she turned to Dan. "Mr. Ford, what are we going to do about the tension in this house?" And Dan would shrug and shake his head and say, "Gladys, what can we do?"

She never again said anything to me, but I could hear her sigh as she went about her work. But nothing ruffled her when she was taking care of little Dan, and she loved to sit by the hour, rocking him to sleep in the old rocker in the nursery. She was always sweet and gentle with the girls, too, exactly opposite from my nervous, high-strung disposition.

No one knew what to do about my worsening condition. No matter how much my husband or my parents begged me to eat, I would not listen. "Please, Cornelia! Please eat *something!*" Mother would say. "Daddy and I think you look much too thin. It's just not healthy for you to eat that way."

"I'm okay, Mom," I replied, each time she would try to coax me.

"You look like a scrawny chicken," my father scoffed. "There's nothing left on you but skin and bones."

What do they know? I'm really fat, I said to myself with my distorted image before me. They don't know anything.

One evening, when Dan was at a business dinner that I didn't have to go to, I was at my parents' house for dinner. They pleaded with me, "If you will just get your weight up to 120 pounds, your father and I will buy you a mink stole," said Mother, as we sat at the dining room table.

A mink stole! They really mean business–120 pounds! That's too much, of course, after I've fought so hard to get down under 110. But–I'd always wanted a fur piece to wear out in the evening.

"Well, I'll think about it."

"No second chances; it's either yes or no," my father answered firmly.

"Okay, 120 pounds you said? I'll do it."

I wanted that stole badly enough that I was willing to eat to get it. It was a matter of will that I had chosen not to eat for several years, and now, with the right button pushed, I chose to eat. Since I was always starvingly hungry, once I made up my mind, eating was not that hard. Unfortunately, eating for a few weeks did not solve the problem. The thing about anorexics is that, like alcoholics, they'll do anything to get their own way—even deceive themselves. If to stay in control of the situation it was necessary to lie to oneself and to others, then so be it. I did not tell my parents, but in the back of my mind was the thought: I can always take the weight off again. And I did. No sooner was the stole hanging in my closet, than the weight started coming off again. And in three months, I was back down to 110, ready for the Junior League Fall Fashion Show modeling.

I *still* did not know there was anything wrong with my behavior, and I definitely did not want any help. Deep down, I knew that Dan was not the only one to blame for the failure of our marriage, but to escape looking at myself, I blamed him for everything. I doubt that anyone suspected there was trouble between us. To all our friends and relatives, it looked like we were a very happy, successful couple with three lovely children. I never, never said a word to anyone about how unhappy and frustrated I was. I went to party after party, always the smiling, fun person—hungry maybe, but certainly fun.

In 1969, when Danny was two years old, we looked at a dream house—a spacious, white frame house situated on five acres of wooded land, atop a hill, overlooking a winding river in Hunting Valley. Looking out the living room bay window, one could see grazing horses around a quiet lake. Ducks and geese made the lake their home, as they flew south from Canada. The house had five large, sunny bedrooms and five bathrooms, as well as a formal living room, den, dining room and family room, plus a laundry and workshop in the basement. We fell in love with it the very day we walked through it. The grounds were beautiful, tall shade trees were everywhere, brick walks led to a flagstone terrace with steps down to the lower lawn. And there was an adjacent two-car garage with room above for a playhouse for the children. Next to the house was a mixed flower garden that was one long bed, the length of the lawn. In addition, there was a formal rose garden with a wooden fence behind it for the climbers. I loved the names of the roses: Tiffany, Queen Elizabeth, Tropicana and Mr. Lincoln. It was altogether more than I would ever have dreamed possible for us to own.

Dan and I talked back and forth about the house. Should we buy in the country or stay in town? What would we do about carpools? Would the children have any friends to play with? Where would we send them to school? Hardly any of our friends could afford to run such a large house. Did we want to make such an important move, now, when we were still quite young? I was not even thirty yet. But Dan's sister had moved out to the country a year before, and we were all excited that once again we would become close neighbors. Our children were delighted to be together and often spent the weekend playing in one home or the other.

"Better grab the house while you can," my father advised us. "A house like that one won't be on the market very long, and if you wait, you might never have another chance." I knew what he said was true, but it was such a big step to make. We took it. And once we made the decision to buy, we only had to wait a short time before our bid was accepted. I knew I would be busy for some time to come, fixing up and redecorating the house. The painting, papering and construction work went on for about nine months, so that it was March, 1969, before we moved in. I was so thrilled, I had to pinch myself to make sure it wasn't a dream! I felt as if I had finally arrived! Now our marriage would change, and our life would be different! I couldn't wait for all our friends to come and see it, so I immediately planned a large housewarming party for later in June, when all the draperies were hung, and the furniture re-covered and in place. Our home was going to be one of the most beautiful in the Chagrin River Valley, and we already had the best view around!

The night of our first big party was a warm evening, so we could be outside on the lawn to enjoy the magnificent view. Mother helped me by making flower arrangements to put around the house. We had bartenders and waitresses to pass the drinks and canapes, and I had set up a lavish buffet supper in the dining room. Having guests was a pleasure, so at my instigation we were constantly inviting people to visit or have dinner, showing off our new home.

More than ever now, I hated being alone with Dan, and the answer was to have parties, have house guests and take trips with the children. Escape! Run away! Don't let yourself think about how bad things are. Join another club, go out to lunch, volunteer to run the school book fair, keep busy, busy, and always look happy, very happy–and thin, very thin!

September was a traumatic month for me. On September 1st, I turned thirty years old–the beginning of middle age. After thirty, it was all downhill. We went to The Homestead, a grand and beautiful old resort in the mountains of Virginia. It was Labor Day weekend and also close to the time of Dan's parents' 44th wedding anniversary, so we were all there to celebrate–Dan and I, Manda and Steve, and Dan's brother George and his wife, Ellie. The time in Virginia was spent on the tennis courts, the golf course, the putting green and in the dining room. And, as a present from Dan's parents, I was given a day in the spa at the hotel. What a treat! I enjoyed every minute, particularly the massage, but I still felt so old and depressed. My life was half over, as far as I was concerned. Here we were at one of America's finest resorts, and I wouldn't eat a thing all day, so that I could eat a little of the five course dinner we would be served each evening. I was in agony!

When we returned home, with plans for the new season under way, a friend told me about a new way to find peace and happiness–yoga lessons!

"Come on, and try it, Camie," she encouraged. "Everyone's doing it, and you can join our group."

"Well," I replied thoughtfully, "that's a new one for me." I had heard about yoga, but had never really understood what it was all about. My friend named several of my close friends who had already signed up.

"Okay, that settles it; sure, why not, sign me up."

A week later a group of young women, all my friends, met together in the living room of Jane's house, where we would start our course in the exercises and meditation techniques of yoga. I was quite disappointed when I met our teacher: she was overweight, dumpy-looking and divorced. Immediately I had doubts; if yoga was going to be the answer to all my problems, why was the teacher fat, unattractive and no longer married? "Well, we shall see," I gasped, as I faithfully tried to copy her positions with my own reluctant arms and legs.

Dressed in leotards and tights, we met once each week to huff and puff away at the exercises which were supposed to strengthen our bodies and clear our minds, so we could handle whatever stress came our way. We also spent lots of time talking about life, our tensions, and our emotions and feelings. We were supposed to reach some level, where we would no longer feel anger—or hurt or joy, for that matter. All the ups and downs of our emotions exhausted the body, said our teacher. Relaxation was the key. Nevertheless, my feelings and emotions did not seem to go away, even though I listened intently to whatever our teacher told us. Each week, I returned home, stuck with the same problems, anxieties and tensions I'd had when I arrived.

The meditation part was much easier than the exercises. We would all lie down on the floor in a comfortable position while she would slowly count backwards from ten to one. We were supposed to pretend we were stepping into an elevator going down from the top floor of a building while she counted.

"All right, I'm in Halle's Department Store," I said, ready for anything. "I've been having lunch in the tearoom, and now I'm going shopping." I could see the familiar bank of elevators with all the smartly-dressed matrons, waiting for the down elevator. The hand on the clock over the old elevator swung up to 10 and then passed slowly down 9, 8, 7, 6, 5, 4, 3, 2, 1. The meditation period lasted for ten or fifteen minutes, and then snap—everyone was to wake up and tell the others what we had seen during this time.

Seen? I hadn't seen anything! Others had all sorts of exciting and interesting visions, but I invariably went to sleep and had a nice cat nap. When it was my turn to talk about my vision, I was frantic! Quick, I thought, I've got to make something up. This is crazy—if I don't see something, she'll think I'm not cooperating. Every week, I had to make up a new vision, until finally I realized that the whole hour was making me feel more and more uncomfortable. "This must be okay; some of my best friends are doing it," I comforted myself, but the uneasiness would not leave.

As the weeks went by, I became quite concerned when several of the girls started getting really seriously involved in yoga. They spent many extra hours with the teacher, and with others at the institute, where yoga students gathered. Eventually, after a couple of years, these friends left their husbands and children and went to India to live for a time to study yoga over there. Not me; when the twelve-week course was up, I resigned from the class, with my troubles just as bad as they had been before.

By the summer things had gotten so bad, that something had to happen, or total disaster would occur. The geographic cure–moving into our new home–had not worked. I began thinking about divorce, which really would be disaster; no one in Dan's or my family had ever gotten a divorce. It was unthinkable–totally contrary to the code that we had been brought up in. And yet I had started thinking about it. Should I seek out a divorce lawyer? But what would I tell him? What would be the grounds? Mental cruelty? If anyone was going to sue anyone for divorce on those grounds, Dan had a much better case than I did. His wife was acting crazy–and I was. Not that I was ready for a mental institution, but I wouldn't mind a few nice, quiet weeks in Hanna Pavilion, our private hospital for the well-to-do, mentally distraught.

As it turned out, something *did* happen–but it was so extraordinary, so unthinkable, that I wouldn't have dreamed of it in a million years!

10

Happily Ever After?

The mountains of New Mexico loomed purple in the distance, as we drove toward them in our Impala. There was little traffic on the road; the only sound to be heard was the steady hum of the engine, or an occasional whoosh when we met some big trailer truck. Overhead, the azure sky was cloudless, and you could even see the heat shimmering on the horizon. We had left the tin cans far behind, at the Jiffy Car Wash in Clovis, which had also removed most of the "Just Married" sign across the side, but the car's carpets were still crunchy with rice. I slid across the seat to sit next to Bud and gave a sigh of contentment. "It was such a beautiful wedding! Can you really believe it? It's like a dream, and I'm afraid that I'm going to wake up and find out that none of it is real."

Bud smiled and put his arm around me. "It *was* a beautiful wedding, and it certainly *is* true. 'Mr. and Mrs. Hale' is beginning to sound familiar after almost twenty-four hours!"

My thoughts drifted back to yesterday–the day that I had looked forward to and planned for almost six years. It had been bright and beautiful, a picture perfect day with just a few fat, fluffy clouds. But it was hot—even at 7 P.M., it was a relief to get inside the air-conditioned church. Standing in the back with my father, I gave him a quick hug. "My, you look handsome in that outfit!" Wrinkling his nose, he pretended not to like the white coat, but I could tell that he was pleased.

Then we heard the organ swell with the strains of the wedding march, and my heart began to beat faster and faster. "This is it, Sunny," whispered my cousin Jane, "straighten your veil!" I took a tight grip on my father's arm and stepped out. Was this really the First Baptist Church? In the glow of candles with white flowers everywhere, it seemed totally transformed. I could see a blur of aqua blue down at the front, where the five bridesmaids waited, dressed in lace and taffeta, but as we walked slowly down the seemingly endless aisle, I could only see Bud's face turning toward me. It was hard to look properly demure; I felt like grinning from ear to ear.

Out of the corner of my eye, I saw rows of filled pews; thank goodness there were some guests here. The church was so large that it would be embarrassing if just a few people had come. The ceremony was astonishingly short; after waiting six years, was that really all it took to get married? Then the joyful anthem pealed forth, and as Bud and I turned to walk triumphantly out of the church together, I was sure that the best part of my life was just beginning.

"Hey, wake up!" Bud said, with a smile. "Stop daydreaming; I'll bet you didn't hear one word that I just said! The wedding was yesterday, but this is today, and we're on our honeymoon, and I'm starving." The small sleepy town of Melrose was coming into view. "Let's see if we can't get some lunch around here somewhere."

"Not in this little place," I said, not bothering to hide my disappointment. "All I can see is a roadside diner—they'd just have greasy hamburgers. You know I can't eat anything like that. I'd rather have a green salad or something light. Maybe there will be a better place down the road." Bud frowned, but didn't argue, and I began to look for a nice restaurant or cafeteria, but we had already left Melrose far behind. Finally, sixty miles farther down the road, Bud stopped the car at a cafe on the outskirts of Santa Rosa.

"Listen, Sunny, this is the last town for miles. We've passed two Dairy Queens, a Lotta Burger, and a Kentucky Fried Chicken, none of which suited you. This is the place that I am going to eat, and you can either come in or stay in the car. But I'm going to eat!"

I don't see why he is so cross, I told myself. I guess he just doesn't care if I like what we eat or not. Well, I can't sit out here; it's too hot, and what would people think if they saw me? Following him into the small cafe, I stopped to check my reflection in the window. The blue-and-white striped sundress looked nice, but I would have to be careful not to gain any weight on the trip. I had weighed 92 pounds the morning of the wedding, and I had no intention of returning home one pound heavier.

Inside, the cafe was neat and clean. A very quiet Bud handed me the menu, which I flipped through quickly. "Oh, I don't see anything here that appeals to me. But I'm not very hungry anyway." I was still following a strict regimen: for breakfast, I allowed myself one-half melon and hot tea, and for lunch, either a salad or one small dinner roll. Then I would feel that I could safely eat a more normal dinner of meat and green vegetables—after all, it was our honeymoon! But I always ate extremely small portions and was hungry almost all the time. Food had already been very important to me on this trip. I could remember exactly where we had eaten and exactly what I had ordered at every meal.

Bud looked up, "Are you ready to order? I'm going to have a club sandwich; you want one?"

"Oh, no, I'm not that hungry," I lied. "It's just lunch; I'd rather eat dinner tonight. No, I'll just have a small dinner roll and a glass of water."

Bud gave the order to the waitress, who couldn't seem to get it right. "One club, one Coke, one–did you say a dinner roll?" We sat in silence until the food was served, and then I tried to make cheerful conversation to cover up the uneasiness I felt. I hoped Bud wasn't mad at me. I had dreamed for so long about this time in our lives; it would be a shame if Bud spoiled it by being angry. But why did I feel so tense and tired and uptight? Oh, well, everyone has a few cross words, now and then. It never occurred to me that I was the one who was spoiling it by my insistence on literally starving.

Our next stop was Santa Fe. Hand in hand, we had walked down to the square and visited an old Spanish mission. Our hotel was lovely, and that evening, we dressed up to go out to dinner. "Now this has got to be something special," Bud said, knotting his tie. "Your Uncle Roy slipped me money at the reception, and told me to be sure to have dinner on him. So where shall we go?" We pulled out the telephone directory and began to do some research in the yellow pages. "Look at this one: BISHOP'S LODGE. TRULY ELEGANT CUISINE. Let's try it!"

At dusk, Santa Fe was unlike any city that I had ever seen. "Look at the houses, Bud! Do you think they're adobe?" I had an impression of flat roofs scattered among low pines all over a hillside, and then it began to get too dark to see. "I think it's starting to rain. Where do you think that restaurant is? Aren't we getting too far out of town?"

Bud peered through the sweeping windshield wipers, trying to read the road signs in the car lights. "Look! Doesn't that sign say Bishop's Lodge? Which way is the arrow pointing?" We wound round and round the hillside in the dark, leaving civilization far behind. "This place had better be good, if and when we ever find it! It's almost nine o'clock." Finally the road stopped at an unpretentious building, and we parked the car and ran through sheets of rain to the door. "This has got to be it, but it looks like some sort of a private club," Bud whispered as we looked uncertainly through the door. "Do you suppose you have to be members?"

It turned out to be a magnificent buffet, or at least what was left of one, and we blew all of Uncle Roy's money on just the cover charge. Nevertheless, in spite of the weather and all the mishaps, we had a delightful time, laughing at everything and feeling very close. In fact, we had so much fun that we drove all the way back out the next morning, to get a look at the place in the daylight and take a picture of the famous Bishop's Lodge for our scrapbook. "Someday we'll want to show this to our children."

After that, Bud was hungry again, so we had stopped for breakfast, and I studied the menu carefully before ordering. Bud had no problem. "I'll have two eggs, over easy, sausage, and biscuits."

The waitress looked at me. "Half a melon, please," I ordered. "Are they in season?" She assured me that the cantaloupe was delicious, and she was right. I ate every bite, right down to the rind, and thanks to the big dinner the night before, for once I didn't feel deprived as I watched Bud polish off his farmhand breakfast. I even felt a little smug. "I wish every meal was as satisfying as this one, with so few calories," I told myself.

It was an auspicious beginning to the day, and I looked forward with excitement to the drive ahead of us through the Sangre de Cristo Mountains to Red River, where we planned to spend the remainder of our week. The fresh scent of the big pines filled the air, as we drove higher and higher, and I rolled down the window so that I could lean way out and see the tops of the trees. "Stop the car, Bud! We've got to take some pictures! Now, you stand right there and look over at that mountain in the distance." The bright green of a flower-sprinkled meadow formed the perfect backdrop, with the darker green of the mountains in the distance. When it was my turn to pose, I felt very trim in my tan pants with my shirt tucked in. I could remember when I had to wear my shirt out to camouflage my silhouette, just a year or two ago. "I am so happy," I said to Bud. "Just one more picture!"

Late that afternoon, with the sun setting on Mount Blanco, we drove down a long hill, and the sleepy mountain town of Red River lay before us. Log cabins dotted the slopes among the towering trees, and from each one a vertical column of white smoke rose lazily in the still evening air. For even though it was August, twilight in the mountains brought a chill. "Smell that wood smoke!" Bud grinned. "Man, doesn't that smell good!"

"It looks very rustic," I said, trying to sound cheerful.

But Bud knew me better than that. "Let's find a place to stay; you'll like it better, when we get settled. Let's try this one, Running Brook Lodge." There was a vacancy, and we soon had the key and were letting ourselves in the cabin down next to the stream.

"Listen to that," Bud exclaimed, opening the window. "You can hear the sound of the water on the rocks."

"Shut the window, Bud, and let's get a fire going before I freeze!" I began to give our new quarters a careful inspection. All three rooms were neat and clean, but somewhat lacking in the comforts of home. Rough finished pine paneling on the walls, a big stone fireplace, and stacks of wool blankets on the high bed gave me the distinct impression that we were almost camping out. Finally I could not remain quiet any longer. "Well, it's really not at all what I had expected."

To be sure, neither Bud nor I had known much about Red River, but we had known lots of people from Lamesa who had vacationed here and loved it. "It's probably a very nice place when you come in July and bring your whole family for square dances, horseback riding and so on, but it really doesn't look much like a honeymoon setting to me. Listen, Bud! What would you think about our driving on to Colorado Springs? It doesn't have to cost a lot more, if we're careful. And we could drive up Pike's Peak, and there are all kinds of things to see and do there. What do you say?"

Soon I had steamrollered any objections he had, we had put all our bags back into the car and were on our way again. It was pitch-black now, and I couldn't make out Bud's expression in the glow of the dashboard lights. He probably wasn't too happy, so I concentrated on Colorado–that would be a great place to spend a honeymoon! Much better than Red River, New Mexico, he would see. He would be pleased in the long run.

We did have fun in Colorado Springs, the days flew by, and we got back, just in time to pack up our belongings for the move to Lubbock. Bud would be registering for his senior year at Texas Tech, and I would be a second grade teacher at Roberts School.

Backing the car carefully into the driveway of our new home, we surveyed the small duplex with satisfaction. It had been difficult to find. Last spring we had spent weeks poring over the classified ads in the Lubbock *Avalanche Journal,* making numerous trips on Sunday afternoons to look at garage walk-ups with pull-out sofa beds, but with no success. And then, almost by accident, we had stumbled on just the right apartment at the right time, and it had been right under our noses all the time. Mr. Bullen, my boss for three years in the Electrical Engineering Department, had a duplex for rent, and the present couple would be vacating at the end of August. Reasonably priced, it was in a nice neighborhood and even had a pink climbing rose on the front porch trellis!

"We're home!" With a flourish Bud picked me up and walked across the threshold.

"Don't drop me," I protested, "and don't hurt your back; I'm too heavy!"

"Are you kidding? You are all bones," he laughed, and safely inside, we both collapsed in laughter in the living room.

"Look at that sofa!" I whispered, in mock horror. "It looks like a jungle pattern with that green fringe and huge purple flowers."

"Well, you can't have everything," Bud chuckled, and we set to work unpacking boxes of wedding presents and arranging them in our new home.

It was so cute–almost like a dollhouse, with a place for everything, complete with small stove and miniature refrigerator in the kitchen. "Let's put up our new kitchen clock right over the table," I said, and on the counter we put out our pink canister set that had been a gift from my Aunt Beth. "Can you fasten that planter over here under this light? Ivy should grow well here over the sink." It was hard to choose which set of new sheets to make up the bed with, and the quilted bedspread from Aunt Martha's family fit the mahogany bed perfectly. Crisp white curtains covered the unattractive windows, and with dresser scarves and throw rugs, the bedroom looked beautiful. "Oh, Bud, I just love it! It's like playing house!"

That evening I carefully set the tiny dinette table with our best china and crystal and silver, and prepared Bud's birthday dinner of homemade pizza and chocolate cake. I watched proudly as he blew out the twenty-three candles on the cake and made a wish. "Tell me what you wished," I teased him.

"Can't do that; it won't come true, if I tell."

"I'll tell you what I wish," I said. "I wish that we will always be as happy as we are right this minute!"

The shrill sound jolted me out of a sound sleep. Where am I? What is that terrible noise? Alarm clock–I felt for the clock and turned it off. Six o'clock! Why had I set it for such an ungodly hour? Then I remembered. I was in my new bed in our new apartment, and I wanted to have a little time before Bud woke up. As much as I loved sleep, I had been willing to sacrifice thirty minutes, in order to carry out my morning routine uninterrupted. Bud turned sleepily over, and I slipped out of bed and groped for the light switch in the bathroom. Shutting the door quietly behind me, I turned to the chrome scale, which I had carefully placed in a corner of the bathroom where it would not be moved or bumped. I had cautioned Bud the day before, "Whatever you do, be sure not to move the scale!" Disrobing quickly, I placed one foot on the scale and then carefully eased my weight on as smoothly as possible. The dial flickered wildly and then settled down at 94 pounds. Hmm–that was not good!

Stepping off the scale, I took a deep breath and started the whole procedure over again. By shifting my balance, holding my breath, and weighing over and over again, I finally succeeded in getting the scale to read 93, just as Bud knocked on the door. "Are you going to be in there all morning?"

"I'll be out in a minute," I snapped angrily, knowing that it was not going to be a good day. 93 pounds was very scary, and I felt very much out of control. If the scale was up one pound, then it might go up five pounds or even ten or fifteen! I wanted to keep my weight below 100 pounds, and the farther below I was, the safer I felt. Today I would have to be very careful about what I ate, and then see what I weighed at my usual after school weigh-in, when I would repeat the whole ritual. I opened the door and brushed past Bud.

"You didn't have to be so rude," I told him.

"Whatever were you doing in there for so long? I've been waiting twenty minutes to get a shower."

"It's my bathroom, too, and I have to get ready to go to school," and without pausing to explain, I hurried past to get breakfast on the table.

I was just finishing the dishes when a car horn sounded in front of the house. "Oh, no, that must be my ride! Tell her to wait just a minute, will you? I have to do something first." Quickly I pulled out the desk drawer and looked for my worn notebook. I flipped through the pages to a blank sheet. "September 1, 1959," I wrote, "Weight 93 pounds.

Breakfast:	1/2 grapefruit	75 calories
	hot tea	0
		75 calories total."

I had done this so many times that I knew the calorie counts by heart. And of course, the entries were the same day after day. Grabbing my lunch from the refrigerator, I waved good-by to Bud and ran for the door.

"Sorry to keep you waiting," I said to Virginia, "I was just finishing up the dishes." It was almost the truth.

Virginia smiled, "Oh, that's okay. I think we have plenty of time." Always calm and unruffled, she was one of the veteran second grade teachers at Roberts, and her room was next to mine in the barracks annex at the school. She had offered to pick me up every day, and we would share the gas and car expenses. We drove down Broadway, past the large department stores and the neatly landscaped banks in the business district, past the Great Plains Life Building (Lubbock's only skyscraper), and then on through a seedier section of the city, dotted with warehouses, rundown bargain basements, and used car lots.

Roberts School, built on the edge of MacKenzie Park, was one of the oldest schools in the system, and its children came largely from the Hub Homes area, a subsidized housing development. We turned into the school yard, and I sighed. I thought it was one of the ugliest, dreariest buildings that I had ever seen. "I'm glad we are out in the barracks," I said. "Maybe there aren't so many mice out there." Inside, I had copied Virginia in trying to decorate the drab walls and brighten the room, and the walls were covered with large cardboard figures of spray painted clowns and circus animals. I straightened the room, set a bowl of flowers on the desk, and sat down nervously to wait for the bell to ring for the first class.

With the bell, the door flew open, and a crowd of noisy children stampeded inside. "Just a minute! Come in quietly, and let's have some order please!" I announced. But it was a losing battle. Many of the children spoke very little English, and I spoke even less Spanish. The Mexican children were bright-eyed and friendly, and many had obviously worn their Sunday best for the first day of school. There were also a few black children in the class, and a sprinkling of threadbare white children who looked out of place. It was not the type of class that I had wanted to teach; what could I possibly offer these children?

"It was my fault for being so honest," I told myself. "I never should have told them at the interview that I only planned to be in Lubbock one year." Roberts School had the largest teacher turnover in the district, and I was beginning to see why.

Student teaching had never been like this. There, for three hours a day, I had taught orderly groups of children from the university section of the city, the sons and daughters of professors. I had made neat lesson plans, and everyone had listened courteously and cooperated, always aware that the real teacher was just around the corner, available to lend a hand should the need arise. Here at Roberts I was strictly on my own, and it was obvious that these children were not accustomed to cooperating with anyone. "Well, I've got to start somewhere," and I called for a group of children to go to the reading circle that I had carefully arranged at the back of the room.

The first major problem was finding a book that fourteen-year-old Juan could read. "What is a fourteen-year-old boy doing in my second grade class?" I fumed. "I won't even try a regular reader," and one by one handed him first grade level books, but even the simplest preprimer was too difficult. Over six feet tall, he had obviously lost interest long ago in the stories designed for six- and seven-year-olds, and besides, he didn't understand any of the words. When I turned back to the bookshelf, he pulled a paper airplane out of his pocket and sent it skimming across the room, where Manuel jumped up and intercepted it to gales of laughter. By the time I turned back around, the room had erupted in chaos.

"Sit down and shut up!" I heard my voice rise until I was almost screaming, and I slammed the ruler down on the desk so hard that it shattered into little pieces. "I don't want any of you to say one single word until lunch! Put your heads on your desks and don't you dare move!"

Finally the hands on the clock reached twelve, and I sighed with relief. The teachers' lounge offered a brief respite from thirty-six totally uncontrollable children; at least there would be only adults around. I sank down gratefully on the sagging sofa and opened up my lunch. "Am I ever hungry!" Carefully I removed the wax paper from the lunch that I had carefully prepared that morning. 149 calories–one slice of Diet Rite bread (79 calories), cut in half and spread with mustard (0 calories), and topped with one-half slice of American cheese (60 calories), and lettuce (10 calories). It was delicious, but the 149 calories were gone in just four bites, and I was still famished. Drinking bitter black coffee (0 calories), I watched the other teachers eat. "You know," I ventured to the other teachers, "I'm discouraged about my class–"

Mrs. Wheeler interrupted with her non-stop voice; "It's a shame. These children can't learn. I just try to keep them in the classroom. Of course, what can they expect us to do in working conditions like these. . . ." On and on she talked, but I was lost in my own thoughts. Maybe I was just not cut out to be a teacher. Barbara had never seemed to feel like this. These were needy kids, but

I couldn't cope with them. Maybe if I just had a little bit more energy, I could stay ahead of them better. Right now I would like to sit here in this chair and never get up. But the bell brought me to my feet. Like it or not, it was time to try again. It was going to be a long afternoon.

"Bye, Virginia; thanks for the ride. I'll see you tomorrow." I hurried into the house, glad to be home before Bud, and with time for a bath and to weigh before I started supper. I had to weigh every day at this time, so I would know how much supper I could eat. 92 ½. Well, that's a little better than this morning. If I can continue to be very careful, everything should be okay. Standing in my slip, I looked critically at my reflection in the mirror. Was my stomach beginning to look a little rounded? I pulled it in as hard as I could, scarcely breathing. There, that's much better.

Monday, Tuesday, Wednesday–the days were almost identical. Go to school, come home, make dinner, iron or clean, and then fall into bed exhausted, as early as I possibly could. "I can get some tickets for the Red Raider game on Saturday," Bud began, after supper on Thursday. "I thought maybe we could go, and first go out to eat somewhere. . . ."

"Oh, no, Bud," I cut him off. "I can't go; I am too tired to go anywhere. Maybe you and some of your friends could go. I just want to go to bed early." At least tomorrow would be Friday, which was the high point of my week.

Right after school on Friday my routine changed for the better. Instead of riding home with Virginia, I had kept the car so that I could drive over to Thirty-fourth Street to the Town and Country Beauty Salon. The minute I opened the glass door and walked inside, I began to feel better. It was a small shop, with only three stations and five hair dryers, and it was usually very quiet so late in the afternoon.

"Hi, Sunny, go right on back for your shampoo. I'll be right with you." It was soothing to sit back and unwind, listening to Aggie chatter while she rinsed my hair clean and then put it up in fat rollers for my page-boy. All the cares of the week disappeared as I sat under the warm, humming dryer, with absolutely nothing to do but relax. I opened the latest issue of *Good Housekeeping* and skipped over the articles to the advertisements. Devouring every word about cake mixes, oven casseroles, and chocolate desserts, I copied down recipes for Whipped Cream Torte and Mocha Macaroons. Each week, I read my way vicariously through the homemaking section of all the ladies' magazines without gaining an ounce, and on Saturdays I would cook.

Each weekend, right after breakfast, I hurried through the housework to get ready for my all-day activity in the kitchen. First, I thumbed through my new Betty Crocker cookbook from cover to cover, looking carefully at all the mouth-watering illustrations, and then I would make my selection. "Today," I announced grandly to the kitchen, "I am going to make cinnamon rolls with confectioners' sugar icing." So engrossed was I, that I didn't even hear Bud, the first time he spoke.

"I'm on my way to class now, but I'll be back early. What do you say we call Bette and Jim and see if they want to go to a movie this afternoon?"

"Oh, I don't think so, Bud. I'm planning to cook all day, and I just don't feel up to seeing anybody."

Bud turned from the door and came back into the kitchen. "I can't understand why you don't want to see Bette. You roomed with her for two years, and she was our maid-of-honor; she's your best friend. I don't understand why you don't want to be with her, or with *anyone*. If you ask me, you aren't very much fun!" And he slammed the door behind him.

Shocked at his anger, I nonetheless had to admit that he had a point. Why didn't I want to be with Bette and Jim? They were two other just-marrieds, and Bette was a beginning teacher like myself. But, somehow the idea of being with other people was just too much trouble and took too much energy. I was happiest all alone, cooking and reading. Once or twice, I'd had the girls over for coffee or had entertained a couple for dinner, and it had been fun to hear their exclamations: "Sunny, you are so thin! Whatever did you do to lose so much weight? I almost didn't recognize you." But as much as I enjoyed their reactions, it just took too much effort to be social. I felt exhausted and irritable all week after school, and finally on the weekend I deserved to get to do exactly what I wanted. Cooking was relaxing, and of course it was really for Bud, I told myself. *I* never ate anything fattening–except that sometimes I licked the spoon when no one was around.

And of course that didn't count, and that morning I had weighed a new all-time low of 88 pounds!

One day in March, we were invited to a cookout in the park with old friends from high school days, and there was no way I could gracefully decline this invitation. It was a little early for a picnic, even in Texas, for the March winds can be raw and blustery, and more often than not, sandy as well. Bundling up against the chill, we set out with the large hamper that Joyce had prepared.

"What are we having to eat?" I needed to plan what I would allow myself to have.

"I've made shish kebobs, and dessert will be brownies with fudge icing," Joyce said proudly.

Oh, no! I would have to use all my will power. I loved chocolate, but it was definitely forbidden. Well, okay, I resolved sternly, I could eat some of the lean beef, and a few of the carrots and maybe a slice of onion. But no potatoes, no bread, and absolutely no dessert! I had to keep my weight below 90!

The trees were still forlorn and bare in the park, and the grass still a winter brown. It seemed to take forever to get the fire going, and strong gusts of wind kept blowing it out. While we waited for the fire to take hold and get hot enough to cook on, Bud, Joyce, and Larry sat around close to its warmth and seemed to enjoy the conversation and one another's company, but I was getting increasingly impatient. Having eaten practically nothing all day so that I could enjoy this picnic, I was very, very hungry, and my feet were freezing. It seemed as if we had been waiting for hours, and I had less and less to say. There they were, laughing and chatting away, and nobody cared about my lunch! If I didn't get something to eat soon, I was going to scream. "When are we ever going to eat?" I finally snapped at the men.

At last, the slightly underdone lunch was served, and we went home shortly afterwards. "It's just not worth it," I steamed, as soon as we were in the privacy of our own car. "I'd rather eat at home! We waited two and a half hours for a tough piece of meat, and then I had to sit there and watch you eat four chocolate brownies! I have never spent such a miserable day!"

Bud looked at me strangely. "Fine, great! Next time, why don't you just stay at home!" And maybe our friends agreed with Bud, for they never called us again.

Something was definitely not right. Oh, it's probably nothing, I assured myself, everyone skips a few periods now and then. But the irregularity continued, until the periods had stopped completely, and reluctantly I made an appointment with a friend's gynecologist for a check-up. The whole thing seemed a little foolish.

"No, I don't really have any other real symptoms," I explained to the doctor. "Sometimes I am just a little tired and cross, and sometimes I cry for no real reason, but of course I have a lot of pressure at school. Other than that, I feel fine," I concluded, smiling brightly. The doctor, obviously under pressure himself, with a waiting room full of paitents far sicker than I, said, "Now, Mrs. Hale, you must remember that the first year of marriage is a time of adjustment. It would seem that your hormones may be a little out of balance. Let me give you some thyroid pills, and you will probably feel better soon. I wouldn't worry about a thing."

I left, wishing that I hadn't bothered to come, and later when Bud and I talked about it, we were relieved that there was nothing seriously wrong. "I think it is just the pressure of school that makes me so emotional, Bud. In fact, I hate teaching school! I really am tired of living in Lubbock, and I'll be glad when you graduate next month. If I can just get through this year, next year will be better." Somehow that rationale sounded awfully familiar. Hadn't we talked this way in the past? Why was next year always going to be better, and never really seemed to be?

It was a sweltering hot June day, but I didn't mind the heat as I ran back and forth to the car, carrying boxes. "Watch that lamp, Bud; be sure that it doesn't tip over in the back."

Once again we were packing the car, and once again my spirits were light. The day before, I had said a very happy good-bye to my problems at Roberts School, and to all the children there. I wouldn't miss them, and I doubted very much if they would miss me, or even remember next year who their teacher had been. With graduation behind him, Bud was dying to get back to Lamesa and to start farming in earnest, and he talked excitedly about tractors and cultivating and fertilizer and other related topics during the hour's drive to Lamesa.

"H'm, that's nice," I said, staring out the window, and not really paying attention. Farming bored me, and as soon as he took a breath, I changed the subject. "You know, it's really almost funny that we are moving back to Lamesa. I always said that when I grew up, I would never live in Lamesa, and now that's where we are going to live. It just goes to show that you should never give yourself orders; they might just backfire! Come to think of it, I always said that I'd never go to Texas Tech, and never marry a farmer. That's not a very good average, zero out of three."

"What's wrong with Lamesa? I think it's a great place to live," Bud countered.

"You just say that, because it's the logical place for you to farm. Oh, well, it's much too nice a day to spoil by arguing. Any town will look good after Roberts School," and I added to myself: Nobody says we have to farm forever.

Moving back to one's hometown had both advantages and disadvantages. We had both been born in Lamesa, and both of our families and relatives had lived there almost forever. If we were not actually related to the barber and the grocer, we had gone to school with their children or had known them at church. At times, I thought that it was very nice to know most of the people you met on the street, and other times it seemed to me that we were doomed to lead totally predictable, boring lives, just like our parents. Not too original–being born in the same town, going to college sixty miles away, and then moving back to the same town. But as much as I daydreamed about what might have been–an exciting career in the publishing field, perhaps a glamorous job on *Time* magazine in New York City, I knew that they were only daydreams. What I really wanted most of all was security. I wanted to marry Bud, to have our own home and lots of children, and to stay at home and be happy. And deep inside, I wondered if I would have been able to handle moving far away from my parents, as my sister had. "You know," I said more to myself than to Bud, "I don't know how Barbara did it. When I think about her not coming home for a whole year after her wedding–not even for Christmas–that was really hard. And then it was just a brief visit on her way to Peru for a year." No, I didn't have that kind of nerve. Lamesa might be boring; but it was familiar, and it was security.

Speaking of security, one of the things I hated about farming, especially in West Texas, was how terribly insecure it was! Farming could be profitable, *if* it rained at the right time, *if* it didn't hail, *if* the young plants didn't get covered up in a sandstorm, *if* the insects didn't damage the young bolls, *if* August was not too hot, *if* there was not an early frost, and *if* the price was right. That was far too many ifs for me. I wanted something more predictable, and I liked the idea of a regular salary every month. "Farming might be okay," I would say, "if we could just have another income to support us. People who have oil wells can afford to farm; I don't think we can." But I was careful not to object too much. I knew how Bud wanted to farm. All his life, he had planned to farm with his father and his brothers, and at this point, not even I could change that. Of course, now that he has a college degree, he won't have to be limited, I assured myself. Perhaps later on, he will want to branch out a bit–say, into banking, or he could be an "ag" teacher, or maybe. . . The possibilities for white-collared careers were endless. But for now, he seemed determined to become a farmer, and I was going to have to go along with it as gracefully as possible.

We soon settled into a tiny duplex, and again I loved the challenge of adding throw rugs, green plants, and ruffled curtains to make it seem like our own. What a relief not to be teaching! I wanted to be the perfect housekeeper. At first I always got up to fix Bud's breakfast, but soon he was getting up earlier and earlier in order to be on the tractor by sunrise. "Sunny, you really don't have to get up so early, if you don't want to," Bud said one morning, when he caught me yawning at the sink. "I can fix a quick bite myself and get to work that much earlier."

I was easily persuaded. "Well, it does seem a bit silly to get up before six, when all I have to do all day is clean two and a half rooms. Maybe I will sleep a little later."

By ten o'clock every morning, the house was spotless, and a little bored, I found myself nibbling leftover cinnamon buns. This would never do; if I ever got started eating, I knew I would never be able to stop. Well, I just wouldn't have any lunch to make up for it. I did seem to have a lot of free time on my hands. There was not much laundry for two people, and the yard was so small and unattractive that all we did was mow the crabgrass occasionally. After Bud's lunch dishes were done, I had nothing to do until the time to start a late dinner. Every day I looked forward to three o'clock when I drove out to my parents' house for afternoon coffee.

The first time, just walking into their familiar kitchen

and smelling fresh coffee made me know that I was home and brought back a rush of memories from my earliest childhood. Mother was putting a plate of Fig Newtons on the table and pouring three cups of strong black coffee, just as my dad came into the kitchen. "Just time for a quick cup, before I go back over to see how the hoe hands are doing."

These days most of Daddy's farming was done from the pickup, as his health was failing. I had always loved to share this special time of day with them, for this was our family time, a time to talk about the cotton crop or the weather, or perhaps just to sit comfortably together in silence. I had never really liked the taste of coffee, but even as a child I had sipped my cup of coffee-flavored milk, liberally sweetened with sugar, and enjoyed the companionship. Sometimes there was a little gossip, "Did you know that Uncle Will's son has left his wife? Poor Nettie is so upset that she doesn't know what to do." It was often a time for dreaming. "You know, I think we might have some bale-an-acre cotton over on the Davis place this year, if we can get some rain before long. It's a real good stand, just as pretty as a picture." If I ever felt down, I could always count on plenty of sympathy: "It's too bad that you had to teach in that terrible school last year. You are a good teacher; they should have had you in a nicer school. All you need is the right class, and you'll do well." Yes, it was certainly worthwhile coming by for coffee; it was home, and I could find solace and companionship and always someone to tell me how wonderful I really was.

Unfortunately, that was not at all how I felt about visiting my in-laws. "Oh, Bud, by the way, your mother called today and asked us over for dinner on Sunday. But I told her that I wasn't sure; we might be going to my folks, and that I'd have to call her back."

"Listen, Sunny, we *have* to go; my brother's family will be there, and besides, I want to have dinner there. We haven't seen them in weeks."

"Well, if you insist, but I hate those huge family dinners. There is always too much to eat—potato salad, banana pudding, everything fattening, and everyone just sits around and eats and eats. It's too hard to go and stay on my diet. And I don't think your parents like me anyway. It's pretty obvious that they prefer their other daughters-in-law."

"Maybe they would like you better if, just once, you acted a little happier to see them! And besides you just sit there with three green beans on your plate and never eat anything. How do you think *that* makes them feel? Or me, for that matter?" As usual, the argument ended in an impasse. We would go to the dinner, but I would punish Bud by scarcely being civil and would make it clear to everyone that I was ready to leave at the earliest available opportunity.

There was also the problem of a house. No one in Lamesa rented houses. There simply weren't any to rent, and our tiny apartment was beginning to feel a bit cramped. Obviously we needed to buy a house, but what were we going to use for money? Just out of college and beginning to farm, we didn't have much to spend. Then one day Bud came home very excited. "Guess what, Sunny? Do you remember the old Jackson farmhouse north of town? The Jacksons are moving, and Dad has offered to help us buy it and move it into town. It's a nice house; I used to go there and play with their son, Eddie. Dad says we can pay him whenever we can afford to. What do you think?"

What I was really thinking, I didn't tell him. It might

have been a nice house when Bud played there as a boy, but that must have been ten or fifteen years earlier. What was it like now? And a farmhouse! But Bud had said we could move it into town, and we already knew of a lot on North 17th Street, which was a nice part of Lamesa. We would have to completely redo the whole inside, but it would be good to have a home of our own. Bud was waiting for an answer. "I guess it's okay," I said; after all, what choice did I really have?

The little white sign said "115"–our first address, our first home. "But, Bud, what's wrong with the roof? It doesn't have any overhang! It looks funny; can't we make it overhang? Why not? Well, you've got to do something to make it look better! And this vacant lot looks terrible. We need some trees–some big trees. I don't want little baby trees that take ten years to grow up."

I did have to admit that remodeling the old house was fun. There was a lot to do, and we wanted to do most of the work ourselves, with a little help from Bud's brothers and father on the painting. Rebuilding closets, putting in new appliances and bathroom fixtures, repainting inside and out, choosing new carpet and curtains, shopping for new furniture–I felt that everything had to be just right. It took weeks and weeks, but when it was finally all in place, even I was pleased. I looked with approval at the maple hutch in the little dining room; our blue and white china looked lovely on display. The cool blue bedroom with its sheer white curtains was restful, and the braided rug in the den was just the right color for the paneled walls. Outside, the grass and bushes we had planted were already starting to grow, and I hardly even noticed the funny overhang any more.

The house looked perfect, and I was determined to keep it that way. "Bud, put your magazine in the rack." I ran around frantically with the vacuum morning and afternoon; everything had to be absolutely spotless. But I was furious when Bud's dad remarked in a half-teasing way, "You know, I really hate to sit down over at your house, because I might rumple something. It hardly looks like anyone lives there."

As fall approached, Bud was busy on the farm, and to pay for all our new appliances and furniture, he would soon be even busier with a second job, working evenings at a cotton gin. The redecorating was finished, and I had begun to wonder what I was going to do now to keep busy. So when the superintendent of schools called, his offer sounded appealing. "We really need a first grade teacher at South Elementary, our newest school. Would you be interested?"

Later, talking to Bud, I thought I might. "I don't know; maybe I should try teaching again. South Elementary is a brand-new school in Park Terrace, and the kids won't be anything like they were at Roberts. The salary is good, and at least it will get me out of the house and away from the refrigerator." More and more I had been giving in to the temptation to eat. I still wouldn't eat at meals, but I was snacking a lot, when no one was around. And I could tell that I was gaining weight, but I didn't want to weigh and find out how much. "Yes, I think I am definitely interested. I need to stay busy. I'll do it."

South Elementary was as different from Roberts School, as night from day. The school was situated on the edge of the nicest residential area in town. Walking into my first grade room, I looked with delight at the big windows and the brightly painted bookcases. And when the children began to arrive, I was even more pleased. Scrubbed and well-dressed, they had nice manners and were properly in awe of the authority figure–me! I didn't know anything about teaching first grade, but I was going to learn. It was a challenge, and I was determined to do well; this was my hometown, after all, and I had my reputation to uphold. I could get lots of approval as Mrs. Hale, the first grade teacher, and my parents were very proud of me. "You know, Sunny, Marge Allen told me that her little granddaughter is in your room. They are so pleased about it." And so I tried even harder. Too, it was fun to go shopping for a new schoolteaching wardrobe, even if I did have to get a size larger.

At Christmas that year, I had an opportunity to get even more approval when I was asked to present the program for the all-school PTA open house. The cafeteria was jammed with parents and guests, and I stood nervously behind the stage, cuing the children on and off and prompting them when necessary. The kids did look like angels in their costumes, even if I knew better! "I just hope that Randy remembers his lines and that his halo doesn't slip," I worried. But even the littlest angel performed well, and afterwards the proud parents crowded around to offer their congratulations. The long hours of planning and rehearsal had been worth it. "Such a nice program, my dear; we are so happy that Alice is in your class," Mrs. Henderson, the banker's wife was saying. "Oh, yes, Tim is enjoying school so much," agreed Mrs. Williams, the doctor's wife. These were accolades and acceptance from the most prominent people in Lamesa, something that I had worked all my life to achieve. Yet where was the satisfaction and fulfillment?

The next day, sitting in the reading circle and listening to Alice Henderson and Tim Williams read, I wondered what was wrong with me. In the past, last night's ego boost would have been enough to keep me aloft for at least a week or two, but something in me had changed. The balloon of approval did not stay inflated as long as it used to. It didn't seem to matter if the mayor himself told me that I was a wonderful teacher.

I looked around at the pleasant setting. The sunny classroom was decorated with Little Bo Peep, Miss Muffet, and a dozen other familiar figures, and the bookshelf was gaily lined with brightly covered books and a variety of plants and flowers, but somehow I felt trapped. Why had I committed myself to a one year sentence in this place? This was the perfect school, and I had been treated royally, but I was still filled with discontent. Was it possible that the problem had not been in my surroundings at Roberts School, but in me? I pushed that unsettling thought aside.

I think I'll stop by the bakery on the way home and pick up some pecan rolls for a snack, I promised myself. The pendulum was beginning to swing from never eating to constant eating, but I refused to face it. I had married my Prince Charming, we were living happily ever after, and I was thinking more than ever about food.

11

I Give Up The Reins

At the end of August, 1970, we were invited to a cousin's wedding in the heart of the Pocono Mountains. It was going to be a family reunion with all my mother's Long Island relatives in attendance, an opportunity to visit with family of whom we were very fond but hadn't seen since David's wedding. I did not want to go, because the sound of it reminded me of those conventions where everyone stood around for hours, drinking and trying to make small talk. On the other hand, I had never been to the Poconos and heard they were beautiful, and it really would be fun to see my aunts and uncles again.

The trip did not start off well. Dan and I were to meet my parents at the airport in Cleveland, to catch the flight to Allentown. Dan was late. When it was time to board the plane, he still had not come, and to make matters worse, he didn't know where we were going. I had told him to meet us at the airport, but I'd forgotten to say where we were flying *to.* "Well, we'll just have to board the plane and hope he makes it," said my father grimly, and so we did. We were in our seats with our safety belts on, when he came rushing down the aisle of the plane. I was so angry, I couldn't even speak, and just glared at him with a frosty look.

Upon our arrival, we drove to our motel, where we met my brother David, and his wife, Barbara, who had driven up from their home in Princeton. We had not seen them for several years, so there was much news to catch up on. I noticed right away that David seemed different, much less nervous and tense, and he was eager to share with us something that had been going on in his life.

The marriage ceremony took place on Saturday morning in a church in the center of the town. Afterwards, we were told that there would be about two hours before the wedding luncheon reception would begin. David took me aside and suggested Dan and I take a ride with him in his car, to find the Delaware Water Gap. There was nothing else to do, and I was intrigued to learn more about what David was doing. He just didn't seem at all like the same old brother I remembered. Barbara was tired and stayed at the motel to rest, but David was anxious to talk, so off we went. What he wanted to do was to talk seriously with me and Dan about his new life–since he had discovered that God was real, and had come to know Jesus Christ. He wanted to tell us all about his conversion experience in New York, and to share the new joy that he had discovered. Dan said that it was all too much for him, but if it had helped David, that was fine with him, and he sort of tuned out. So David concentrated on me, telling me that he and Barbara had been headed for divorce, but that God seemed to have them in a holding pattern now, and while Barbara had not yet made the same "vertical connection" that he had, he was confident she would, if he, David, kept trying to become the person that God wanted him to be.

Whew! I was stunned, to say the least. But as he talked, I seemed to sense a ray of hope at the end of Dan's and my tunnel, where it had been totally dark for so long. Maybe David *had* found something that could help. So I proceeded to pour out to him all our problems and to tell him just how badly things were with Dan and me. We drove on and on, looking for something that I thought would look like a miniature Grand Canyon—we never did find the Water Gap, and in the process of looking we were almost late for the reception!

I felt bad, when I looked around the room and saw everyone seated at his appointed place. Mother glared at me for my rudeness at her brother's child's wedding. Oh, dear, now I've really blown it! I'll hear about this when the party is over. I hoped there would be lots of champagne and no one would remember. But in the meantime, I had so many things to think about! David had told me in great detail about this incredible thing that had happened to him, and was continuing to happen and to affect everything in his life. I wasn't sure if I understood, and I had trouble believing some of his comments, but he gave me a book which I promised him I would read, a book that had helped him tremendously, *Beyond Our Selves* by Catherine Marshall. I kept my promise and took the book home with me to read.

After the reception, we drove down to Princeton to spend Saturday night with David and Barbara. The weather was perfect for supper on their terrace and a long evening chat. David had so much more to tell us about those past few months in New York and about his new circle of Christian friends. Our conversation went on late into the night and continued again at breakfast. At last, it was time to go to catch our plane back to Cleveland. I could hardly wait to find my seat and start my new book, as David's enthusiasm was contagious.

Scarcely had I arrived home than a box appeared in the mail from Logos, a Christian publishing house in Plainfield, New Jersey. David, who had been an editor at Doubleday, had left after his conversion and was now executive editor at Logos. He began to send me a steady stream of Logos books, written by Christians about their Christian experiences. I read each one when it came, and continued to wonder about the personal relationship these authors had with Jesus, Jesus Christ the very Son of God. I knew who He was, because I was a confirmed Episcopalian with years of Sunday School behind me. But to know Jesus as a friend? As a person who answers prayers? Never!

Another long, cold winter passed, without any change in our marriage from the usual state of silent warfare. As spring approached, I had another real estate convention to look forward to, this one in the Rockies at a fabulous hotel called The Broadmoor. Colorado Springs in May was supposed to be lovely—but that spring it snowed for the entire week we were there. It was numbingly cold—much too cold for the swimming, walking, riding or tennis advertised in their lavish brochure. Dan did manage a round of golf, as the snow swirled down, while I, in my most unpleasant mood, stayed inside our room, read my latest novel, and seriously contemplated divorce. Because at this point I liked the thought of being alone. And yet, I knew deep down inside that a divorce would not solve my problems. And then I looked at something I had never faced before: My biggest problem was me.

This particular trip seemed to drag on forever, even though each day was planned, with activities from breakfast speakers until long after the banquet dinners. We were taken to the Air Force Academy to tour the facilities, to the ice arena to watch the skating stars of tomorrow practice their routines, and on drives to see the spectacular scenery. But I remained as cold inside as it was outside.

Later in the month, one other event took place that really set me on the path to finding out some answers to my personal problems. We were invited to Richmond, Virginia, to visit with an old friend, Dan's roommate from college and usher in our wedding. Woody and his wife, Leith, had become good friends over the years. We had not seen that much of them, but when we were together, we always had a lot of catching up to do.

We drove down to Virginia, and spent most of the ten-hour drive in frosty silence. Oh dear, here we go again. Another trip like the one to Colorado. This time, the temperature outside rose steadily as we approached our destination, but inside the car the icicles remained the same. I loved Richmond with its pretty old houses built in soft, rosy-red brick. We passed one gracious home after another as we drove to our friends' house.

As we pulled up in their drive, Leith and Woody came out to greet us and introduce us to their two children. "We're so glad you came," they said, giving us welcome hugs. After a delicious dinner, that warm Saturday evening, we relaxed outside on their patio, enjoying their garden. Leith began to talk about problems that she and Woody had had, and how she had found help and support from their Episcopal parish priest. She had gone to him for counseling help and later had become very active and involved in her church.

I was surprised; I could have counted on one hand the number of times I had voluntarily been to our church, but then we had just moved to Gates Mills, and our church was new to us. Later in the evening, Dan and Woody took a walk, and I talked with Leith about my own unhappiness. Her love for her husband was very obvious, as was his for her. I was extremely jealous of their relationship, for in my usual pattern, I turned against Dan with great resentment when, after a few drinks, he made a put-down comment about me. We were both masters at putting each other down with sharp, critical judgments–well-aimed thrusts straight to the heart.

By the time we returned to our motel for the night, I was so fed up and angry, I could hardly speak. All the emotions of the past ten years welled up inside me. I was absolutely furious with Dan, who had fallen into bed and begun snoring, even before I had taken my shoes off. I didn't know what to do, except that I certainly didn't want to stay one more minute in that room with that man. If I had been home in Cleveland, I would have gone into Liza's or Lexa's room to sleep in one of their extra beds, but no such luck tonight. I finally decided to spend the night in our car in the motel parking lot. Ten years of feelings were bottled up inside me, because, never, in all our marriage, had I spoken one word to anyone about how I felt. My despair, frustration, and hurt I had expressed only in generalities to my brother, and I certainly hadn't let on to my parents that things were less than perfect between Dan and me. They thought he was terrific, amusing, fun to be with, and oh, so successful!

That night was the longest night of my life. I smoked cigaette after cigarette, until the first crack of dawn appeared in the sky. I would have loved a cup of coffee and a doughnut, but I was afraid to go alone to an all-night coffee shop. I was also afraid someone would see me, sitting by myself in the car, and I wondered how safe it was to be out there. Well, what am I going to do now, now that this wretched night is over, and I've had no sleep, thanks to my dear husband who is snoring away as usual. He makes me so mad I could scream! Who does he think he is anyway–Mr. Downtown Cleveland?

As it got lighter, I finally decided it would be better to go back into the motel than to be seen by anyone coming along. The rest of Sunday was a blur, seen through sore, red eyes after my sleepless night. Our drive back to Cleveland was even frostier than the one coming down. There was no point in even discussing the previous night; Dan had never woken up, so he never knew I spent the night in the car, and I was not about to tell him. Besides, our fights never came to any resolutions, just bitter silences.

Once we arrived back in Cleveland, I was somewhat happier, because I was always glad to get home and see the children again. At three, seven and nine years of age, they seemed very young, but they sensed something was very wrong between Dan and me. Did they worry? Did they understand? Or were they afraid that we would split up, as a number of our friends already had?

Monday morning, as soon as the children were off to school and the dishes done, I sat down by the telephone to get up my nerve to call the rector of our Episcopal church. I did not know what I would say, except to ask him for the name of a marriage counselor. My hands were wet with perspiration, as I dialed the number. "Good Morning, St. Christopher's Church," said a cheerful voice. It was the church secretary, who told me the rector was off on Mondays, and would I please call again tomorrow. My stomach was in a knot, and I was trembling when I put the phone down. I was both relieved and disappointed not to get it over with. Now I would have to get my nerve up all over again.

Tuesday morning I tried again, this time with success. Mr. Shively was very understanding. He told me that he would be happy to see me himself, since he was a marriage counselor as well as a priest. Why didn't I stop by the next afternoon, and we could have a chat? I could hardly wait for Wednesday to come, and at the same time I was very nervous about what to say, how much to tell him. And what would he say back to me? Oh, well, I don't care what he says! I've got to tell someone what's going on; I'm about to explode! I am so tired of pretending everything is okay between Dan and me, when it's horrible! I hate him, and he must hate me. I'm so nervous and tense and hungry–well, at least it's summer, and I can eat more because I'm playing more tennis again.

Monday was Hospital Board day; Tuesday was tennis in the morning at a friend's court, and the Garden Club for lunch or tea. Wednesday was tennis at the club; Thursday was golf, and Friday I played Ladies' Day tennis in the morning, then got my hair done. That was my schedule for this June, as soon as school ended, and the children began their summer camp. I thought it was healthy for them to be at camp with children their own age. And it meant that I would not have to cope with them and feel guilty every time I got angry and spanked them.

My appointment with Mr. Shively was for 4:30 P.M. that first Wednesday, and then, as it turned out, every Wednesday for the rest of the summer. Once I found someone who would listen to me, I lived from one Wednesday to the next. That first afternoon I drove slowly to the church and reluctantly parked my car in front. The church was directly across the street from The Hunt

Club, and I was so afraid one of my friends would see my car or me, and wonder what was going on. Mr. Shively's office was air-conditioned, so we could sit in comfort, while I got everything up and out. I decided not to waste any time and was very straightforward.

"Our marriage is a total disaster, I'm always angry at my husband, I'm terribly unhappy, and I don't know what to do." And then I burst into tears and cried and cried and cried. Thank Heaven for the comforting hum of the air-conditioner! Mr. Shively sat there quietly, offering me Kleenex and didn't say much. But he was not shocked by a thing that I said. In the hour that we had that first Wednesday, I just rattled on and poured out all my pent-up angers, frustrations, and hateful feelings. It was funny, but once things came out into the light, they didn't seem quite so terrible. As the weeks went by, he would gently and patiently probe and question me, but mostly he let me talk, talk, talk, until I had said everything I could think of to say.

In the meantime, my brother David was continuing to send me an assortment of Christian books from Logos. Along with the books came a few phone calls to find out how I was doing, and what I thought of the books. I didn't know what to make of an Episcopal priest named Dennis Bennett, who prayed about getting a parking place when he went to the shopping center. His book, *Nine O'Clock in the Morning* was one of the most fascinating I had read. I almost never prayed to God, but if I ever did, it would never occur to me to pray for a parking place!

In August my parents went East to visit friends. They decided to stop off on Cape Cod to see David, Barbara, and their daughter Blair who were living at that time in a Christian community in Orleans, Massachusetts. While

Mother was there in the Community's guest house, she became acutely ill with severe back pain and could not get out of bed. She was in such pain, the doctor said she could not be moved for three days—so there my parents stayed, in the retreat house, until Mother could be taken to the airport to be flown home to the hospital, where she was placed in traction. Upon her return, I went to the hospital to see Mother, but found her heavily sedated for the pain. She spoke over and over again about this wonderful place where she had been, where everyone was kind and loving, and where there was such peace and joy all around. She just kept talking about love and joy—I listened, but wondered, what kind of a community *was* this?

One September night, a couple of weeks later, David called to ask me if I would like to come East for a retreat that his community, The Community of Jesus, was going to have in New Hampshire, at a retreat camp known as Brookwoods. If I would fly to Hyannis, on the Cape, he would meet my plane. "I can't wait for you to see this place and to meet Cay and Judy, the directors!" he exclaimed over the phone. "Mom and Dad liked it, and you will, too, so please come!"

"Wait a minute!" I laughed. "Slow down! who are Cay and Judy, and what's a retreat?" David explained, and I said, "Okay, I'll come." I laughed, when he started in all over again. I still didn't know what I was going to do, except take a plane to Hyannis. I said good-bye to Dan and the children with a great sense of anticipation. I had never done anything like this in my life, flying off alone, to heaven only knew what.

I arrived right on schedule that sunny, warm, September Thursday, the 23rd. I looked about for my brother whom I had not seen for a year—since our trip to the Poconos. A tall, lean, tanned and very handsome man came forward to greet me. This thin man couldn't be my brother who had been close to 250 pounds only a year ago. What had *happened* to him? What kind of a place did he live in?

We went straight to his car, to drive the half hour from Hyannis to Orleans, arriving at his house just in time for lunch. I loved David and Barbara's new home the minute I saw it, right on the water off Cape Cod Bay. We ate lunch in the sun porch, from which we could see the charter fishing boats bobbing up and down on the horizon. Later in the afternoon, David took me on a tour of the Community, and introduced me to all the members who regularly gathered for coffee and tea at 3:00 on the back lawn of the retreat house.

I was amazed that everyone stopped what they were doing to have coffee hour together. I looked around the circle at all the happy, smiling faces and recalled Mother's comment about the peace and joy she found here. I, too, felt a sense of peace and quiet and order amongst these people. We spent about an hour, and then I was taken to see more of the homes. In one kitchen I found large pots of freshly-picked tomatoes stewing away, while in another kitchen vegetables were being prepared for freezing and canning. I thought of my own kitchen, empty at four o'clock, because I was always so busy on the telephone, organizing another committee.

Barbara planned a surprise birthday party for David that night complete with his favorite cake and ice cream. His birthday was actually the next day, but we would be driving up to New Hampshire for the retreat, so she wanted to have the party early with all the family.

After the delicious birthday dinner, I went off to the guest house, but I was too excited to sleep. I climbed into my comfortable bed and tried to remember all the events of this day. I remembered especially the feeling of contentment that prevailed everywhere we went, in spite of all the activity that I saw going on. I had no idea what tomorrow would bring, but somehow I knew even then that something wonderful was about to happen. It was all connected with my brother, this new place he and Barbara had moved to, and my tenseness, my tired, thin body, my husband and children–I sensed that we were all going to be affected by the events of the next three days.

Friday morning, I awoke early to the smells of breakfast eggs and homemade bread just out of the oven. The September sun was shining, and the birds were gaily singing their welcome to this new and glorious day, as I dressed quickly, anxious for our trip to begin. But first I sat in the dining room, watching the fishing boats riding at anchor at the Rock Harbor dock. Breakfast was every bit as good as the aromas that had drifted up the stairs to my room. I had no trouble eating the lovingly prepared meal, just as I had enjoyed the special birthday dinner the night before. Everything tasted wonderful–my rigorous diet was forgotten for this trip. I waited impatiently for David and Barbara to come with their car for the six-hour drive to the retreat center. Already my thin, nervous body had quieted down after just one good night's rest in that place and all the nourishing food, and I looked forward to the next three days. We arrived at our destination shortly after lunch, in time to help set up all the chairs for the evening meeting. The camp buildings were just as I had imagined–rustic, wooden structures with beamed ceilings and large picture windows overlooking a sparkling blue lake. The air was crisp and clear–perfect weather for a weekend in the woods of

New Hampshire.

It was in the midst of this afternoon activity that I first met Cay Andersen and Judy Sorensen, the two women David had told me so much about. He explained to me that they were the founders and directors of the Community of Jesus which had formed around their joint ministry of counseling, teaching, and leading retreats. David took me over to introduce me. I saw two very different women and yet at the same time, they were like one. Cay, in her late fifties, was older by several years and had softly waved blond hair, while Judy, in her mid-forties, had shorter, dark brown hair and dark eyes. These two smiling ladies welcomed me with a kiss and a hug. "We're so glad to meet you, Camie." I told them how glad I was to meet them, too, after hearing so much about them. We only had time for "hello," but I felt a warmth and love from them immediately. They were very nice ladies, I thought–and so friendly. I couldn't wait to hear them speak after dinner.

We walked into the large meeting room where at least 150 men and women had gathered together from all over New England. Why had they come? What had drawn them here? Did they face the same horrible problems I did? I glanced around the spacious room nervously, not quite sure what would happen next. Then I relaxed and felt my tensions slowly slip away, as we started singing some familiar hymns to the accompaniment of a rickety old piano. "Stand up, stand up for Jesus," I remembered from Sunday school days, and "Dear Lord and Father of Mankind," was another one I knew, from boarding school. This wasn't going to be so bad, after all. I enjoyed singing along with everyone and let my voice join with theirs. After about fifteen minutes of singing, I saw Cay and Judy walk forward to stand in front of the assembled retreatants. They stood side by side with Cay on Judy's right, both in quietly attractive dresses. They reminded me somewhat of my mother, not so much in appearance, although Cay was the same age, but in their dignified presence.

Judy started off by asking the Lord to bless our time together, praying that His will would be done, and that the Holy Spirit of Truth would prevail. After that, they took turns speaking, and I later learned that while one talked, the other prayed for her. I found myself leaning forward and listening intently as they taught about Jesus and our ever-present need of Him. I didn't understand all of the message, but I knew I was attracted to the vibrant life that I could see in their faces. They laughed a lot and told many humorous stories about themselves to illustrate points. I laughed too, and felt myself relax more and more, as the night went on. They also told us stories about their husbands and children, so that by the end of the evening I felt as if I had known their families for years. There were times I just didn't know what to make of everything they said, because so much of it was new to me, but I never lost my excitement or sense of anticipation.

The next morning, Saturday, dawned bright and sunny. I lay there on my camp cot with thoughts swirling through my head. I liked what I had heard and wanted to hear more about Jesus, but I had so many questions. Maybe Barbara would answer them at breakfast. I was very disappointed, when Barbara said to me: "Camie, it would be better for you not to sit with David and me at meals. Why don't you pray and ask the Lord where you are to sit?"

What? Pray and ask the Lord where to eat breakfast? Was she crazy? And yesterday, she had prayed about which bed to sleep in–the whole thing was too much for me! I stood for a minute in the doorway, surveying the cheerful dining room filling up with hungry retreatants. What am I to do now? I don't know anyone here! I marched into the room, furious that I could not eat with them, and nervous about what to do next.

Well, there wasn't anything else to do, so I prayed to myself and said, "Okay, Lord, show me a table." I started walking then, towards the back of the room, when I actually heard a voice inside me say, "Right here." With goose bumps on my arms, I stopped short–the table in front of me was empty, but soon filled with chatting, smiling people, including two nice-looking men who sat next to me. Remembering my training in social graces, I turned to them and asked, "Where are you from? And what do you do?" They both replied, "We're ministers, from Farmington, Connecticut."

"Oh, my!" I exclaimed, "That *is* a coincidence! I went to school there." I sat for a minute wondering, and then I added, "I was at Miss Porter's for three years. In fact, I went to one of your churches on Sundays!"

They just smiled. "Funny thing, isn't it?" Then, one of them asked me to tell about myself. I told them about my husband and three children, where I lived, who my brother was, and that this was my first retreat.

"Why did you come all the way from Ohio for a retreat?"

All of a sudden, tears welled up in my eyes, and I fumbled in my purse for a Kleenex. Why did I come? Because my life was such a terrible mess, and I didn't know what to do about it! I started to cry, as I searched for an answer. "To find peace," I finally replied.

"Good," they said, looking first at me and then at each other. To my utter astonishment, they then told me that they would pray for me this weekend–that I would indeed find the peace I was looking for so desperately. I couldn't believe my ears–what a breakfast! And all because I was willing to pray to know where to sit. Was this really happening?

The day went by quickly, with more teaching by Cay and Judy during the morning, then lunch followed by a quiet time for reading or walking in the silent woods, or to the sun-dappled, sky-blue lake nearby. Around 3:00 P.M., we gathered in smaller groups for a question-and-answer time. My discussion group was led by a team of ministers, and retreatants like me were able to ask questions about the teaching we had heard last night and that morning. I had felt very uneasy, tearful, and all mixed up inside, as the afternoon went on. I just didn't know what I thought about all the things I had heard about the reality of Jesus and God. I felt better, though, after my new friends from breakfast waved "hello" and encouraged me, "We're praying for you," they called to me, when I passed them on a walk.

After dinner, we had another teaching session with Cay and Judy. Once again, I sat there, wondering and questioning, not really knowing what they were talking about. It all had to do with Jesus, His love for us, our obedience to Him and the blessings of knowing Him as Lord and Savior. I couldn't get over it–Jesus, the Son of God, as our friend!

When the meeting was over, refreshments were served in the dining room. I started out the door, as two ladies, strangers to me, came up to me and said that the Lord had told them to ask me to have hot chocolate and doughnuts with them. They were so friendly and loving, I started to cry again and sat at the table with tears streaming down my cheeks. I didn't know why.

The next thing I knew, I looked up and there stood Cay and Judy, smiling at me. "Would you like to come outside with us?" they asked. I nodded yes. Then they gently led me out the door into the warm September night. I felt quite undone, totally out of control, and an emotional wreck, as we walked toward some tall evergreen trees. We were standing under the spreading branches, when they said: "Would you like to give up the reins of your life? Are you tired of carrying all your worries and burdens by yourself? Would you like Jesus to take charge?" Again, I nodded yes. "Then, why don't you hand over control of your life to Jesus, and let Him be your Lord and Savior?"

"Yes, oh, yes!" I sobbed with great relief. "I would like to have Jesus come into my life." I did feel very tired, very burdened, as if I had the weight of the world on my shoulders.

So Cay and Judy prayed with me and laid hands on my head and shoulders, as I asked Jesus to take over my life, to become the Lord of my life. I was laughing, crying, and praying all at the same time with these two ladies who were telling me that Jesus could help me, and that it was safe to give the reins of my life over to Him, that He would carry my load of troubles and problems. And, as they talked, I felt the very real presence of Jesus, standing right there next to me, and I felt the weight being lifted from my shoulders. It was the most marvelous feeling! I felt light-headed and giddy with relief!

I don't know how long we were outside, but then we returned to the meeting room, to join with the others for the closing service. I was so happy! And I felt so free, so joyful! That night there was much rejoicing in our cabin bunkroom. I was so excited that I hardly slept the whole night. I felt—I *was*—a completely new person! And, the next morning, after breakfast, there was a time of sharing, when people could say what the retreat had meant to them. I stood up in front of all those 150 people and told them what I had done the night before. Once again, I was in tears, but this time they were tears of joy.

Sunday, at lunchtime, I prayed again about where to eat, and ended up sitting with the chaplain of the Community, Father Arthur Lane, who was also very warm and friendly. While we were talking, Cay and Judy invited me to come back to the Community for a few days for a rest and time to relax. This threw me into a state of panic, because I knew that in a couple of hours my husband would be leaving for the airport to meet my plane from Boston. How could I not go home? What about the children? Could they get along without their mother on such short notice? I had always been very organized–lists made, meals fixed and carpools arranged–before leaving town. How. . .

This day would be my first lesson in how to trust God in my life. Now I could practice turning my life over to Jesus, then standing still and watching Him move. Father Lane was very encouraging and suggested that my new lunch table friends pray, while I called Dan to tell him I would be staying on with David and Barbara for a few extra days. So I called–and was in tears again, while I talked on the phone. Poor Dan! He could not begin to understand what on earth was happening to me, but he was pleased, because in spite of my tears, I seemed happy to him.

I drove back to the Community with David and Barbara, and spent the next two days reading the Bible, and seeing everyone and everything with a new pair of eyes that suddenly were opened up to a whole new world, thanks to the new life I had found in Jesus. David gave me a copy of the New Testament, and I spent hours sitting in a lawn chair in his backyard, looking at the sun glinting on the waters of Cape Cod Bay, reading different Scriptures, and thinking about all the events that had taken place during the past weekend. I was a bit nervous about going home to Cleveland. How in heaven was I ever going to explain to Dan and the children what had happened to me?

I needn't have worried a bit! Jesus was in charge, now. Dan met me at the airport and took me out to dinner, before we went home, so that I would have a chance to tell him more details about my experience. I don't know how much he understood, but he saw me happy and content and eating, and that in itself spoke volumes. And when I got home, I gave each of our children a big hug and kiss, and told them how happy I was to see them, and that spoke volumes, too!

12

The Battle to Stay Thin

I was very sleepy. I could hear voices nearby, as I floated somewhere above the bed, and it seemed that they were talking about me. As the anesthesia wore off, I recognized the voice of our family doctor. "Let me be very honest, Bud," Dr. Perkins was saying. "I don't usually tell any couple that it's impossible for them to have a baby. But in my experience, I must say that I've never seen more discouraging tests. They show absolutely no signs of ovulation, nor have there been any menstrual periods for several years. It seems like some sort of hormone imbalance. To be absolutely frank, if I ever saw a couple who should accept the fact that they will have no children of their own, you and Sunny are that couple. I'll be glad to give you the names of several good adoption agencies, and I want to help you in any way that I can."

Keeping my eyes closed, I pretended to be asleep. I didn't want them to know that I had heard until I could get my feelings under control. And later on, when Bud and I did talk about the doctor's report, I pretended to be very matter-of-fact. I insisted that Bud go ahead with his plan to go to the out-of-town football game in

Midland: "You should go! Really, I'm perfectly fine. Go and have a good time, and we'll talk about adoption tomorrow." When he had gone, I turned out the light in the bare, impersonal hospital room and wept bitterly in the dark.

No children of our own! That had to be impossible! How could such a thing be? Our hoped-for family was the one subject on which Bud and I were still in total agreement. We both wanted a big family of at least four. Earlier that year, we had started eagerly planning. "A baby," we had agreed, "it's time for us to start our family." We had been married for more than two years, we had a home of our own, and I was certainly more than ready to stop teaching. We even had a room set aside to be the nursery, with polished hardwood floor, pale pink walls, and white ruffled curtains tied back at the windows. Our perfect plan had just one flaw: Mother Nature had not cooperated. After several disappointing months, I had finally gone in to see our family doctor, who had scheduled an overnight stay in the hospital for minor surgery and diagnostic tests.

And now it sounded as if those dreams were totally and completely smashed. If there was a God, He was heartless and cruel! What had I ever done to deserve this? It was so totally unfair! Adoption! I wanted to have a baby of our own! I wanted to be pregnant and to experience motherhood firsthand. I wanted to see who our babies would look like–would they have the Hales' Roman nose or the pug nose from my side of the family tree? I thought about the grandchildren on both sides of the family, and the way that our parents adored them. My sister already had two little girls, and Bud had two little nieces. The perfect family *had* to have children! It was in the script that I had so carefully planned out for my life–and now it was never going to happen. The tears continued to flow.

Finally, I resigned myself to adopting–and soon discovered that adoption was no easy matter. Even when abortion was far less prevalent, there were far more prospective parents than available babies, and there was an enormous amount of preliminary work to be done, just to get on the waiting lists. First, we sent out a flood of applications with references from ministers and former schoolteachers who spoke of our character in glowing phrases, and then we went in person to be interviewed by some of the adoption agencies.

In the fall of 1961, I took a long weekend from school, and Bud and I drove 300 miles to Fort Worth to visit two agencies. I had been to the Dallas-Fort Worth area only two or three times in my life, and it should have been an exciting trip. The fields were white with cotton, ready to harvest, and the mellow autumn sunshine played on unaccustomed red and yellow foliage as we drove into East Texas, but none of the surrounding beauty lifted my spirits.

"What if they don't like us? What if we have to wait a long time? Who will the real parents be?" On and on I went. "What if we get a baby that we don't like? Are there return privileges?"

Finally Bud had heard enough. "Will you stop!" he exploded, and I sat in wounded silence the rest of the way.

The next morning we drove through Fort Worth to one of the nicer parts of the city. The main building was a gracious residence, set back from the street amid sloping lawns and tall shady trees. In the waiting room were about ten couples near our own age or a little older, some of the husbands already a little thin on top.

Assembling for a tour of the grounds, we eyed one another nervously, as we waited to hear more about our chances of becoming parents. At best, it did not sound very promising as the social worker began to talk.

"Of course we want to make every effort to ensure that our babies have happy, secure homes," she told us. "We have many more applications than we can supply, and we carefully match each baby to the parents in background, physical characteristics, and so on. We will put your name on our waiting list, but it will probably be at least a two-year wait for the right baby to come along."

Bud seemed grateful to have been accepted, but my own thoughts raced round and round as we drove back to the motel. Two years! That's forever. I can't wait that long. I don't see why we couldn't have had our own baby like everyone else! Maybe our parents had been right. While they had not actually said anything against adopting, I could tell that they were not wildly excited about the idea. "Don't be in too big a hurry," had been their counsel.

Today I just felt depressed and disappointed. "Let's get something to eat, Bud; what about that Holloway's Chicken Inn up ahead?" Soon I was consoling myself with one homemade roll after another, topped with butter and honey. Who cared if the sleeves on my dress were feeling a little tight?

Slowly, almost imperceptibly at first, I was gaining weight. I could no longer deny it to myself, even though I avoided the scale. It was becoming more and more difficult not to eat. I still wanted to look thin and worried about it constantly, but the supercontrol–the old power to will myself not to eat–was weakening. Morning doughnuts in the teacher's lounge at school, apple pie in the school cafeteria–one day I would eat everything forbidden, and the next day, guilt-stricken, I would have nothing but a glass of liquid Metrecal. The pleasure in eating was shortlived, for it made me feel like a failure. Oh, well, I had failed everywhere else—and then, even more unhappy and depressed, I would have something else to eat.

Often driving home from school, I would turn in at Campbell's Bakery. "I'll take six pecan sticky buns, please, Mrs. Campbell." Then feeling embarrassed, I added, "My husband just loves them!" The truth was, I just loved them and planned to eat every one myself. At home, bored with the long afternoon that stretched ahead until Bud would be in from the farm, I would lie on the sofa in the den, reading a book and eating one sticky bun after another. Bud wondered why I usually wanted no dinner. "Oh, I'm just not hungry," I said vaguely.

It was no longer any fun to go shopping. The size 7 dresses from my trousseau had long since been outgrown, and I went through size 9 in just a few weeks. When the newly-purchased 11's began to feel a bit snug, I had stopped weighing altogether. "Well, after all, a size 11 is not too bad. It's still a junior size," I tried to convince myself. "Maybe the sizes run a little smaller than they used to."

But the mirror could not be convinced. "I hate you! You are fat, and you are ugly!" I cried out loud at my reflection. "I hate you, I hate to teach school, I hate to live in this town, and most of all, I hate farming!"

Maybe that was the problem. After all, I had never wanted to farm, and now here we were, tied to a farm and to Bud's family and to mine. It was Bud's fault, and so I told him how unhappy I felt at every opportunity. "You don't get home until 8:00 at night! What am I supposed to do until then? You don't care about me at all. All you think about is cotton and tractors; you never think of me. We don't have any friends, and I hate this house; I never wanted it anyway. It has a terrible yard, all sand burrs, and yesterday I ran over a horned toad when I mowed the grass. I wanted a house with big trees and a pretty yard, and this one has the ugliest roof I've ever seen!"

Bud listened and said nothing. Then he abruptly turned, and murmuring that he had forgotten to check some equipment, he got back into the pick-up and drove away. And the following morning, he left for work even earlier and came home still later.

But still sometimes he would try, in spite of me. "Who was that on the phone, Sunny?" he asked one Saturday afternoon.

"Oh, it was just the Turners. They wanted us to come over and play cards tonight. But I don't want to. I don't have anything to wear; nothing fits anymore."

"Now, come on, you can find *something* to wear. We're going! It will do you good to see some people, and besides he's your principal. You can't refuse." I could tell that his mind was made up and there was no use resisting, but I spent a miserable evening, just as I knew I would. I had pinned my waistband over because it would no longer meet, and it was impossible to have a good time when I knew I looked absolutely awful.

Christmas finally came–a welcome break in the monotony of days all exactly the same, at home and at school. I could forget our differences as I threw myself into decorating the house. It was going to look just like the pictures in *Good Housekeeping.* I sewed little elves with cotton beards for the living room mantel, shopped for pine cones and candles for every table in the house, and hung homemade wreaths on all the doors.

Then came the cooking, and as this was going to be the first year that I actually ate the goodies that I made, I tried recipe after recipe. Chocolate-dipped Martha Washington candies, date loaf, bishop's bread, fruit-cake–the cupboards and the freezer were stocked to overflowing, as I cooked and ate, and cooked and ate some more.

Sitting on the living room floor, surrounded by yards of red felt, I suddenly felt a little queasy, as I pinned tiny reindeer and Santas on the Christmas tablecloth that I was making for the round dining room table. Even the smell of the material made me feel nauseous. "Guess I've overdone it," I thought. "Never should have eaten those last pralines." A little fresh air might help, so I walked out on the front porch to get the mail. The long, blue envelope postmarked Fort Worth caught my eye, and I ripped it open eagerly.

"Dear Mr. and Mrs. Hale," the letter began, "We are happy to tell you that we will be visiting you in your home within the next six weeks, in order to make the final arrangements for the placement of a baby, probably by the end of February." Waving the letter, I ran outside to meet Bud, as he pulled into the drive.

"It's here! The letter has finally come," I told him. "We're going to be parents!"

But even that excitement and anticipation could not dispel the unhappiness I felt about my weight. It hung like a dark cloud over even the brightest moments, and I could never forget about it. Everything was so tight now that I could scarcely breathe, because I refused to buy anything larger than a size 12, no matter how uncomfortable it felt. It got to the point that even my mother had discreetly hinted that I seemed to be acquiring a rather ample waistline.

"Well, okay," I thought angrily, "that's just great! After all these years of trying to get me to eat! As if I don't know that the whole situation has gotten out of hand!" But Mother's comment was the final straw. Gathers and pleated skirts could no longer camouflage my round tummy, and finally in desperation I knew that I had to get help.

Right after school that day, I headed for the office of our family doctor, arriving breathlessly at the receptionist's desk. "Listen, Joan, I know I don't have an appointment, but this really is an emergency. Do you think the doctor could see me?"

Soon, seated in one of the small examination rooms, I wondered what I was going to say to him. I hated to admit that I could not control my weight. It was a matter of pride to me, especially since his daughter was one of my first grade students. But pride or not, I needed help, and I was going to have to ask for it.

"Hello, Sunny, what can I do for you today?"

"Dr. Perkins, you've got to help me! I've just got have a diet or something. I feel like jumping off the roof," I exclaimed, only half joking. "I've started gaining weight, and I can't stop."

The scale in his office soon confirmed my worst fears. The iron weight on that big scale kept moving farther and farther to the right–past 120, 125, and finally settling at 130! I had never weighed that much in my entire life, even in my "Chub" days! How could this have happened? From 88 pounds to 130! Fighting back tears, I followed the nurse back to the examining room for a thorough physical, and then back to his office to hear the verdict.

I sat opposite his desk, while he looked at me with a

puzzled smile and shook his head. "Sunny," he said, "unless you have the largest tumor I've ever seen, I'd say you are about three and a half months pregnant!"

"*What?*" And he repeated his diagnosis to my incredulous surprise. Suddenly the whole world looked different. Bud and I were so excited that we drove all over town, visiting everyone we could think of, sharing the good news. It was a miracle, and one we just had to tell to parents, relatives, neighbors, and schoolteaching friends. Everyone rejoiced with us. It was like a wonderful dream, the most exciting time of my life!

When we calmed down, we called the adoption agency to remove our names from their list of prospective parents. Then I took a shopping trip to the Maternity Shop in Lubbock for a brand-new wardrobe. How I loved all the clothes! The loose smocks, the stretchy-topped skirts—everything felt marvelous! All the pressure to be thin was gone; it was okay to be fat! I was not a social outcast, after all; on the contrary, I was going to be a mother! The next stop was the local bookstore to stock up on reading material. *Life Before Birth, The First Nine Months of Life, Prenatal Care*—I wanted to read everything in print on the subject. Giving birth was the most fascinating subject in the world, and it was happening to me! At long last, I had found my reason for being.

The news of the expected baby brought Bud and me together in a new way. We had lots of important decisions to make: Did we want a boy or a girl? Should we paint the nursery blue or leave it pink? Should he or she go to Texas Tech or Texas A&M? Then, too, there was the all-important subject of names. For hours we discussed the relative merits of Jim (short for James, Bud's name as well as my grandfather's), Stephen, Michael, or Jon (spelled without an H). We would make up our minds, and then the next day I would find another name that sounded very nice with Hale, and we would start all over again.

Even teaching school now seemed more fun. All the children and their parents were excited about the news, and of course everyone knew right away, because I immediately appeared in my new maternity clothes and was happy to explain my weight gain of months past. The due date was expected to be around the Fourth of July, so I would finish the year, hand in my permanent resignation, and stay home and be a mother. There were showers and gifts, and how I loved being the center of attention! It was even more fun than a wedding.

Weight-wise, I felt that I had been given a reprieve, a new chance, and this time I was not going to blow it. I started out right away to turn over a new leaf; there were more exciting things to think about than food anyway. The night after we received the big news, Bud and I went out to celebrate with dinner at Allen's Galley. "I'll have a chef's salad," I ordered. I had already gained the recommended twenty pounds for an entire pregnancy, and I intended to draw the line right there.

When Michael James was born, I felt very, very grateful. I seldom prayed, but this time I just had to say, "Thank you, God, for letting us have this baby of our own." He was big (8 pounds, 12 ounces) and healthy, and the most beautiful bald-headed baby I had ever seen. He was real, he was ours, he had tiny perfect fingers and toes, and I adored him.

Bud and I were not the only ones thrilled with our new son; at the nursery window there was a steady stream of grandparents, aunts and uncles, cousins and friends, and my room looked like a florist's shop. My mother was especially happy; Michael was the first boy in our family in two generations. My sister had girls!

Even in the midst of the first joy and wonder of it all, I still had to look good. Visiting hours were 4 to 6 in the afternoon, and at 3:45, I jumped up, smoothed the covers, changed to a frilly gown, and put on make-up. It was hard to really rest because I wanted to be ready all day, just in case someone should stop by. The first thing I did on the morning of July 12 was to walk down to the nurse's station and weigh. The scale had only dropped to 120; I still had a long way to go.

Once the baby and I were home, I had other pressing problems, most important of which was: What in the world was I going to wear? It was fun to take care of the baby, and I could wear loose robes around the house or maybe even a maternity top, but sooner or later, I would have to get dressed and go out, and none of my clothes fit. Maybe I could pick up a few things in a larger size down at Baldwin's, just to tide me over. I went, and returned home in tears, my morale shattered.

"What's the matter, hon?" Bud asked, as I ran into the bedroom and slammed the door behind me.

"Go away! I don't want to talk about it!" But I finally stopped crying long enough to share the terrible news. "It was that awful clerk down at Baldwin's," I wailed. "She asked me when was our baby due. She couldn't even tell that I had already had it, three weeks ago! Oh, Bud, I look horrible! I've got to lose weight!"

The next morning I took myself in hand. "Okay, Sunny, this is it: Nursing mothers use a lot of calories, and this is one mother who is not going to eat much. All the books say that the most important thing is to drink a lot of liquids, which is fine; I love Diet Dr. Peppers."

The strategy seemed to work, and the pounds slowly began to melt away, as I stopped eating. It was worth having just an apple for lunch, if I could get into my clothes again. Lucy, the cleaning lady, came in regularly, the grandparents were always available to babysit, change diapers, and give baths, and I began the serious work of getting thin again.

"One, two, three, bend," I groaned, trying to touch my toes. Even with all the exercise and cutting my calorie intake drastically, I could not get my weight as low as it had been the first year of our marriage, and I was forced to set a new "upper limit." If I could keep my weight between 105 and 110, I would be okay, I told myself. But if I wanted to go on wearing slacks, I simply couldn't weigh any more than that!

All was right in my world again. I was thin, Bud's farming was expanding, I worked hard at motherhood, and for the next few years life seemed to be what I had always wanted. But sometimes after dinner, I would restlessly take a walk in the cool Texas twilight, often stopping by Sam's little drive-in grocery to buy Tootsie Rolls. After a day whose menu consisted of one piece of toast for breakfast, one apple for lunch, and meat and green vegetables for dinner, I would stuff my mouth full of Tootsie Rolls, when no one else was looking.

One day, I announced to Bud that I thought it was time for another trip to Dallas-Fort Worth. "But this time not to an adoption agency; I want to see a specialist."

"What in the world for? We've had one baby; why are you so worried about the next one? Just relax!"

"I can't relax! I think we should go and see a specialist. I think we can have another baby, too; but the question is: why aren't we? I want to find out why. I hate the waiting and the uncertainty and the disappointments. I want to have another baby *now*!

So we went. Baylor Hospital in Dallas was well-known for its excellence, and I had confidence in the doctors who practiced there. Dr. Taylor was younger than I expected, but I liked him at first sight. I felt I could trust him, and I poured out all the frustrations and fears of the past few years.

"Your physical symptoms are interesting," he said. "You have many of the symptoms that were seen in women liberated from Nazi concentration camps at the end of World War II, symptoms that were the result of severe malnutrition. Loss of menses, loss of weight—these days we see it again in models and ballet dancers. It's a psychological condition called *anorexia nervosa.* But just to be sure that there is nothing organically wrong, I'd like you to enter the hospital here for a full battery of tests. It would take about a week; can you stay?"

The whole idea was scary. I had not been away from Bud since we were married six years before, but I was willing to try anything. Bud went home to check on Mike and the cotton crop, and I went into the hospital to room with a lady from Amarillo, who had leukemia. When her family came to visit, I felt very much ashamed of my petty problems. She had so much courage and optimism, and although her leukemia was presently in remission, she knew that she was probably going to die within the next few years. "How can she be so cheerful and loving with her children and husband?" I wondered. "I could never be like that."

It seemed like Bud had been gone forever, when Saturday finally came, and I checked out of the hospital. Together we drove over to Dr. Taylor's office to hear the verdict.

"Mrs. Hale, I believe that it is a simple matter of your being too thin. If you bring your weight up eight or ten pounds at least to 115, then I believe you will start ovulating again and be perfectly normal. That's probably what happened when you gained weight before your first pregnancy."

I could feel myself begin to panic; I almost wished that he had said that I was physically sick. "But, Doctor, you don't understand! If I ever let myself start gaining weight, I just can't stop!"

"That's because you are so far under your normal weight," he assured me. "When you reach a normal weight for your height and bone structure, you should start to level off."

"At 115 pounds I'll look like a blimp! And I feel so guilty when I eat. Maybe I could just take vitamins instead of actually gaining the pounds. Would that help?"

Dr. Taylor was very patient. "Mrs. Hale, you are going to have to change your whole way of thinking. You have a truly distorted mental picture of yourself, a *Vogue* idea of what is attractive. I can't tell you how many models we see here, who are also malnourished and anovulatory. I hope that your problem is not psychologically deep-seated and that with this high-calorie diet you will be able to gain at least two pounds a week. If not, then you may need the help of a psychiatrist. But right now, I am going to prescribe some tranquilizers for you to take, which should help your anxiety."

"Okay, I'll do it. But just to 115, and if I gain any more than that, you'll have to give me a low-calorie diet."

I wanted to be pregnant, so I was going to be obedient–for a time. I threw away the Librium, but I did try to eat more. "Maybe I have to gain this weight to have a baby, but I don't have to stay there very long. And I certainly don't need to see a psychiatrist." I went down to the public library and photostatted all the references to anorexia nervosa, which turned out to be not very many. It was an interesting but obscure condition, first identified by some doctor in the nineteenth century. An occasional case had been seen here and there in recent years, but it was definitely a rarity. Evidently the name was something of misnomer, because the patient often was really very hungry and willfully refusing to eat. "That's all very enlightening, but it doesn't have anything to do with me at all." I dismissed Dr. Taylor's diagnosis as nonsense. "Maybe I like to be thin, but I'm certainly not crazy enough to starve myself to death."

Slowly I gained a pound or two a week, until the scale hit the magic number of 115. I assuaged the guilt I felt when eating with the thought that the weight gain would be only temporary. And just like clockwork, within a few months I was pregnant with our second child. This time it was not a surprise, and this time I had no intention of letting my weight get out of control.

Again, I really loved to be pregnant, although this time it was not quite the cloud nine experience that it had been before. For one thing, I had a toddler to take care of, and it seemed that I was a lot more tired. Of course I was much more strict about what I did or did not eat. I took vitamins and tried to eat very small, nonfattening meals. Somewhere I had read that there really was no danger of depriving a baby of nutrients, for it would take what it needed from the mother's system. That, of course, was exactly what I wanted to hear.

But sometimes I got *very* hungry, and often I had an almost irresistible craving for potatoes or something equally starchy. When the urge was overpowering, I would cut up one potato, cook it in a small amount of water, and devour the whole thing as my lunch, liquid and all.

Weighing in at the doctor's office each month was very important. "Mrs. Hale, you're doing so well." Cora, the nurse there, was very complimentary. "Just half a pound this month! I wish all our patients tried this hard not to gain too much." Now the medical profession seemed to approve of my weight control, so I felt more right than ever about it.

Our baby was due in August, and I spent the whole last part of the summer sitting at home with the air-conditioner blowing full blast. Everything was ready, the bassinet was hopefully ruffled in pink, and on the appointed day I was packed and ready to go, but unfortunately I did not seem to be having any pains. Finally I did manage to have a few contractions, and Bud and I arrived at the hospital just as the breakfast trays were being wheeled down the hall–not quite as exciting as a middle of the night entrance!

In the delivery room I held my breath until I heard the doctor say, "It's a girl!" I had wanted a daughter just as much as I had wanted a son the first time. When later that day, the first visitor arrived with a tiny little dress embroidered with little pink flowers, I was ecstatic. Now we had the perfect storybook family–strong father, loving mother, sturdy little son, and sweet baby girl. Who could ask for anything more? And an added bonus: this time I made it down to the nurses' station that same afternoon, and this time I was already back down to 110 pounds. I had gained only six pounds during the whole nine months.

A storybook family needed a storybook home, and it was time for a move. I left the house on North Seventeenth Street without a backward glance, for I had never liked it. We moved only one block over, but our new home was directly behind the high school, a much better location. We bought the house from a family in our church that I admired, and the backyard was lovely. On the first day after we moved in, I woke to a gentle rain, and lay there, eyes shut, listening to the sound of the raindrops hitting the leaves of the big tree outside our window. Mike had his own bedroom across the hall, Leigh's room had pink carpet, and I felt *very* content. Two children all our own, and now we even had trees!

Euphoria unfortunately turned out to be an all too short-lived phenomenon; before I knew it, my life had settled back into its dull, predictable routine. Redecorating the house and shopping for a closetful of little girl's dresses could only take up so much time, and soon I found my days hard to fill. By the time that Leigh was two, I was restless.

"Maybe I should get a job," I told myself. "Maybe I'm home too much; when I get bored, I want to eat." I was thin again, and wanted to stay that way, but I also wanted to eat and had to fight the constant temptation to nibble all day long. It seemed like a good idea to get out of the house, but at the same time the prospect of working and leaving the children made me feel very guilty.

"I know! Maybe I could get a *part-time* job! I'll try to find something for just half a day. Lucy comes in to clean, and maybe I can find a reliable baby-sitter who will come here to the house, so that I won't have to take the children out. Then I won't feel so bad about leaving them. After all, Mike is almost old enough for kindergarten; maybe they'll take him a little early."

I had soon convinced myself, but I felt compelled to keep explaining my reasons to friends and relatives, as neither my mother nor Bud's had ever had a job with small children at home.

"After all," I said to Bud's sister, "it's only *half* a day at Dr. Perkins' office. I'll pick up Mike at school and be home in time to fix lunch for everyone. I think it will do us all good for me to get out a bit. I won't be quite so nervous." She looked at me, and it was obvious that she did not see it the way I did. The guilt returned, but I pushed it aside and took the job.

It was fun to dress up in the white nurse's uniform with white shoes and to show patients to their rooms, take their histories, pulse, and blood pressures. Before long, Dr. Perkins had taught me to give a few simple shots and there was always something new to learn. After the busy morning, I enjoyed being home in the afternoon, getting dinner, and just being with the children. Sitting in the white rocking chair in Leigh's pink room, rocking her before her nap, I sang her to sleep with a silly little song that she liked, "Bye, Bitsy, bye, Bitsy, bye," the same nonsense tune that I remembered my mother singing to me. Fiercely I hugged the sleeping little girl to myself, my eyes filling up with tears. "What is *wrong* with me? Why can't I be like my mother and want to stay home? Why can't I ever be content? Leigh won't be little very long. I hope that I won't regret this later." And that day I spent some extra time with Mike and Leigh, reading stories.

Each week, the drug salesman came to the doctor's office, leaving behind boxes of new drug samples to be stored in the cabinets in the hall. The other nurse and I put them away carefully, and Dr. Perkins would give them out to patients and friends when needed.

One afternoon, a new red box caught my eye. "Appetite suppressant," I read. Intrigued, I read all the small print and possible side-effects. They didn't sound too bad. "That would really be a help! I wish I could suppress my appetite." It took constant will power to keep from eating, and I knew from experience that if I ate three meals a day I would gain weight. Furtively I put one of the packets in my pocket. "What would be the harm of trying a few? After all, Dr. Perkins had given me Dimetane and Novahistine samples when I had a cold. It's really not stealing; they're just samples."

I took the brightly colored capsules home, and they really did work! Taking them three times a day, I found that I wasn't hungry at all. The only problem was that where I was nervous before, now I was supercharged. At two o'clock in the morning, I was still up polishing the silver. I didn't want to eat, but I didn't want to sleep, either.

When the pills were all gone, I found myself standing in the hall at the doctor's office, looking at the cabinet. It was a quiet morning, the doctor was in with a patient, and it was Cora's day off. No one would ever know . . . but *I* would know. "I can't do it. It is stealing. I can't let myself depend on pills to stay thin. I don't trust myself; it's too tempting." I did not open the cabinet door again.

But while appetite suppressants were definitely wrong, in my mind diuretics were a different matter altogether. After all, Dr. Perkins had prescribed them for me when I was pregnant. Certainly they couldn't hurt me. I had discovered that if my weight was up in the morning, I could take a diuretic and weigh two or three pounds less by afternoon. "And if they were harmful, the drugstore certainly wouldn't have let me refill the prescription so easily," I reasoned. Also, I didn't lie about them, as I had been tempted to do about the appetite pills. Anytime I was asked what medication I took, I always said, "Thyroid pills and occasionally a diuretic." That wasn't lying, I assured myself. It all depended on what one meant by "occasionally." I did try not to take them too often, but I took them every time my weight went up. And of course it was all right to take thyroid pills every day, because once I had been tested low in thyroid. Too, I knew that thyroid secretion affected metabolism, which in turn affected weight. I had once known someone with an overactive thyroid, who was really skinny, so I never forgot to take my thyroid medication.

After about a year, the novelty of the nurse's job began to wear off, and I decided that I was not cut out for the medical profession. "You know," I thought aloud, "I've been a teacher, librarian, soda jerk, tax office clerk, and several other things, and always I get tired of it. Maybe it's time to be a housewife and mother again."

For some time, I had been thinking about how much I would like to have another baby, and Bud and I liked the idea of spacing our children about three years apart. One thing I knew; I did not want to see Dr. Taylor again and be told to first gain up to 115 pounds! There had to be a better way!

One Sunday morning, leafing through the paper, an article in the Living section caught my eye. "Listen, Bud: there's a new fertility drug being used around the country. It's called Clomid, and it triggers ovulation. Maybe that's the answer to my problem!" If I could take a pill to cause ovulation, then I wouldn't have to spend weeks gaining that hated weight.

The more I thought about it, the more excited I became. The only question was how to get the Clomid, for certainly no one in Lamesa had ever heard of it. But the article mentioned a doctor in Arlington who was involved in this type of treatment. "Well, here we go again, Bud. Everytime we decide to increase our family, we have to make a trip to the Dallas-Fort Worth area."

Dr. Herbert's office was filled with photographs of children. Tiny infants, cute two year olds–the inscriptions from satisfied customers certainly boosted my confidence. "To Dr. Herbert, with love and gratitude," and "Thank you so much for all you've done." I nodded, as I read. He must be doing something right.

I liked Dr. Herbert at first sight. Kindly and gray-haired, he looked like a grandfather, tapping his glasses thoughtfully on his desk as he listened.

"From your test results and from your history, it sounds as if we may be able to help you. You seem to be in good health, although you are depleted in potassium from taking too many diuretics. We can remedy that with lots of bananas and orange juice. Now if you do feel that you would like to take Clomid, I want you to know a few thing about it: It is a relatively new drug, and we have had very good results with it for the most part. But as perhaps you've read, quite often it results in multiple births. A woman in Wisconsin recently had quintuplets after Clomid therapy, and twins and triplets are not uncommon. How do you feel about that?"

Not waiting for Bud's response, I blurted out, "It's worth it!" Even this possibility was not going to deter me. The important thing was that it worked, and that I not have to gain those dreadful ten pounds!

Going back to Lamesa with a three-months' supply of Clomid, a basal thermometer, and all kinds of charts and graphs, I felt very confident. I followed all the instructions very carefully, and each morning eagerly took my temperature before raising my head from the pillow, later plotting it on the chart. Monday 97.8, Tuesday 97.6, Wednesday 97.8, Thursday 97.7, Friday 97.7. If ovulation took place, the temperature would drop slightly and then shift to a higher level, and maintain the higher level if pregnancy occurred.

Day after day, the line on the chart remained depressingly flat. "It's not working!" I felt like crying, but tried to pretend that my hopes were still high. "It *has* to work!"

The second month began. 97.7. 97.8. 97.8. 97.4 And then one morning I looked at the thermometer in astonishment. The mercury registered 98.2. Unbelieving, I took it three more times, and it stayed the same. "Bud, look at this graph. It dropped yesterday, and it's up today! It's working–the Clomid is working!"

But then there was a sharp temperature drop a few days later. "There's only one more month left," I groaned to myself. "Dr. Herbert said that I can only take the drug for three months, and two have already gone by." I tried not to let Bud know how disappointed I felt, as day after day I recorded the same low temperatures. One day the thermometer registered 98.3, but I refused to let my hopes rise. The next day read 98.4, then 98.3, 98.5, until finally it had remained high for twenty whole days.

"What do you think, Dr. Herbert?" I finally reached him on the phone.

He was cautiously optimistic. "It's a little early to be sure, Mrs. Hale, but the chances are good that you are pregnant. Why don't you drop in to see your local doctor in the next few days and let me know the results." His long distance diagnosis proved correct, and Bud and I were thrilled about the good news.

But the crisis had not all passed. Early in the third month I began to feel unwell, and a visit to Dr. Perkins was not reassuring. "I don't want to take any chances. It could be absolutely nothing, or it could be a threatened miscarriage. You should go to bed and stay off your feet altogether." I spent the next two weeks in bed, reading, worrying, and trying to supervise two small children from my bedroom. Often I plunged into self-pity, and the tears flowed.

"Why does everything have to be so difficult? After all we've been through trying to have this baby, I don't want anything to happen to it." I felt that fate, or God, or whoever was in charge, had been unfair and unkind to me. What had I done to deserve all this? Other people had their children and thought nothing of it. "Fertility drugs are so risky anyway; it makes me mad to have to depend on something like that. I don't see why my hormones have to be so messed up. Why can't I have been like everyone else?" All that Dr. Taylor had said at Baylor Hospital three years before, about my deliberately starving myself, had been conveniently forgotten. I refused to recognize that the problems we had had conceiving had anything to do with my demand to be thin. But even if I had remembered, I would have made the same choices. As much as I wanted to have children, it had to be on my terms.

The gloomy days passed, and soon I was on my feet again, and the rest of the pregnancy passed smoothly and uneventfully. I worked hard at not eating and kept my weight very low, and by the January due date I weighed just a little less than 120. Kathy Lynn Hale arrived on schedule, and her weight of 7 pounds, 11 ounces confirmed my rightness. What did all those books know anyway? All three of our children had been heavyweights; 8 lbs. 12 oz., 7 lbs. 13 oz., and 7 lbs. 11 oz. "I knew it didn't matter how little I gained!" With Michael I had gained the twenty prescribed pounds and eight or ten more, and with the girls I had gained less than ten. Now I knew that I *knew* best!

This time I wanted to be sure not to make the same mistake I had made after Leigh was born. I would be sure that we had some outside interests, so that I would not get bored and restless. I had learned that there was no lasting satisfaction in a job, and staying home all the time wouldn't work, either. "Guess what, Bud? I have a great idea!" I announced at dinner one evening. "It's time for us to have a social life!"

Bud put down his fork in amazement. Could this really be his wife talking? "I thought you didn't like to go places," he said.

"Well, anyone can change their mind. There are a lot of new couples in town, not just the ones we went to school with. I think we should try to make some new friends."

Still in shock, Bud nodded. "I couldn't agree more."

"The only catch is that we will have to learn to play bridge!" I absolutely hated the game because I had never played well. Normally I avoided anything that I couldn't excel in, but if we planned to have any social life in Lamesa, we would have to learn to play.

Soon I was meeting regularly on Tuesday afternoons with a bridge club of twelve young mothers, all about my age. We alternated homes, and the first time that I was to be hostess, I was in a panic. There was so much to be done! Everything had to be absolutely perfect! First I frantically cleaned the house from top to bottom (with Lucy's able help, of course). The curtains had to come down and be washed, the windows and the woodwork cleaned. The silver must be polished, and the yard cut and edged. Then there was the search for just the right recipe–something spectacular that no one else had ever served and preferably had never before tasted.

When the appointed Tuesday arrived, the house sparkled, and I was exhausted. Three bridge tables had been set up in the living room, with small bowls of nuts and candies and decks of decorative cards carefully arranged on each. In the refrigerator my Angel Delight dessert waited triumphantly–surely everyone would ask for the recipe! Mike, Leigh, and Kathy had been shipped off to Grandmother's for the day; I couldn't be bothered with children underfoot, while the important preparations went on. Their rooms were in perfect order, with every book and toy neatly aligned on its shelf, because, of course, there would be a tour of the house. The family's dinner would not be a problem–Bud could pick up hamburgers on his way home from the farm, and I wouldn't be eating anyway.

I took a quick look around. Yes, everything was ready. Just back from the hairdresser, I quickly dressed in a pink pants suit and nervously swallowed some antacid for my terrible stomach ache, as I waited for 2:00 to arrive. "Maybe I'm just hungry." After all, I hadn't eaten all day just so that I could have a small portion of dessert. "The Maalox should help." The doorbell rang, and I hurried to let Joan inside.

Tall and willowy, Joan walked like the model she was, and she dressed to show off her pencil-slim figure. She, too, was determined to never gain another ounce, but it did seem much easier for her to stay thin. She had become my best friend, and I was incredibly jealous of her. "Oh, Joan, come in! You look marvelous! I just love that outfit!" The others began to arrive, and the afternoon began, with talk of children, household help, diets, and new furniture. Occasionally someone would bid, but the cards were always secondary to the conversation.

Furtively I compared my size to everyone present, and always I felt fatter. "Isn't this fun, Joan? I'm so glad I started playing bridge!"

The ladies' afternoon bridge club was such a success that we decided to include our husbands, and soon Bud and I were hiring babysitters and going out two or three nights a week for dinner parties and bridge. There were parties at holidays, tennis on Sunday afternoons, and trips in the summer. I just watched the tennis games, and I resisted the summer water activities as long as possible.

"But, Joan," I had protested. "You know I don't like the water, and I'm terrified of lakes."

She was persistent. "You and Bud simply have to come and try our new boat. The Allens, the Millers, and the Pattersons are all coming. You'll love it, and the kids will have a ball."

"Well, okay, I'll go, but I definitely draw the line at water-skiing."

In spite of all my protests, I soon found myself sitting in the middle of Lake Brownwood, with a yellow life-belt holding me up in the water, and with the bar handle tightly clenched in my hands, as the boat and safety moved farther and farther away.

"Just relax," someone called from a million yards away. "Keep the tips of your skis up out of the water. When the line feels taut, stand up!"

"Stand up? In the water? They've got to be kidding!" The boat would speed up, and with a swoosh, I would lunge forward, my skis would porpoise, and I would be flat on my face, letting go of the rope to keep from being pulled through the water on my stomach. Only my pride kept me from begging to be let back on board the boat, and then we would go through the whole humiliating process again, with me promising that I would never,

ever get within a hundred miles of a lake again. At last, I made it to my feet and began to skim across the water, terrified of going on but even more afraid of letting go. Finally I got tired and had to let go—and sank slowly, gratefully into the water.

"You did it!" I received the congratulations back in the boat, wrapped in towels and trying to ignore Bud, who was gliding along effortlessly behind us. "Wasn't that fun?"

"Oh, yeah, terrific!" I agreed weakly. "A real blast! I can hardly wait until tomorrow."

In the winter, there was snow skiing. That had to be better; at least there was no water. Four couples with our assorted children drove up in the mountains of New Mexico to a ski lodge at Cloudcroft, and I loved the old-fashioned hotel with its gingerbread trim and high-ceilinged rooms. The first morning we met downstairs by the huge fireplace, and Joan was an absolute knockout in her black, formfitting ski suit. I felt like an elephant at 108 pounds, and was glad that my parka was long and bulky. That evening we played bridge in our rooms, and then took turns baby-sitting while the others went down to listen to music in the lounge.

It was a romantic evening, with a big fire roaring in the background and a trio singing old favorites, but I was silent and moody, while the others laughed and talked. I could hardly believe Bud; he seemed like another person, so happy and animated and joking. And once again, he was everybody's favorite. I felt as if I were looking at a person I hadn't seen in a long, long time. I had always kept him tucked away in the background of my life, as necessary to my well-being as air, and food, or shelter. He was the leading man in my carefully staged drama—popular boyfriend, convenient date, strong husband, devoted father. But who *was* Bud, as a person? I really didn't have the faintest idea.

After midnight, back in our room, I slammed the closet door. Bud looked up, startled. "I don't want to go on any more of these trips," I announced abruptly.

"Why not? I thought you were having a good time."

"It's much too expensive, and besides I'm getting tired of these people."

"But I thought you liked them."

"Well, I'm tired of all of them now, and I'm tired of the way that you ignore me," I finally blew up. In the morning, the incident was forgotten, and we pretended that it had never happened.

Bud was farming more and more land, and in addition he had begun a farm chemical business. It was very hard work at first, and he worked long hours getting it established, but after a few years it was beginning to be successful. At first, I resented the time and attention that Bud gave the business, but I liked the security that a second income provided. "Of course I want him to be successful," I thought, "after all, what benefits him, benefits me." But I felt uneasy when I saw how uninvolved I was in this part of his life, and how little he needed me.

There were, however, definite side benefits. The first was a trip to the Bahamas, and the next year to Jamaica—all expenses paid by Elanco Chemicals. The third year, the trip was to Acapulco. From the moment we landed and drove to the hotel, I was disappointed. On the left was the beautiful blue bay, lined with plush white hotels, but on the right stretched a dry and desolate looking hill dotted with small shacks. It seemed depressing, or maybe the landscape only mirrored what I was feeling myself. Anyway, nothing was right. "I liked Jamaica better than this. Everything was lush and green there, and there were those beautiful mountains in the distance. And why aren't we staying at the Princess Hotel? Did you see it? It's built like a pyramid."

"Sunny, there's nothing wrong with this hotel, and it's a free trip, don't forget."

"How can I forget? We have dinner every night with those dull chemical people, and I don't know any of their wives. I wish we had never come." I looked out the window at the shining beach, and the gentle breakers curling in to shore. The scene was breathtaking, but I was not going to give in to it. "I hate Mexico! Maybe it's too close to Texas to appreciate," I went on and on.

Bud had finally had enough. He looked at me and said in a low voice, "I wish you would quit saying that you hate everything. Do you realize how often you say that?" The conversation ended abruptly.

The last night I stood angrily by the pool, watching Bud, enjoying himself, deep in conversation with the other farmers. Good old Bud, successful Bud–and what a bore it was to watch everyone drink, when I, in great self-righteousness, disapproved of it. It made me even angrier when Bud accepted a drink from a tray the waiter offered. "What do you think you're doing?" I hissed at him under my breath. "You know I hate drinking!"

Finally I couldn't stand being in that boring place with all those boring people another minute. "Why don't we go for a buggy ride?" I suggested. I had seen couples in horsedrawn carriages pass by in front of the hotel all evening. It had looked very romantic.

As we clip-clopped along in the moonlight, my anger was still seething. We sat in total silence, staring unseeing at the shimmering bay, oblivious to the beauty of the night. This was far from romantic. "I think I'm ready to go in," I said stiffly. And back in our hotel room, we had the fight that I had been spoiling for ever since we left home. "It's obvious that you didn't want to go for a ride with me," I stormed. "If you had wanted to be alone with me, *you* would have suggested it, not me."

"Sunny, what in the world is wrong with you? Why can't we just have a good time on this trip?"

"A good time? Do you think that it's fun to stand there on the beach this afternoon and watch you go floating off in the sky over Acapulco Bay, pulled along by that motorboat? What if the parachute broke? What am I supposed to do then? And do you think that it's any fun to stand around and watch you talk to people that I don't know and don't want to know! I'm glad we're going home tomorrow."

Bud stood in silence, and his stony expression made me angrier still. My voice rose to almost a scream. "What's wrong with us is that I don't even know you any more!" I took off my wedding ring and threw it at him, and then waited for him to pick it up.

He didn't.

13

What Now, Lord?

The day after I got home from the Cape I went to see Mr. Shively, who had been such a caring counselor all summer. Bubbling over, I shared my conversion experience with him, and together we rejoiced at my newfound happiness–that I had given up hope of ever finding. I knew my troubles were far from over, but at last there was dawn's early light on the horizon! Mr. Shively thought it would be a good idea for Dan and me to continue seeing him (for Dan had started coming, too), and I readily agreed; we needed lots of help in learning how to communicate with one another. He also suggested that we take a weekend away together. "Take a trip, just the two of you, and this time let it be what it should be–a time to relax and enjoy yourselves."

I was not too sure about that idea, since our previous trips together had been such disasters, culminating with the one to Richmond, in which we hardly spoke at all, ten hours down and ten hours back, and I spent the night sitting in the car. Yet it was a new life I was living, I reminded myself; I had Jesus now, and I was a different person. But did Dan know that? Well, I would make the suggestion, and when he got home, I did. “Mr. Shively thought it might be a good idea for us to get away together for a weekend,” I said hurriedly, steeling myself for his telling me that this was the busiest season of the year at work, and he couldn’t really get away.

“That might be a good idea,” Dan said, smiling. Goodness, had he forgotten about Richmond?

“Well, um,” and I was suddenly shy, “I thought it might be nice to look at the fall coloring in New York or Pennsylvania. But of course, if that’s too far, we could always–”

“No,” he interjected, “that sounds fine. Why don’t we drive through Allegheny National Park? I’ll bring my camera.”

Tears started to come to my eyes, and I turned quickly away to look out the window, so he wouldn’t see them. I hadn’t counted on his being so nice.

“We can try that steak house in Olean that the Ladds told us about,” he said, enthusiastically, and I nodded, not trusting myself to speak. I couldn’t believe what I was hearing. Maybe it *was* going to be different.

But on the first Friday morning in October, as we climbed into the car and headed out the driveway, I was not so sure. All I could think about was the last time we had been in a car on a trip together, knifing each other at the outset with words so hurtful that we rode in bitter silence the whole way. I snuck a sidelong glance at Dan; was he nervous, too? If he was, he didn’t look it. “Couldn’t ask for a more gorgeous day!” he exclaimed, and for the first time I noticed that it really was breathtaking. I didn’t know about upper New York state, but fall had certainly come to eastern Ohio with a vivid palette! There was not a cloud in the sky, and the air was just crisp enough to be invigorating without being chilling. I got comfortable in my seat; this was going to be a good trip!

I looked over at Dan; there was so much I wanted to say to him. I wanted to ask his forgiveness for my being such an incredibly spoiled brat all my life, especially about the time he devoted to his business, of which I had been so jealous. I wanted to thank him for being so incredibly patient with my rotten disposition and my monstrous selfishness. I wanted to say how unfair I'd been, demanding that he be some kind of Prince Charming, and then punishing him vindictively whenever he failed to live up to my impossible ideal. But how could I begin? Mr. Shively had helped us to start talking to each other, to start to dismantle the high walls we had erected between us, but we had only just started. That had been fine with me before, but now I wanted to smash the walls flat.

And yet there was still a part of me that didn't. It was that wretched company's fault–No! Stop thinking that way! It's *your* fault, all of it. Well, isn't he wrong, too? I mean, if I'm the only wrong one, then he wins! Then let him win; it's not supposed to be a contest. But that was too much for my stubborn pride. Well, then at least be pleasant. But it had been so long since I had been pleasant in any situation with him, I had almost forgotten how. Talk about the children; they're good kids and we both love them. So we talked about the children and many miles passed, as I brought up one non-antagonistic topic after another. I still wanted to take his hand and hold it and ask him to forgive me for having been so awful for so long, and I sensed that that was what God expected of me, yet part of me still refused.

"Why don't we stop for coffee and a doughnut?" I asked, after we'd been driving for a couple of hours.

"Seriously? You're going to eat between meals?"

I laughed. "I'm going to enjoy myself this weekend, and not even think about my diet."

"Hey, that's a switch!" he exclaimed, slapping the steering wheel. "I'd just about given up hope that you were ever going to eat normally again." I was surprised; it had never occurred to me that Dan would be bothered by my peculiar eating habits, that he did not like eating alone or ordering a steak dinner while I sipped black coffee.

Off and on, throughout the afternoon and then over a delicious dinner–I had forgotten how good steak and mushrooms and a baked potato with sour cream, bacon bits and chives could taste–Dan asked questions about my time at the Community. What were the people like? What did they say about Jesus? I didn't know what he was thinking, but he, too, was trying to be interested and pleasant. The evening passed quickly, and it was fun to relax in our room, put our feet up, watch TV and just spend time together without children, telephone or friends dropping by. In fact, the whole trip was exactly what it was supposed to be–a chance to relax and just enjoy being together.

One Saturday morning, not long after my return from the Cape, I picked up the morning paper and began to read the religion section. There was an article about an Episcopal Church in Mentor, Ohio, that had a prayer meeting on Tuesday evenings. A prayer meeting–what would that be like? Maybe I ought to drive out there and see that church. The sun was shining, and it was a beautiful fall day, so off I went in search of St. Andrew's. Twenty minutes later, I found the church and several members who were out raking leaves and tending the grounds. Someone waved and that gave me courage to get out and go over to them, which wasn't like me at all.

I showed them the newspaper article and explained that I would like to meet the rector. "Why, he's gone home to lunch," a man said. And a woman added, "Here, we'll show you the way," and so saying, got into her car and led me in my car to the rector's house.

What am I doing? I must be *crazy,* to go to a stranger's house to ask about a prayer meeting! Mrs. Worman, the minister's wife, opened the door and invited me into their home. I introduced myself and showed her the newspaper, apologizing for the intrusion. They didn't seem at all surprised, however, that I would just drop in out of nowhere. "People come to our church from all over the area," they explained. "Tuesday nights the church is packed with young and old, who come for prayer, especially prayer for healing." We talked further, and I learned that Bill Worman and his wife Alice were good friends of the minister who had married Dan and me. While I was there, they called another couple on the phone, to ask if they would bring me to the next meeting the following Tuesday. "Of course," said Les Hallet and his wife. He, too, was a minister who happened to live near our house and could pick me up on his way to the prayer meeting.

The first Tuesday evening was a new experience for me, and I was extremely apprehensive about the whole idea of a Charismatic prayer-and-praise meeting. And, indeed, though the Hallets couldn't have been more gracious and considerate, I was still the most inhibited, uptight, self-conscious Episcopalian in the church hall that night. Somewhere between fifty and seventy-five people had gathered there, to sing and praise the Lord, and they prayed together and sang, and read from Scripture. Some shared exciting things that the Lord had done in their lives the previous week, and others asked for special prayers, for friends or relatives who were sick or about to have an operation, or for situations at their work. There was such a warm, "family" feeling to the group, and they made me feel so welcome, that there was no reason for me to feel the way I did. Nonetheless, it was all I could do to sing a little; there was no way I was going to pray out loud. They seemed to understand, though, and I felt no pressure, just acceptance. And a few weeks later, I did ask for prayer–out loud.

In addition to Tuesday nights, God arranged some very special fellowship for me. I had told a friend who had noticed a difference in me just a little of what had happened to me, and she suggested I call a friend of hers named Anne Ostrander, saying that we might find we had a lot in common. I did, and we did. Two hours passed before Anne and I hung up from that first phone call. She had gone to the same school in Shaker Heights that I had, a few years ahead of me, and I could vaguely remember her as a pretty, blond, very popular girl. As it turned out, she lived close by, so we spent a great deal of time drinking coffee in each other's kitchens, or on the phone. She had experienced the same sort of conversion that I had, and was a great source of encouragement.

Moreover, she and her husband Don attended Christ Episcopal Church in Shaker Heights, where Dan and I had gotten married. She introduced me to the ladies in her prayer group, some of whom I was already distantly acquainted with, and I joined them, too. And Mr. Shively, it turned out, led a weekly Bible study, which I added to my schedule. He also suggested to me a small group of women who met once a week to share, with as much openness and honesty as they could muster, the problems that they were facing in their lives. The group met under the guidance of our church's Christian

Education Director, Rita Wolf, and I fit that in, as well. And of course Sunday church now had a top priority, where previously it had held no priority at all. The children were enrolled in Sunday school, and we all went every Sunday that we were home.

With all of these Christian activities crowding into my already crowded schedule, something had to give. I was able to weed out some of the things that I had joined out of boredom, or because I couldn't say no, and I resigned from a few of the committees that I had joined primarily for approval and acceptance. But I did keep up my charity and volunteer work, so my life was still every bit as busy as it had been before, only now, instead of seeming so futile and frustrating and pointless, it began to take on new meaning and depth.

Pausing to look back, I couldn't believe the change that had come over me since September! Religious activities of the sort I was now involved in would have ranked near or at the very bottom of my social scale, and now they were among the most important things in my life. Those of my old friends who knew of my changing interest may well have regarded such pursuits exactly as I had before, but I didn't care. For I had had the faintest glimmering of true happiness–not all the time by a long shot, but I had never been truly happy in my whole life before. I was also beginning to know a tiny measure of peace and fulfillment. But most importantly, I had found something that *worked.* In the bottom of my heart, I now knew our marriage was going to be saved, even though it was still a mess and there were still many rocky rapids to go down, before it could become what God intended it to be–and what I had given up hope of its ever becoming.

But, for now, it had a long way to go, and so I found myself in the small sharing group, finally summoning the courage to speak after attending for several weeks. And then Rita asked me: "When you look in a mirror, what do you see?"

"Nothing!" I blurted out, and that was exactly what I meant: absolutely nothing. I was still extremely thin, weighing somewhere between 110 and 115 pounds so that physically there was little to look at. For despite my new life, I still believed that "thinner was better," and still struggled to diet day after day. Spiritually I had been totally dead inside before that September night in New Hampshire when I finally came face to face with my need for Jesus Christ. Where I had looked at myself, really *looked,* as I did once, there was only emptiness, a big zero as far as I was concerned, and that had frightened me.

Who was Camie Ford? What did she look like? I didn't know, and I started to cry—I felt lost, without any identity. I was the good, polite little girl my parents raised to shake hands firmly, look their friends in the eye, and say "How do you do." But now I was 32 years old and the mother of three children, and what did I have to show for it? A woman who was a nervous wreck with a wreck of a marriage. But Rita and Mr. Shively understood my feelings of despair and gave me much encouragement to continue my walk with Jesus. As the weeks went by that fall, and I came to know Jesus better through the Bible studies and prayer meetings, very slowly a new Camie began to emerge. My friends were somewhat taken aback by this new Camie Ford, who couldn't stop talking about Jesus to anyone who would listen. It was quite obvious that something had happened to me, but I was too naive and insensitive to realize I should keep quiet and let my actions speak for me. I had a big mouth, and now I was driving people crazy, telling them all about my "born-again" experience.

One evening, at a party we were attending, a girlfriend came up to me and said, "If you're a Christian, why are you still smoking and drinking?" I stared at her and then at the cigarette in one hand and the cocktail in the other. She was absolutely right! I never thought about drinking and smoking as being off-limits for me, but suddenly I knew that God was speaking to me through this friend. I put the drink down and put out the cigarette in the nearest ash tray. This Christian life was not going to be easy; I had been smoking ever since I was fifteen in boarding school, and it helped to keep my weight down. I couldn't imagine reading the morning newspaper without my second cup of coffee and a cigarette. Well, it had to go. But then I made a tremendous discovery: if I asked Him, Jesus would help me. When I prayed for Him to take away my desire to smoke, He did! I still, even today, from time to time, in a restaurant after a good meal, or at a party where others are smoking, have an occasional craving for a cigarette. I could easily start smoking again tomorrow–but I won't!

Now a rather startling development took place. Having given up cigarettes, I began to gain weight! All of a sudden, I could *not* stop eating! It was awful! I would sit at the bridge table and pop candy after candy into my mouth, while my friends puffed away. I ate Fritos and potato chips by the bowlful, and then went into total panic each time I stepped on the scale and saw the needle moving slowly up past the 120 pound mark.

That winter I dreaded the thought that I might not be able to get my skin-tight ski pants zipped up. Jesus was helping me not to smoke, but what about my diet? It never occurred to me that He might not agree with my ultimate goal: to get below 110 pounds. And now, thanks to no cigarettes, I was up over 120 with no end in sight.

"Enough of this!" I rebuked myself sternly. "Where is your famous self-control?"

I had turned control of my life over to Jesus, but I certainly didn't mean to include my weight, too! Jesus could help me with all the rest of me, except my figure; there I drew the line. In desperation to stop the upward creep of the needle on the scale, I joined Weight-Watchers. I was determined to lose those pounds I had gained over the winter. "This is ridiculous. I will just get out on the tennis court and play every day if necessary! I will never cheat on the Weight-Watcher diet," I said aloud, as I drove over to the nearby college auditorium where the sessions were held.

The ladies at the Weight-Watcher session that I attended once a week did not take too kindly to me. Looking me over, they must have wondered what on earth I was doing there. I told the lecturer that I had stopped smoking and wanted to get rid of the extra pounds I had gained. Each week I went home armed with literature to read, recipes to try, and with a new resolve to diet.

Just because I had found a new life in Christ did not mean my days were carefree. In fact, the exact opposite was the truth. It seemed that I was busier than ever. And I was still running away from what I considered an intolerable life. Dan was entrenched in his work—more so now than ever, because he had become president of his company and was working hard on deal after deal to lease office space. His salary was enormous now, and his commissions were even larger, but what good did all that money do when I was miserable? We both tried to maintain the rapport that we had achieved that fall weekend, but our schedules were so hectic, and I was always so tired that we still weren't very good company for each other. And when I was perfectly honest with myself, I realized that *I* still came first in my life–not Jesus, and certainly not Dan or the children.

The one positive change was that my obsession with being superthin had come to an end. I had known in my heart for some time that where I had come from was wrong, destructive and not pleasing to God. And as I finally accepted the fact that I would never again be as thin as 110 pounds, I seemed to quiet down inside. I did not lose my temper so quickly with the children. I did not flare up at them, as I had when I was starvingly hungry, though I still struggled to keep my weight below 125 pounds.

On the marriage front, Dan and I were not doing too much better, although we didn't seem to fight as much. I was still very jealous of Dan's business success and his immense popularity with his office staff, as well as with all our tennis and social friends. Everyone adored him and I was still emotionally and physically exhausted with my constant striving to make a name for myself! I did not want to be "Mrs. Daniel B. Ford, Jr." or "Dan's wife" or "Cornelia, daughter of Mr. & Mrs. David B. Manuel." I wanted to be important for me!

During the winter of 1972, I returned to the Cape for another retreat and a visit with David and Barbara. I loved going to the Community and talking with the members. They were so friendly and loving to me, and I always felt calm and peaceful there, in spite of my inner turmoil. I had made plans that winter to bring our three children for a visit next summer. "Why don't you rent Bethlehem cottage for a couple of weeks?" David suggested. "It's right here on the Community property–a small, cozy cottage just right for your family."

"All right, sounds good to me," I replied, and booked

the cottage for the last two weeks in August. I was hoping I could persuade Dan to join us.

In July, 1972, Billy Graham came to Cleveland for ten dynamic days at the Cleveland Stadium. It was a hot, humid week as he stood under those bright TV lights and encouraged us one and all to come to Jesus, just as we were. One evening, at the end of his talk I joined the slowly moving crowds of men, women and children that found their way to the infield. As Billy prayed, we each gave our hearts to Jesus, and once again I asked Him to take over the reins of my life. When my Crusade Counselor spoke with me after the meeting, I told her I was a "born-again" Christian who was rededicating my life to Christ. I faithfully filled out the Bible Study booklet and followed the lessons in the pamphlets I was given. I really wanted to stay on this straight and narrow path, and I wanted to be obedient to go in whatever direction I felt God leading me.

Where He seemed to be leading me that summer was into a new relationship with my husband. Dan and I were not much closer together than we had been. The only difference in my life was in the new ways I spent my time. I went to prayer groups, Bible studies, prayer-and-praise meetings, and at night read Christian books instead of watching television. But I still didn't know how to live day by day with Dan.

I was perpetually angry at him for what I thought was the uncaring way he treated me, without ever seeing where I had been so uncaring for him. Instead, I escaped into my Christian books and activities and resented Dan all the more, because Christ seemed to be making so little difference in his life. I thoroughly enjoyed reading late every night and eating when and what I pleased, but I knew I couldn't dodge the issue forever. I stuck closely to my diet in one last attempt to lose those few extra pounds, because in August I had asked to rent Bethlehem Cottage. I knew I couldn't diet while there; David and Barbara would have us over for dinner. The food at their house was so good.

Before we knew it, summer was almost over, and it was time to head for the Cape. Dan agreed to come for the Labor Day weekend at the end of our stay, and then we could all return to Cleveland together. The children and I had a blissfully restful two weeks in the Community, in our little Bethlehem Cottage.

In 1972, the Community consisted of Bethany, the large white retreat house that overlooked Rock Harbor on Cape Cod Bay; Bethesda, which housed the Community's seven Sisters, and Zion, the home of the directors, Cay and Judy, and their families. Close by this complex were several other homes each with the name of a Biblical location, such as Nazareth, Damascus, Gennesaret, Gethsemane and a rectory called the Ark. The Community was made up of married couples, young children, teenagers, single women, as well as a small Sisterhood and smaller Brotherhood. All together, there were about fifty people, all living within a five-minute walk of each other.

Each morning we attended Holy Communion with all the members of the Community in their tiny chapel that was once part of the old three-car garage. After chapel we returned to our cottage for breakfast. Then Liza, Lexa and Danny joined their cousin Blair, who was David and Barbara's daughter, and went to the children's activity of the morning, while I spent my day at Gennesaret, their home. There was always plenty to do around the house, dishes to wash, laundry to fold, gardens to look after, and always someone to sit and talk with over a cup of coffee. Slowly I unwound and found that I could express my feelings, no matter how negative or ugly, without being thought ill of; someone would understand. In fact, I never felt judged or condemned for the anger I had or the bitterness I showed, when I talked about our life back in Cleveland.

David and Barbara helped me to look at my feelings and understand why I had them, and why it was important to give them up and not hang on to my negativity, my depression and anger. In situation after situation, I needed to see where I was wrong, and that it was okay to be wrong. It was okay to be angry and to express it, but then I *must* give it up and not wallow in it. Back in Cleveland, I would punish Dan with my silence for days if he had crossed my will or had been particularly unresponsive and preoccupied with business. And there were days where absolutely everything he did irritated me. But now I had to look at my jealousy of his success and popularity, and it was not much fun for me to see where I had hurt Dan over and over again because I was jealous of him.

Labor Day weekend soon arrived and Dan came, as he said he would. The children and I couldn't wait to show him around and introduce him to all our new friends—I say "our," because by now the children felt as close to the Community kids as I did. Dan seemed rather taken aback by our enthusiasm. He was definitely quiet and reserved about his comments, and it was impossible to discern what he was thinking.

Saturday of Labor Day weekend we heard on the radio that a hurricane watch was forecast. September was the month for hurricanes, but it had been many years since the Cape had been hit by one. Yet the warnings became more prevalent and the barometer started to fall. The Community was prepared, with plywood sheets standing by to be nailed over picture windows, fresh water put in containers, candles ready, and everything loose outside either stowed away or lashed down. But they were also praying for the Lord to alter the hurricane's predicted path towards the Cape, so that there would be no damage or loss of life. During the day, it couldn't have been more beautiful–sunny and warm, with the Bay a light milky blue. To look around you, as you walked from Bethany through the wooded glade to Gennesaret, it was impossible to believe that a hurricane was coming–except for two things: overhead, the clouds, white and fleecy, were nevertheless racing across the sky from the south, like time-lapse movies. Down where I was walking, there was no more than a gentle breeze which came from no particular direction, but up there, there was already a full gale going on. The other uncanny thing was the quiet. Normally, there were all kinds of bird songs, and crickets and all the other rural buzzes of summer. Today it was eerily still. The animals knew.

Sure enough, toward the end of the day the ground-level wind began to pick up. By supper time it was really blowing hard. The children and I were safe and sound at David's house, but Dan had gone to our cottage to read a book. David and I suspected that he was trying to avoid the whole scene, so David went to get Dan for supper. The wind increased in strength steadily until it finally read 75 mph on the windspeed indicator. I could imagine those little ice cream scoops on the roof, whirling around at purée speed. What a night! To help Dan to relax, David had arranged for a couple of the Community men to just "drop by" after they had gotten done helping to save the fishing boats in Rock Harbor. The men stopped by, dressed in heavy-duty raingear.

"Just checking to make sure you all are secure over here by the water."

"Come on in and have a cup of coffee," David said, ushering them into the living room after they'd shed their outer garments. As the winds roared and howled outside, Buzz Elmer told Dan how he had left his brokerage firm in New York to answer God's call to come to the Community. And Rick Pugsley, whose family was living at Gennesaret, told of his leaving his position on the faculty of a Connecticut college to come here, also in answer to a call of God on his life. As they talked in a low-key way, I could see Dan's face soften and change. And then Father Lane, who had been a high-powered and very successful salesman for Swift and Company, told how he received a call into the ministry relatively late in life, had turned his life over to Jesus, had pastored two thriving churches and then been called to the Community as its chaplain. I was thrilled to hear these stories myself, and I prayed that God would touch Dan's heart. He did.

When the worst of the storm had finally blown out to sea and we returned to the cottage for the night, without telling me what he was doing, Dan suddenly knelt down by his bed and prayed to ask Jesus to come into his heart. I was so excited I went over and gave him a big hug. Before leaving for Cleveland that Labor Day, we made plans to return to the Cape in three weeks for a Community retreat at Craigville, a retreat center on the Cape.

On the retreat Cay and Judy prayed for Dan to receive all that God intended him to have, through the fullness of the Holy Spirit. As the retreat was breaking up on the final day, and everyone was saying good-bye, we asked Cay and Judy if they would be willing to come to Cleveland to teach and talk with some of our friends. Anne and I would be so pleased to be able to have a retreat with our prayer group, with Cay and Judy as our leaders. "Why, certainly, we'd love to," they replied, having checked their calendar, "but the first chance we'd have would be next February."

I left Craigville with wings on my feet, counting the days from September until February. The minute I walked into our house, before I took my coat off, I called Anne on the phone to tell her that Cay and Judy were coming to Cleveland. After that we were on the phone practically every day that fall, praying together–and helping each other to see the truth as best we could in each situation that troubled us. Grace, one of the members of our prayer group, offered her spacious home for the winter retreat. There were twelve women in our group, and we all hoped to bring our husbands. When I wasn't talking with Anne on the phone, I was talking with a psychologist at the Cleveland Clinic. In between the Billy Graham Crusade, and my two weeks at the Community, I had been seeing a doctor recommended to me by a friend. I continued to go down to the Clinic hospital with hopes that through professional therapy and counseling, I might find out why I was so negative and unhappy. I took all kinds of tests, answered hundreds of questions, and spent hours telling the doctor my problems. This process went on weekly all fall, until the man decided that the next step for me would be hypnosis. I had a strong negative reaction to that; hypnosis reminded me too much of my yoga classes. I was not about to turn over control of my mind to anyone! And I ended my visit to the doctor then and there. Evaluating my therapy in retrospect, in all those hours I had not learned one new thing about myself that I had not already learned during the retreats and counseling sessions I had had at the Community. For me, depression came from repressed anger. I was just plain angry that my husband did not love, honor, worship and adore me!

In November, we took a two-week trip to Hawaii. We were going to Honolulu for the annual fall meeting of the Society of Industrial Realtors. Going to Hawaii had been one of my dreams, ever since I read James Michener's book *Hawaii* and seen *South Pacific.* To me, Hawaii was the most beautiful and romantic place in the world. The only problem with my golden dream was that Dan and I were not getting along very well. "Well, okay!" I decided, "I will just be on my best behavior." Whether I was tired, hungry, angry, or whatever–I was *not* going to blow this long-awaited trip to Paradise. Those two blissful weeks were going to prove that I could set my will to do *anything,* if it was important enough. Just as I had wanted that fur stole, so I wanted my trip to Hawaii, and I would set my will to be pleasant, positive and agreeable as well as being determined to follow Jesus and His will for me. One *can* choose to be pleasant or not, I told myself.

And for once, it really worked–not through my efforts, but because in this instance, my will happened to coincide with God's will for me. We both wanted me to choose to be pleasant, instead of ugly, cheerful instead of miserable, agreeable instead of hateful. And He gave me the grace to stand against myself whenever my will was crossed, or when I had to do something I didn't want to do and was on the verge of letting Dan have it, to punish him, just out of jealousy or sheer vindictiveness. Often I had to ask His help, especially when I felt that rage rising up in me, but "Jesus help me!" is one of the fastest, most effective prayers a person can pray, and right behind it is, "Lord, change my heart!" The point was, I could not have done it without Him. All the self-motivation in the world would not have been enough. Sooner or later I would have blown it. Look at all those New Year's resolutions I had made to be nicer in the coming year, or how hard I had tried to cut down on my eating when I gave up smoking. You cannot permanently modify your behavior by sheer strength of will. But–if *God* wants you to change, and you want to, too, then you can be sure that the grace will be there to do it.

Those two weeks turned out to be the honeymoon that our first honeymoon was not. In fact, we had such a marvelous time we seriously considered saying good-bye to Cleveland and moving our family to the Islands. At that time, I still thought the cure might be more geographic than spiritual. We visited four of the islands, staying in deluxe hotels everywhere we went. On each island we rented a car so that we could take picnics and explore at our leisure. We found lush tropical gardens, splashing waterfalls, and soft, white sand on quiet, private beaches. We traveled alone for once, choosing not to join real estate friends who were also touring the Islands, and for once we actually preferred to be alone together! Only much later did I realize that this honeymoon was a special gift from God, and was also a foretaste of what our marriage could be like, when we were both determined to live in and for Him.

One of the highlights of our trip occurred one afternoon, when I was walking outside to the beach. I saw a familiar figure, reading a book on the veranda of the Royal Hawaiian Hotel. It was Billy Graham, who was staying at the hotel with members of his family. I knew he was to be the guest speaker at a prayer breakfast for the Realtors on Sunday morning.

Oh, Lord, I would so like to go up and talk to him and tell him how much his Crusade in Cleveland had meant to me. But I suppose people bother him like that all the time, and he probably doesn't get any chance to just rest and relax and be by himself, so I won't–*go ahead,* came the thought. And so, with a bit of fear and trembling, or at least shyness, I walked up to him, introduced myself, and told him that I had gone forward at his Cleveland Crusade this past summer, and that my husband I were here for the convention. He stood up and was very tall and shook my hand with a firm grip. And he had the bluest eyes I've ever seen. He said how nice it was to meet me, and he wondered if we would like to join him and his family for dinner that evening. My eyes widened, and I couldn't speak; I could hardly believe my ears! But I was crushed, because I knew we were already commited to go to a large reception and dinner with our group of Industrial Realtors. And that, after all, was why we were in Hawaii–to do business and make contacts. Finally, I managed to find some words and declined, and I don't think I have ever in my life been so disappointed at having to turn down an invitation.

But the next day I saw Dr. Graham again. He said how sorry he was that we were unable to join him. We talked for a while about how to lead a Christian life, and what it meant to follow Jesus in this day and age, and then we parted.

Early the following morning, Sunday, at about 6:00, the phone rang, and I sleepily answered it. A man's voice asked, "Is this the room of Mr. and Mrs. Daniel B. Ford, Jr.?"

"Yes, this is Mrs. Ford speaking."

"I'm Billy Graham's secretary, and Dr. Graham asked me to call and invite you and your husband to be his guests at the prayer breakfast. If you could come right downstairs, there is a car waiting to take you to the Honolulu Civic Auditorium."

"Oh, my goodness! Uh–we'll be right there!" I hung up.

"Dan, wake up!" I punched him. "Get dressed! Quick! We're going to have breakfast with Billy Graham!" Dan thought I was kidding at first, then realized I was serious and without a word leapt out of bed and into the bathroom. Ten minutes later, we flew out of the room and down to the waiting car and drove across town. I will never forget walking into the private dining room for special guests. There was the Mayor of Honolulu, the Governor of Hawaii and the Commander in Chief of the Pacific Fleet, and many more men in white uniforms with wide bands of gold on their sleeves. We were given name tags and shown where to sit. Seating myself carefully, I tried not to gape in awe at the scene around me. The lady across from me peered at my name tag and asked rather condescendingly, "Who, my dear, are you?" I looked right back at her and said casually, "Billy invited us."

Our two weeks in Paradise ended much too soon, as far as I was concerned. In my naïveté I hoped we would be able to bring home some of the island romance, but, before I knew it, we were immersed in our respective schedules and snapping at each other again as the Christmas season approached. I was in despair; I really thought that I had changed out in Hawaii, but now I was back to my usual, nasty self. I had been a Christian for a year and still had not experienced the fullness of a life lived in Christ. There had been a few brief mountaintops with long, deep valleys in between. Hopefully, I would find some nice, small foothills and broad plains, if I could just learn the secret of a joy-filled life.

February was here before we knew it, and it was time for Cay and Judy's visit. We had decided to begin the weekend with dinner Friday evening. Anne and I went to the airport that February afternoon to meet Cay and Judy, and were so happy to see them that we talked their ears off all the way to Grace's house. We told them our plans for the retreat to be Friday evening, all day Saturday, Saturday evening and Sunday through lunch. We knew God would bless this time, and we were excited.

The weekend was even more than we had hoped for. Cay and Judy talked about Jesus in a way we could all identify with, whether we were Episcopalian, Methodist, or Presbyterian. These two ladies told funny story after funny story about themselves! It was impossible to keep a straight face, and we often dissolved in laughter. "We take ourselves too seriously," they explained, "and God not seriously enough." One of the teachings that particularly impressed me that weekend was about haughtiness. I knew that I wanted desperately to be perfect, to be the best, the top. Whenever I made mistakes, I was down in the pits, full of self-condemnation and self-pity. Cay and Judy reminded me that "if you get discouraged about who you are, it shows who you think you are."

I found out that weekend that it was okay–and safe–to be wrong, because that's who Jesus came for: the wrong ones, the weak and needy. The more Cay and Judy talked about themselves and their two families, the easier it was for us to let our guards down, to push aside the protecting walls we had built and to be real with each other.

I tried hard to concentrate throughout all the teaching times, but I found my mind wandering to another situation that I was struggling with. Just before Cay and

Judy arrived, we had learned that there was a small house for sale at Rock Harbor, just across from David and Barbara's house. I was very intrigued at the thought of buying it and going there for vacations, where we could be close to the Community and Cay and Judy, with my brother practically next door–but Dan wasn't so sure. What would it mean in the way of commitment to the Lord? Buying a house in a Christian community must imply a more serious commitment in trying to lead a Christian life; would having a home on the Cape mean that we would have to spend all our vacations there? What about our Spring vacations in Florida? Could we do both? These questions swirled around in my head, with no answers in sight.

We finally made a date to fly to the Cape for a weekend in May to look the house over and hopefully find the Lord's will for us. But by the time the weekend arrived we were no more settled in our decision than we had been in February. The Bethany retreat house was as peaceful as ever, of course; you could feel your pace slowing down almost as soon as you drove in the driveway. That was one of the most amazing things about the Community–the extraordinary sense of peace that seemed to pervade the place when you visited. Of course, there was so much activity behind the scenes, that when you mentioned this to a Community member, he or she invariably looked a little surprised. Nonetheless, it was true, and one of the blessings of the Bethany Retreat House was to just go there and relax and let a little of God's peace seep into one's own inner turmoil. Not much peace, however, was able to seep into my turmoil that weekend. I was too busy praying fervently for God to give us a sign, a nudge, a direction to go in.

Saturday night neither of us slept very soundly as we

tossed and turned with our decision; nevertheless, as the sun peeped in our window Sunday morning, we were both in accord. I rolled over and looked at Dan, and his eyes opened. "I had a thought last night," I said. "It was about that parable of how hard it was for the rich man to get into heaven. It seems to me the Lord is telling us not to worry about money, or where it will come from and how we would have enough. The truth is, we do have enough to buy this house, and I think we're supposed to."

Dan nodded sleepily. "Yes, I think we are supposed to buy the house." Once again, at breakfast, there was much rejoicing around the table with Barbara and David. They were as thrilled as we were with our decision. We talked with Cay and Judy, told them our plans, and said that whenever we weren't there, the Community was welcome to use the house for whatever purpose they needed. We also talked about a name for the house and, at Cay's suggestion, decided on Nineveh. The house, as it was, was very dark and gloomy and crying out for bright, cheerful redecorating. So we made plans with Cay's husband Bill, a building contractor, to put on an addition in the fall. We only had time this visit to talk about the changes; actual work would have to be done later. But we were soon to find that owning a house in a Christian community did not make one a Christian of great faith and deep commitment.

Meanwhile, the summer was very busy and full for me. I struggled in vain over my weight, in preparation for swimming pool season. As I looked around the poolside, I could no longer claim to be the skinniest of my friends–a year of no smoking had added inches everywhere. I still tried to follow a diet, mostly Weight Watchers, but usually ate whatever struck my fancy.

There were many plans to be made and suitcases to

be packed in preparation for our trip to the Cape for the month of August. I arranged to bring Lexa and Danny with me, and Liza would fly up from her camp to join us. I had asked Dan to come, too, but wasn't surprised when he couldn't get away from work for that long a time. We would be separated for four weeks that summer, and that was okay with me; I knew I needed that much time to get some real help with all my feelings. Hopefully, at the Community I could begin to see why we continued to hurt each other so much, and be so angry and hateful. For at that point, in my mind, Dan was just as nasty a person as I was, even if he didn't think so (or any of our friends, for that matter). My jealousy of Dan's immense popularity with everyone made me all the more desirous of putting him down. After all this time, I still wanted to be on top, the best at something–anything!

There are not words enough to describe what I learned about myself that August, living in "The Ark," the home of the Community chaplain, Father Lane, and his wife Lenny. With us was another Community family and several other "live-ins" like myself. A live-in, I learned quickly, is someone who joins into the full life of the Community for short periods of time. For the month that I was in the house, I helped with any and all household tasks, such as cooking, or cleaning, dusting and ironing or taking an after-supper bike ride to see the sunset over at Rock Harbor.

As part of the Ark household, I was treated as a member of the family. People were very frank and candid with me, in helping me to see areas in my life where God might want me to change. For instance, practically the first day I realized how much I hated being told what to do–not just didn't like it, hated it! Practically my entire adult life, I had been boss, deciding what and when I wanted to eat, or whether I would go for a walk or a swim after lunch. The minute someone said, "Let's see–we'll need sandwiches for eight in time for lunch at noon," I reacted. I didn't want a sandwich for lunch; I wanted a salad! My whole day, from breakfast until bedtime, was out of control for me, and I couldn't stand it. In all the years I had been married, I had been in charge of running the house. Now, I had the experience of listening to Lenny make out the schedule for the morning work and the menu for lunch and dinner, for I was there to listen and learn and to take directions, rather than give them. I knew perfectly well before I came that this would be the case, but I had no idea the depth of rebellion that it would bring up in me, this business of not being the one who made the decisions. Father Lane, Lenny and others were very loving, patient and understanding, as they helped me to see the extent of my self-centeredness, willfulness and my consuming desire to always be right.

I was devastated if anyone else in the kitchen mentioned that my cake was dry, or the vegetables were overcooked or, as happened one morning, that the eggs were not scrambled properly. I had forgotten to add any milk–me, the gourmet cook !

Then there was the time that all the shirts I had ironed were returned to the laundry room–"*What?* What do you mean, they weren't ironed? Of course, I ironed them! Use spray starch? Oh, I didn't think they needed any starch–Yes, well, they do look a little limp. . . . "

Then again, one night at supper: "These blueberry pies ought to be good–it took me all day to make them! What do you mean, they're tart! There's nothing wrong with the pies! Oh, um, yes, now that I taste them, I see what you mean–whew! I guess I just didn't want to put in all the sugar that the recipe called for. Well, yes, I usually do follow the recipe, but I thought blueberries were naturally sweeter. I guess I didn't think it was that important to be obedient to a recipe."

After I got over the exhaustion of my first week, we had a lot of fun together, and the time flew by. And I learned some things I never knew before–how to clean a house properly, iron a shirt, and bake a good blueberry pie. I fell into bed each night with every bit of energy used up, but I was happy and more relaxed than I had been in years. There is something very freeing about simply doing what you are asked to do.

One warm, lazy afternoon towards the end of our stay, I was sitting outside in the backyard in a lawn chair, trying to do some reading, but also dozing off in the warmth of that sunny afternoon, in the comfortable lounge. All of a sudden, I looked up and saw Nineveh, our house. The one we had bought, sitting right there next door to the Ark. What have we done? I thought with panic in my heart and a knot in my stomach. What did it mean? There was no turning back on God now! Dan and I were called to follow Jesus *today*, just as those disciples on the beach by the fishing boats had been, so many years before. "Oh, no! This is all too much for me, for Dan, and for the children!" And I burst into tears and cried and cried and cried. "Jesus help me! Please help me, because I don't know what I'm going to do!"

At the end of August, we all returned to Cleveland together as planned. Dan had come and joined me at the Ark for my birthday and Labor Day weekend. The month passed by so quickly and, for the first time, I was not eager to return to the hectic fall season that awaited me.

❧ *Sunny* ❧

14

The End of the Fairy Tale

We were in the car again, and I was in a bad mood again. "Okay, okay, I know I have to go, but I'm just telling you: I think the whole thing is ridiculous, and it's all your fault. It's not exactly what I would choose to do on Friday night–why did you ever agree to be the chairman of this whole thing anyway?"

Bud and I were on our way to the First Methodist Church on a Friday night, a most unusual occurrence. Sometimes we were there on Sunday morning; more often we were not. Always conscious of my image, I included church attendance as necessary for a well-rounded family life, but I didn't let it interfere with anything that I really wanted to do, and secretly I didn't believe most of the things that I heard there anyway. Sometimes I had looked around at other people sitting complacently in the congregation and wondered if most of them didn't feel the same way that I did. "If any of us really *believed* that God was real, it would turn our lives upside down." No, I decided that most of them must feel exactly as I did about the whole thing.

And now Bud agreed to be in charge of a whole

weekend at the church–something called a Lay Witness Mission–and we were stuck for all day Saturday and most of Sunday as well. "I don't know why you ever let Richard talk you into this," I went on. Richard Scott was the minister, a very low-key, likeable person, not at all the standard religious type. He liked golf and football and had a casual way of just dropping by the house to chat, and we were very fond of him. He had asked Bud to serve as Superintendent of Sunday Schools, and I had even agreed to teach a third grade class. But this was too much; now Richard had gone too far!

The March wind nipped at me as I opened the door to get out of the car, and I pulled my scarf lower to keep the dust out of my face. We were in a full-fledged West Texas sandstorm and with a shrug, I went inside; with such depressing weather, we might as well spend the weekend in church as anywhere else.

Detached, I sat toward the back as an observer. I had no idea what to expect–the name "Lay Witness Mission" conjured up images of embarrassingly emotional testimonies from revival services of my youth, and I wanted no part of anything like that. After a few choruses of such familiar songs as "Showers of Blessing," along with a few new ones, a genial department store owner from the small town of Ralls was introduced as the mission leader, and he presented his team–a group of couples and young people who had come from many different towns in the West Texas area. It looked like a fairly ordinary group, and I relaxed. So far no one was getting emotional.

Suddenly I felt Bud's elbow in my ribs, as one of the couples from Lubbock stood up. "Look, that's Gary Powell!" he whispered. "He was a Phi Delt at Tech. What in the world is he doing at something like this?" He chuckled. "I played basketball against him, and believe me, he was no saint!" Bud began to listen intently, but I sat there only half aware of what they were saying, more interested in what the ladies were wearing and evaluating their various figures and hairdos. I had to admit that they were an attractive group, for the most part, and they certainly seemed to enjoy what they were doing.

I felt a little uncomfortable as the Powells walked to the rostrum and began to talk, for first the husband prayed for his wife, and then she prayed that God would give him the words to say. They seemed to be talking about the void that had been in their lives, and the difference that it made to know Jesus and to want to live for Him.

"I've heard all this before," I told myself. In my distant Baptist background, I had memorized a lot of Bible verses. "And why all this talk about Jesus?" But on the way home in the car Bud was very quiet, and I could see that he was still thinking about the evening.

The next morning I was up early, surprisingly eager for the meetings to begin. In fact, Bud and I even called a few of our friends who had not been there the night before. At the noon salad luncheon I watched the faces of the ladies who were talking about their lives. There was so much life there, so much vitality and enthusiasm. Their faces were positively shining. I wished I felt like that. They were talking about things that I knew about: problems with their children, an emptiness at the center of their busy lives, a disappointment in their relationships and in the way their lives were turning out. But they went on to say that they had found the answer to their problems in Jesus–and there was the stumbling block for me. Intellectually it was hard for me to accept the part about Jesus. I wanted to know God; I even had a yearning to reach out to Him. But they kept talking about a living, invisible person named Jesus. All day long, I puzzled about it.

After dinner we divided into small groups, and I raised my hand to voice some of the questions I had thought about throughout the day. The words were scarcely out of my mouth, when in a flash the whole thing connected for me. It was as if the pieces of the puzzle suddenly fell into place. And it was so simple! I had missed the forest for the trees. "*Jesus is God!* If I want to know God, it's going to have to be through knowing Jesus." I didn't know how to do that, but later that night, Bud and I knelt together at the altar and prayed together for the first time. "If it's real, Jesus, if You are real, and I hope You are," I whispered, "please help us. Our lives are such a mess. Please take our marriage and make it what You want it to be. Please help me."

On Sunday morning just before the last session began, I pulled Annette Powell aside. "I wonder if I could talk to you for just a minute." I really didn't know how to ask the question. "You see, I have this problem with the scale. I have to weigh every day, and it's making me really unhappy." Annette told me that whatever the problem, Jesus could help me with it, and we walked down together to one of the most glorious worship services that I had ever attended. Nothing really very new or different, but I was new and different. I was *hearing*, and I was *seeing*, and my heart was singing.

The next day I woke up scared. What if this new awareness of Jesus wore off, and everything was no different than it had been before? We had said a very reluctant good-bye to our new friends on Sunday afternoon, and now we were on our own. "Tell me what I do"—I had begged for last minute advice, as they were leaving.

Libby Keith had smiled. "Don't worry! Jesus will be staying with you, even if we go." Somehow that wasn't terribly reassuring to me. I was not at all sure how well Jesus and I were going to be able to communicate without a little outside help.

I really ought to pray, but how should I go about it? Then I remembered that someone had talked about something called a quiet time, and they had even given me a little sheet of paper, explaining how to begin to talk with God, just as you would with your own father. I slid out of bed to my knees and began very self-consciously to try to talk and listen to Him. I felt very uncertain and needy, very much like a little child taking faltering first steps. "Lord, if this is really going to work out, You're going to have to help me, because I don't know what to do next."

Later in the day the phone rang. It was Toni Caviness, one of the young women in the church whom I knew slightly. "Some of us have been talking about the weekend," she said, "and we're anxious not to lose what we feel has been a new beginning in our lives. We're thinking about getting together, perhaps for a Bible Study, or just a talk about what has happened. Do you and Bud want to come?" Did we ever!

And so we found that there were others, maybe twenty or so, who had felt much as we did. It was as if a wind had blown through the First Methodist Church of Lamesa, leaving many of the members as they had been before. But for others of us, the wind had been a small tornado, turning our lives upside down and drawing us close together.

I had to admit that we were an unlikely assortment of people. Looking around Toni and Joe Ben's tasteful living room, I wondered what we were all doing together.

What could we possibly have in common? Of course we had all been members of the same church and were Sunday acquaintances, but few of us had ever shared similiar interests before. David and Anne Harris, the forty-ish bank president and his capable wife, certainly didn't seem to have any needs. Jack and Sue Garner appeared to be the epitome of success; why were they here? The Ellysons and the Daniels were farming couples with grown children; surely they led full, busy lives with many interests. Most of them I had admired and looked up to, never dreaming that on the inside, they felt just as I did about many things. But week after week, as we came together and began to really know each other, we found that we had had a common experience that drew us together in a closeness that I had never known before. We had met Jesus, and our lives would never be the same, and we felt a deep sense of kinship.

Suddenly Bud and I were very busy. There was no time for bridge club, because we went to a prayer group that night. The services of our church seemed to hold new meaning for us, and we were there Sunday morning, Sunday night, and Wednesday evenings, too. There was so much to learn, so many books to read, so much Bible to study. Often we would drive an hour or more to hear a Christian speaker–first to Midland, then to Lubbock, next to Brownfield. The people whom we had met on the Mission kept in touch, and we began to correspond and visit regularly with many of them.

We were still very much brand-new, beginning Christians, when the phone rang one evening. "Hello, Sunny? This is Jerry Hanson from Ralls." I recognized the voice of the young man who had been such a dynamic influence in our church just a few weeks before. "I am going to be coordinator for a Lay Witness Mission at

Trinity Interdenominational Church, and I'd like for you and Bud to be part of the team."

Although pleased and flattered at the invitation to one of Lubbock's largest churches, I protested. "I don't know if we are ready to do anything like that, Jerry. The whole idea scares me to death." We were just beginning to find out who Jesus was; how could we stand up and tell anyone else about Him? Yet at the same time, I wanted very much to be part of what was happening.

"Don't worry, no one expects you to have all the answers. Just be willing to share what has happened in your own lives these past few weeks."

The weekend at Trinity Church was tremendously exciting; and soon we, along with the Garners, Ellysons, Daniels and many of our other new friends, were accepting invitations to go to churches all over the area, and then during the next year, on to Dallas, Oklahoma, and beyond. I loved it! I loved being part of "the team," being with our new friends, and having a sense of belonging. I loved having something to *give,* something worth giving, that could help other people. What a change–to be giving, after a lifetime of taking!

And at last, Bud and I shared a common interest. Now we had goals and a real purpose and fulfillment in our lives. "Thank you, God, for healing our marriage," I prayed. "And thank you for filling up my empty life."

We were still leaving our children with baby-sitters, but of course it was much better to leave them for a Christian meeting than a dinner party. There were still times when I didn't understand why Bud seemed angry, when I was just trying to be helpful, but most of the time our lives seemed much better to me, and I was grateful for the improvement. Of course, I still wanted to be thin and look good; after all, a Christian should try to have a good appearance in order to be a good witness. I kept a close watch on my diet and on my size, but somehow it didn't seem quite as important as it had before.

Sometimes I had doubts to contend with: "If I really do know Jesus and have become this new person in Christ, then why do I still act so much the same way? Why am I still the same on the inside? Why does it still worry me, when I can't keep my weight below 110? Why did I lose my temper and scream at Leigh and then feel so terrible about losing control? Why am I so preoccupied with the way I look? A Christian shouldn't be thinking about herself all the time. And why did I feel so devastated at that Lay Witness Mission in Pecos, when, for the first time, we were not asked to give our testimony in the evening meeting?" I had a lot of questions and very few answers, but on the surface things were going well.

The best thing that happened was our new house. I pulled the station wagon into the driveway and just sat for a moment, looking. I couldn't believe that it was really ours; it was a dream too good to be true! I had loved the house from the first moment that I had seen it. Of course, it was twenty years old and needed a few improvements here and there, but basically it was the house that I had always wanted. The ivy climbed lushly up the red brick walls, the floor-to-ceiling windows brought the outdoors right inside, and the underground sprinkler system would make the beautiful yard easy to keep.

I remembered the day that I had heard that it might be for sale. "Bud, guess what?" I tore in the door excitedly. "You'll never guess what I heard at Bible Study today. Jack and Sue Garner are going to build a new house, and their old one will be for sale. Quick, we've got to call them right away and tell them that we are interested." The Garners had become good friends after the Lay Witness Mission, and their house on Hillside Drive was in the nicest section of Lamesa. Most of the town was flat, but we had taken many Sunday drives through the winding, tree-lined streets of Park Terrace, and I had always dreamed of the day when we would live there ourselves. The Garner house would be perfect–not too big, not too pretentious, but comfortable, roomy, and respected. There was a long wait until their new house was built, but their old one was worth waiting for; I had to have it. Bud agreed, and we finally signed the papers.

I threw myself into the redecorating. It had to be perfect! It took weeks to pick out the wallpaper for the kitchen, and before deciding for sure, I drove all the way to Lubbock to see it on the wall of a new house there. Carpet samples were stacked in a corner of the living room for months, while I kept changing my mind. "This is a nice color, but it looks funny at night. What do you think about this one? No, I think it's too light. I really would like to find a green the color of spring grass," I told Bud. "What one do you like?"

"What difference does that make?" Bud had learned that although I might ask other opinions, I still made the final decision myself. "For heaven's sake, just make up your mind and stick with it!"

Who would have thought that choosing a white paint would take so long? But there were dozens of shades of off-white; the whole thing was very confusing. "Do we want Oyster White, Creamy White, Egg-shell White, or Dover White?" I pondered. "Bud, why don't you paint a strip of each one on the wall so that I can look at it?"

More than once I had the workmen take out an entire wall and then put it back again. "I'm terribly sorry, but I've changed my mind. I think I liked it better before. Would it be too much trouble to put it back just like it was?"

Slowly the house took shape. The day that the carpet was finally laid, I was almost afraid to look. Had I made the right decision? Would I like it? What about the Karastan carpet in the living room; was it too dark? No, it was perfect! I walked slowly from room to room, admiring my handiwork. What did it matter, if we didn't have much furniture yet? I had sold the maple hutch, and all the Early American was gone. This house was very contemporary; we would furnish it piece by piece, carefully selecting just the right thing for each spot. I loved the bright hues of blue and green, different shades in different rooms, but basically the same color scheme throughout. I loved looking out the big windows, and the feeling of space and light within. Often I would just sit in a room, just looking around and savoring it.

"Maybe it's wrong to love a house so much," I excused myself, "but it's more than a house to me. God understands. Somehow, this house is *me.*"

One special evening in May, 1974, the house looked particularly lovely. I always preferred to entertain on Fridays, because Lucy came in to clean on Thursdays, and everything would still be fresh and spotless. Walking from room to room, I made a last-minute check.

It was hard to say which room I liked best, but certainly the dining room had turned out well. Now with the pale yellow chandelier casting a soft glow on the painted brick wall, the vivid blues and greens in the abstract painting picked up the color of the carpet. The table was carefully set for five, and I stopped to straighten the centerpiece, which didn't need it. How nice the china looked on the new linen cloth! Bud would be arriving soon with our guest, Peter Marshall, and I wanted everything to be absolutely perfect. It was too bad that our other dinner guests had to cancel at the last minute, but that would give us more time to talk to the visiting speaker. Bud seemed rather indifferent to his coming, but I had a million questions I wanted to ask him.

The kitchen clock showed a few minutes before 6:00–still plenty of time. Dinner was waiting in the oven–baked ham with Jezebel sauce. There was nothing left to do, so I wandered on into the den to sit down for a minute to look out the big windows onto the patio and the garden beyond. What a find Señor Martínez had been! Even if he couldn't speak a word of English, we were able to communicate perfectly about the ivy and the vinca–the whole backyard was lush and green, with hanging baskets of petunias swaying gently from the branches of our big Carolina poplar. It was a perfect May evening, mild and soft, with the scent of honeysuckle in the air. Thank goodness the sand wasn't blowing! An Easterner would never understand a Texas sandstorm.

We had done a lot of entertaining during the past twelve months. As chairman of the local laymen's group called Maranatha, Bud had served as host to the different speakers who had been invited to Lamesa as part of a series, and it had been fun to meet and talk with them. Maranatha had invited one wellknown Christian to come to our local auditorium each month to speak, and we were sure that revival would sweep Lamesa as a result. Nicky Cruz, well-known from the book *The Cross and the Switchblade,* had started off the series to a standing room only crowd, but since then the attendance had dwindled, with only a hundred or so of the same old faithful group attending each meeting. Some of the speakers had been rather disappointing, I had to admit, but I had high hopes for Peter Marshall. Of course, I had heard of his late father, the former Senate chaplain, and everyone had read his mother Catherine's books. I had been surprised to learn that there was a minister son also named Peter, when I had stumbled on one of his tapes through a lending library in Arizona. The tape was poorly recorded, and after I heard it once or twice, it broke; but I had heard enough to know that he said things about Christian maturity that I hadn't heard before. "Bud, let's see if we can get Peter Marshall to come as part of the Maranatha series," I had urged. We had invited him months ago, and now he was finally arriving. I had the feeling that tonight was going to be something very special.

I jumped up as a car turned into the driveway. "There they are now!" I opened the door to admit a smiling, blond young man, who was easily an inch or two taller than Bud's 6'3". "My," I thought, "he's not at all what I expected. And he certainly is tall!"

The dinner conversation that evening was not exactly what I had expected, either. We touched on many different topics, such as baseball, the cotton crop, Christian writers, and an unusual sounding place on Cape Cod, where Peter said that he often went for counsel. Then the conversation turned to the Hales.

"Tell me about your family," said Peter, pleasantly.

I was always happy to talk about our children. "Well, there is Mike, of course, and then we have two daughters, seven and four, who are visiting their grandmother tonight." I always preferred to have the children safely out of the way when company was expected, but after some deliberation Michael had been allowed to stay.

"How old are you, Mike?" Peter asked.

"Ten." Michael was a boy of few words.

"Why didn't you eat your broccoli, Mike?" Peter went on.

"Oh, he never eats broccoli," I interrupted, hurriedly changing the subject. What did broccoli have to do with anything anyway? I much preferred to talk about religious subjects. "It's almost time for the meeting, Peter, but first tell me what you think of Watchman Nee's books."

The weekend teaching mission went very well, and I took pages and pages of notes. I was very interested in this practical approach to applied Christianity. "Don't you think that this has been a great weekend, Bud?" I asked. His response seemed a little noncommital, and I was disappointed in his lack of enthusiasm. Oh, well, perhaps he didn't like this particular speaker.

The weekend was soon over, and I tossed my notebook in the drawer and went on with the routine of early summer. The children were out of school, and June was my favorite time of year. One day, as I drove the children home from a busy morning at Vacation Church School, my mind was racing ahead to plans for the afternoon. "Let's throw a quick lunch together and then go to the pool until time for Leigh's piano lesson and Mike's Little League practice," I suggested. This was often the daily routine; we loved the private neighborhood pool which was located just a block away from our house.

"That's funny," I murmured, as I noticed Bud's pickup truck already parked in the drive. "It's a little early for your father to be home for lunch. Oh, well, I'll fix him a quick sandwich. Maybe he's on his way to the farm."

Walking through the kitchen, I left my load of books and pictures on the table and went on through the house, finding Bud in the bedroom. "Oh, here you are. I didn't expect you home this early. We're on our way to the pool; do you want a sandwich?" Then I noticed the pile of clothes on the bed and the open suitcase. "Oh, no! Don't tell me you've got to go to Tulsa again for another business meeting!" And then I saw his face. "Bud, what's the matter?"

He walked over and shut the bedroom door. "Listen, Sunny, I want to talk to you," he said, his voice very quiet. "I'm going away for a few days. I have to have some time to think. I just feel mixed up; I want to be by myself for a while." He filled the suitcase, shut it, and picked up his jacket, and headed for the back door.

"Bud, wait! What's the matter? What have I done? I'm sorry if I've made you angry about something. Won't you come back and talk about it?"

The only answer was the sound of the outside door shutting, and the pick-up engine starting. I sat on the edge of the bed, too stunned to think. I had no idea what was happening, but something was terribly wrong.

"Hey, Mom? What's for lunch?" I could hear the normal sounds of children in the kitchen, but my whole world was spinning.

"Just open a jar of peanut butter, Mike, and fix the girls a sandwich. I have a headache, and I'm going to lie down for awhile. You all run over to Grandmother's when you finish your lunch; I don't feel like going to the pool today. Just take the girls and leave me alone."

During the long hours of that afternoon and on into the night, I went over and over in my mind what had happened. I felt totally numb–how could everything be fine one moment, and the next my world was collapsing? What was wrong with Bud? He was always so steady, so reliable. Was it some kind of sudden illness, like an emotional breakdown? He had been working very hard with the farming and the chemical business, but the last year had been more successful than any other. Maybe he was just overtired. Maybe he had been working too hard. And where could he be? Surely he would come back right away. At least he would call, when he realized how worried I must be. Maybe it was some kind of spiritual crisis that he was going through–yes, that must be it; some kind of rebellion against God. If he could just talk to someone he'd be okay.

Unable to sit still, I paced the floor back and forth. I called my mother to please give the children dinner, and I stayed close by the phone. He's got to call soon and say that he is sorry, that he just got angry over something I said.

Then I tried to think of what I might have said or done. Of course, our marriage wasn't perfect, but we didn't fight much. And almost always I was the one who got angry, not Bud. But we hadn't had any quarrels lately, at least that I could remember. In fact, it was even hard to remember what Bud had been doing recently. His interests were chiefly the farm and his business; while I was totally involved with the house and the yard, plus chauffeuring the children back and forth and keeping up with their schedule. Not only had we not fought much lately; our paths had hardly crossed at all.

Why doesn't that phone ring? The silence was maddening. It was a relief when the children came bouncing in. "Where's Daddy," Leigh demanded. "He promised to fix my bike today."

"He had to go out of town suddenly," I exclaimed. "He'll be back soon. Now one hour of TV and then straight to bed."

Mechanically, I helped the girls through their evening ritual of toothbrushing and pajamas, glad of so mundane and ordinary a diversion. I felt frozen, numb, unable to cry. This cannot be happening! In the morning, I will wake up, and this will all be a bad dream. But sleep would not come, as I reached out to Bud's side of the bed. What if he's been in an accident? What if he's in a hospital room somewhere? Maybe I should let someone know— but who? I certainly didn't want to talk to my family or his about something like this. I didn't know where to turn and finally I did doze for a few hours with the phone on the bed beside me.

One, two, three interminable days passed. I tried to keep busy with the normal routine of Vacation Church School and household chores. He would *have* to call sooner or later. If the phone would just ring. *Please* let it ring!

And finally, it did ring–around ten o'clock in the morning, four days later. "Bud, is that you? Where are you? Are you all right? Don't you know how worried I've been? When are you coming home?"

His voice was so low that I had to strain to catch the words. "It's no use, Sunny. It's all over. I've tried. God knows, I've tried. I didn't want to hurt you, but married to you, I feel like I'm suffocating. I have to get away to where I can just breathe. I don't even feel like a man anymore; I don't know who I am. I'm dying on the inside. I have to leave, before I go completely crazy. I'll be home tomorrow to get my things, and we can try to make some decisions then. But I *am* going to leave."

There was a soft click, and I stood there, looking at the receiver in my hand. Who *was* that on the phone? It didn't sound like the Bud I knew. It was a totally defeated person, a stranger. Oh, my God, what has happened to Bud?

I made it into the bedroom before the feelings hit. Then the sobs started, and they wouldn't stop. They were coming up in waves from somewhere in the pit of my stomach. "I don't want to scare the kids; I've got to have some help." I could see them hovering frightened by the bedroom door. "Mike, take the girls over to Gramollie's right away, and call Sue and tell her that I'm sick, and can she come over right away?" And when he went out and shut the door, I fell across the bed and cried, "God, please help me, please help me."

When Sue came, she sat by the bed and waited. At first I couldn't talk at all, but when the words started, they came out in a torrent, and she just listened. "How can Bud be doing this to me? We've been married fifteen years! We've known each other over twenty years, and then he calls me on the phone and tells me that he is leaving. What has *happened* to him? He's the only person that I have ever cared about; I know he really cares about me. He has to. He must be sick–but he doesn't sound sick." I squeezed Sue's hand. "Can you tell me what's happened? What's gone wrong? I thought we had a good marriage; I thought we loved each other. I won't believe this is really happening! We are Christians! Maybe this could have happened a few years ago, but why is God letting it happen now? Things have changed. This really can't be true. It's impossible! I won't believe it." And on and on, until finally Sue had to go. After she left, I kept going over and over the same things to myself: Bud is going to have to come to his senses; this simply cannot be happening to me.

That night I couldn't sleep at all. I walked from the bedroom into the living room, to the kitchen, to the den, and back into the bedroom, back and forth, back and forth, restlessly seeking comfort from the things that had once brought me so much pleasure. Finally exhausted, I lay down flat on the living room floor on the carpet I loved so much and had spent so many hours picking out. But what difference did the beautiful blue carpet make, if I had to live in this house alone? Without Bud, the house had no meaning at all. It was just wood and brick and paint and paper. And how could I raise three children alone? Bud had always been a much better father than I was a mother. I couldn't believe that Bud could consider leaving the children; maybe he could do without me, but never without them. But what was I going to do? I had to talk to someone who could help me.

Somewhere in the gray hours of early dawn, I thought of our guest of three weeks before—Peter Marshall. He had been to our house, he had met us both, and he was far enough removed to confide in, surely he could tell me what to do.

The hands on the clock seemed to drag, as I forced myself to wait until six o'clock to call the Massachusetts operator and get the East Dennis number. I wanted to talk before the children were awake, so I placed the call, knowing that in the East it would still be only seven o'clock. A sleepy voice answered the phone, "Marshalls' residence."

"I'd like to speak to Peter Marshall," I whispered, not wanting the children to overhear.

"Who's calling, please?" the woman's voice asked. "Do you know that it is just seven o'clock?"

Soon Peter picked up the phone, and in bits and pieces I poured out the whole story, hardly making any sense at all. He listened a long time without comment, and then he said, "Well, Sunny, I'm sorry to hear what has happened, but it sounds to me as if God is trying to tell you some things about yourself."

"Anything, I'll do anything!" I promised, "if you can help me!" But instead of comforting words of sympathy and consolation, Peter began to tell me the truth about me.

I sat down on the hard, cold kitchen floor to listen. He talked on and on, totally frank and honest, but never unkind. He spoke of my control that would strangle the life out of any man; he spoke of my demand to be served and cared for, and the way that I used people and loved things. He talked about self-centeredness and the unloving, thoughtless hurts that I had inflicted on Bud over so many years. It never occurred to me to wonder how Peter knew so much about me after just a few hours together, because in my heart I *knew* that everything he was saying was God's truth. I didn't understand all of it or take it all in, but I listened as hard as I could, because I knew he was throwing me a lifeline. Every word that he said seemed to bring some picture or memory from the past, and gradually I began to get a glimpse of the enormity of what I had done to Bud, and what it must have been like to live with me.

At length, he stopped, and then he said, "So now you have to decide: what do you do now? You and Bud will have to make that decision together, but if you do try to make your marriage work, *you,* Sunny, are going to have to change. Never mind Bud; God will deal with him. *You* are the only person that you can do anything about, and you have a lot of repenting to do."

Somehow, when I hung up the phone, I felt much calmer. Though it would be years before I would know the full depth of what had been said, I knew that God had used Peter to speak to me–and maybe, for the first time in my life, out of sheer desperation, I was willing to listen.

I did a lot of thinking in the hours before Bud came home. I thought about our years of courtship, of the feelings of superiority I had always had, and the way that I had taken Bud for granted. I thought about college and the way that I had demanded my own way, totally ignoring anything Bud had wanted to do. Everything had to revolve around me–*my* wants, *my* desires, *my* plans. With something akin to nausea, I recalled the details of our honeymoon–I had acted like a spoiled brat! I thought about our first house and how I had punished Bud when things didn't turn out exactly the way I wanted. How hateful I had been to his family and friends, and how mean and hurtful I had been to Bud himself! When had I ever listened to a word he said? When had I ever been interested in anything that he cared about? When had I ever been sensitive to *his* feelings, *his* needs?

The awful, sickening truth was that in thirty-five years, I had never cared about any person but myself. As the light of this truth began to illuminate my heart, I began to see many, many more things that I had never been willing to look at before, and what I saw was ugly. I saw now that the real question was not why had Bud left, but rather how had he ever endured as long as he had! My tears of self-pity dried up, and now God gave me the grace to do something I had never done before: to weep because of the terrible things that I had done to someone who loved me and cared for me. "Oh, God, I am a cold, hard, selfish person. I am sorry for who I am, and for what I've done to Bud. Please, Lord, give me another chance. Please don't let it be too late."

About mid-afternoon, I heard the children call out, "It's Daddy! Daddy's home!" And after a while, the door opened, and Bud came inside. But it was a different Bud, or maybe I finally had eyes to see things I'd been blind to before. He looked older, somehow, and very tired, and there was no light in his eyes at all. He stopped in the doorway, and we just looked at each other for a long time. Then we were holding each other, and we were both crying, and I saw how much this man was suffering, because of what I had done to him, and how much I had hurt him. "Oh, Bud, please forgive me, please forgive me. I promise I'll be different. Please, please don't go."

He was quiet for a long time. "I won't go," he said.

And so we started over—or at least, we tried to. Bud tried hard to make things work, and I tried hard to be different. But old ways die hard, and things were not better overnight. Bud seemed distant and preoccupied, and then I would wonder, "What is he thinking? He doesn't really love me. If he did, how could he have left?"

Sitting across the dining room table from him and letting the children's chatter fill up the silence, I thought: I don't know what to talk about. We are total, complete strangers. How long, how many years, have we been this way?

Maybe it would help to pay more attention to how I looked—so I made an extra appointment with the hairdresser, and, of course, paid more attention than ever to my weight.

In front of the children, we tried to pretend that everything was fine, but there was still a terrible deadness between us, and we could both feel it. And gradually I began to forget all those places where I had seen my wrongness, and I began instead to look at Bud's. That first flash of truth, after talking with Peter, had been like a bolt of lightning, illuminating everything in almost blinding light for a split second; but all too soon I was unwilling to stay in that place of repentance. The dark clouds of self-righteousness closed back in, and I could no longer remember what I had seen so clearly.

"Maybe I've been wrong, but Bud has been wrong, too. How could he have done this to me? Maybe I haven't been the perfect wife, but I didn't deserve *this!*" And the more I began to let the anger and self-pity go round and round in my head, the more I became depressed. It was hard to think about anything else, and I was acutely restless, never able to sit still or stay in one place.

Maybe it would help to get out of the house for a few hours. "Do you know what's showing tonight at the movies?"

"No."

"Let's go anyway!" Anything to occupy my mind!

But sitting in the darkened theater, I found it hard to follow the plot. Bud's heartless and cruel, I thought. He has no idea how much suffering he's caused me, and he doesn't even care. Tears of self-pity began to stream down my face, and ignoring the children's worried glances, I went into the lobby to wait for the movie to be over. The evening was a disaster.

June was hot, and July even hotter. The weather was almost unbearable, and my thoughts were even worse. Once again, I was totally consumed with myself. How could Bud have rejected me? How could he have hurt me so much? Didn't he know how this had humiliated me? How could I ever hold my head up again? He had no right to do this to me! He had destroyed my world. I thought about it day and night, and then on the Fourth of July, I exploded.

It had been a sultry night, and now in the early afternoon, the temperature was well over the hundred mark. There wasn't a sign of a breeze blowing. Here and there around the neighborhood the pop-pop of firecrackers could already be heard. Bud had switched on a baseball game, and the children were downstairs in the cooler basement playroom. I didn't know what to do with myself. I felt fidgety; I couldn't settle down to do the laundry or even to sit down and look at a magazine. Maybe it would be cooler out in the porch swing, but it was no better there. I hated those firecrackers! I wandered back in the house, lost in my thoughts. "I feel so alone. Nobody cares about me; nobody loves me. I thought being a Christian was going to help our marriage; in just three years it has totally fallen apart. How can Bud sit there and watch television, as if nothing had ever happened?" But when I looked at Bud, I could see that though he was looking at the screen, his thoughts were a million miles away.

"What are you thinking?" I demanded shrilly. "I think this whole thing is hopeless. I know you don't want to be here; you don't love me at all. I know you only stayed because of the children. If you hate me so much, why do you bother to stay?"

I had forgotten that he had stayed only because I had pleaded with him not to go. And yet, even as I spewed out all my venom, I desperately wanted him to tell me that I was wrong, and everything was going to be all right, that he really loved me, and that we were still going to live happily ever after.

He said nothing. With a look of infinite sadness, he got up, switched off the television set, picked up his cap, and walked out the door. Only the fact that the children were in the basement kept me from picking up a vase and throwing it against the wall. I couldn't go on like this. I was going absolutely crazy!

15

Press Towards the Mark

Had our trip to Hawaii been just a dream? No! It was proof to Dan and me that our marriage *could* work, but our pattern of relating to one another was going to have to change radically. And what I should have seen then, but would not see for several more years, is that it only takes one person willing to be wrong and to change to start things going. *I* had determined on that trip, and by the grace of God, that I was able to change. And Dan had responded positively to my new personality; in fact, he could hardly believe it!

But—I was not yet ready to be the only wrong one. I was willing to be wrong, *if* he was also willing to be wrong. So I told him that we would both have to stop expressing our negative feelings to each other and stop scapegoating on each other. Over the years I had taken out on Dan all my tensions, frustrations, and angers, whether they had anything to do with him or not. This was particularly true where my weight was concerned. If I had gained, which I usually did over the weekend, then I was a bear on Sunday morning, snapping at the children and growling at Dan. In fact, I made Sunday the most miserable day in the whole week. By Tuesday, after starving myself for two days to drop those weekend pounds, my disposition would have improved. I could be very cheerful on an empty stomach, if I had managed to lose a couple of pounds.

If I was angry or upset about any incident during the day, I would retire early in the evening to avoid any conversation with Dan. And there were days when anything Dan did or said irritated me. On the other hand, the more vocal and outspoken I was, the quieter and more passive *he* became. I used to wish Dan would speak up, take charge, make decisions, instead of leaving everything to me to do. But whenever he did try to voice an opinion or make a decision, I would ignore him and go ahead and do what I wanted to anyway.

My weight had stabilized at around 120-125 pounds that November, depending on how many parties I had been to. My social life was so hectic that I was perpetually exhausted from the effort of trying to be everything to everybody–super Mom of the Year, driving my children all over town to lessons, dancing school, Girl Scouts, choir practice, and after school sports; "Hostess with the Mostest," entertaining at least once a week for dinner, lunch, bridge party or family; Volunteer of the Year; and Chairman or Board Member of the Children's Hospital, the Day Nursery Center, the Garden Club, Church Vestry and Alumnae Council, while still trying to play tennis at least once or twice a week and attend my Bible Study and weekly prayer group meetings. My temper, which was usually short, depended on the pressures of the day, and the amount of food I had or had not eaten. I ruled the kids with an iron hand, because I simply had no time for misbehavior. Either I was very strict, or, consumed with guilt at being so harsh and ugly, I would let them have their own way and do as they pleased.

The three children were the focus of my life after 3:30 P.M., when school was over. Conversation at dinner and any afterwards was invariably centered around the activities of their day. Dan and I did not talk much, because I was still jealous of the place that business had in his life. I did not want to hear about the ins and outs of the downtown Cleveland real estate. I was much more interested in what happened in school or at gymnastics practice or at the Girl Scout meeting. The girls were very active and got along well together. They would play by the hour inside with their dolls, or outside in the acres of woods surrounding our house.

Danny, however, was having trouble growing up emotionally, and it showed up in school. Upon completing first grade, his teachers and the head of the Primary Department suggested that we keep him back a year and let him repeat first grade. I can see now that I had kept him a baby to be a comfort to me, for it was right after his birth that I realized how much I hated to be with his father. I also knew that Danny would be our last, so I poured all my loving attention on him as a baby and a toddler. I needed to love someone and, since I didn't love my husband, the baby got all my stored-up affection. When he was just walking, he would cry every Sunday in baby nursery at church, and an usher would have to come and get me to go to the nursery. Though I was embarrassed by his behavior, part of me was secretly delighted that Danny missed his mommy and said so. He was so lovable, with his brown curls and sweet smile. I took him everywhere with me–to the market, or shops, or waiting for the girls to have a piano or ballet lesson. Dan learned how to play by himself, because there were no other children his age living near us, and later on, when he got older, his sisters allowed him to join their games.

During January and February, with great anticipation and excitement, Anne and I planned another visit by Cay and Judy. Once again, we organized a weekend retreat that would take place at Anne's home this time. The rest of the week, they would spend in personal counseling and talking to friends in small groups. For weeks, all we discussed were the details of this special visit—what we would have to eat, who would meet the plane, how many chairs to borrow, how many invitations to the retreat to be mailed.

At last, the long-awaited day arrived. Anne and I went to the airport to meet Cay and Judy and, as usual, chattered away all the way home. We settled them into Liza's bedroom, where they would stay for the week, then sat down to dinner. How wonderful to see their smiling faces again at our table! The best part of their visit was the precious evening time, after the meeting was over and everyone had gone home. Each night we would get a cup of coffee or a cold drink and a snack, and then, with shoes off, we would talk with them until the wee hours. It was so easy for Dan and me to share our troubles and problems with them. For once, the two of us were able to be totally honest, and after living in our home for a week, Cay and Judy got to know us very well. They could see how frantic and uptight I was, even though I tried to cover it up as best I could. I didn't like my schedule altered, so it always upset me if anyone called and changed an appointment, or just dropped in unannounced. I had each day organized just so—alterations were not welcome. And yet I tried to always keep a smile on my face, regardless of what was going on in the kitchen or on the phone.

Cay and Judy were terrific houseguests—nothing

seemed to bother them. They didn't try to straighten us out with advice; instead, they mostly listened to what we said and then gently helped us to see where we could change—where we accused each other and blamed the other for our problems. They talked a lot about Jesus as a person who cared for us, as Someone we should lean on and turn to in our need.

Where *was* Jesus in our lives? Not very close by, it seemed, in spite of all my Bible studies and prayer groups. I was still trying to do everything in my own strength, still bent on making a name, securing a place, and proving to the family and myself, most of all, that I had at last succeeded. I never prayed about what to do each day. I never turned over my day to Jesus. I just did whatever I thought needed to be done, or more often, whatever I wanted to do. And always before me was the image of the perfect homemaker I was striving to be. Cay and Judy could see all this, and they tried to help me to see the state I was in. But, I was not entirely sure I agreed with them. I had problems, but I thought I could handle them. After all, my friends seemed to keep similar schedules, and they managed to survive.

Dan and I made a maximum effort to be more loving to and caring for each other. And for a few weeks after the visit of Cay and Judy, life did seem more peaceful. I knew my attitude towards Dan was still rotten, but now I fought against saying many of the hateful remarks I was tempted to make. Even so, it didn't last, and before long things were worse than ever, and inside I was a wreck. What was worse, my thoughts were starting to make no sense at all. And that was scary. By the end of May I knew I needed help badly, so I called my brother David. He suggested that maybe it was time to come East again. Cay and Judy were leading a retreat at Craigville Conference Center in the middle of June. "Fine," I said, "I'll make plane reservations, if you'll meet me in Hyannis. I really need to talk to someone again. Dan and I are at each other constantly, and I know this hurts the children." Also, I wanted to do some landscaping for our Cape home, Nineveh, so this would be a good time to buy the plants, bushes and flowers.

When I arrived on the Cape, I found myself most of the time dissolved in tears. I went through the retreat weekend with ears only half open to what was being said–I wanted to hear the message that was being taught, but I was in too much turmoil inside. For I had come to the conclusion that all my troubles were because I was married to the wrong man. Those two weeks in Hawaii were only a dim memory now. When the retreat ended Sunday afternoon, I returned to the Community, planning to stay two or three extra days to try to gain some measure of the peace I'd previously found there. Monday morning, I talked with Cay and Judy, and after a while it seemed to me that what I really needed to do was to stay on, until I got myself sorted out. I had no idea how close to the emotional brink I was at the time. I just knew that I either cried or felt like crying all the time, and nothing that marriage counseling or any psychiatrist could do seemed to help.

I called Dan to see what he thought of the idea of my staying on at the Community. Young Dan would be welcome there, and the girls would be off at summer camp. I knew I was leaving him with a burden, but I also knew how close I was to coming apart at the seams.

"Well, sure, I guess so," he replied, stunned by what I had said. "Of course, I'll look after things here, if you really think it's the right thing to do."

I tried not to cry. "I don't see any alternatives. I'm a

mess, and obviously I don't seem to be able to help myself. Maybe this time I'll learn something."

"I won't be able to stay there with you, you know," said Dan. "There's no way I can be away from the office in the middle of summer for very long. Maybe I can join you for a couple of weeks later on."

"Okay," I said, trying to sound cheerful, "let's plan on it. I'll see you whenever you can come. Kiss the girls good-bye for me and tell them I miss them very much. They can fly up to Boston from camp, and I'll meet them," I said, my voice breaking.

So it was settled: I would stay for the summer in Damascus, the home owned by Buzz and Belle Elmer. During those weeks of June, July, and August, I helped to supervise, look after, and be "mother" to an assortment of teenage girls who came to the Community to live in that summer. It was my job to organize the girls' household cleaning assignments, supervise the cooking of breakfast, lunch and dinner for our extended family, and help take care of the flower garden. But my first responsibility was simply to keep my eyes and ears open and watch out for my young charges.

At the end of July, Liza and Lexa arrived from camp all full of excitement and enthusiasm. They loved community life, especially since there were so many children their ages. In Cleveland, the girls were really isolated, because we lived so far away from neighbors.

The weeks flew by, and then Dan arrived for a visit. I was glad he was coming. I had written to him every week, telling him of my experiences keeping a dozen teenagers busy and out of mischief from morning until night. Just keeping their bath and shampoo schedules straight was difficult! But now he would see for himself what I was talking about.

No sooner did he arrive, than he caught the flu and had to go to bed for several days. I was so disappointed, because I had hoped he would be able to spend time with the Community men and get to know them. I wanted so much for him to like this place and feel comfortable around these people, who had come from all over the United States and from all sorts of backgrounds, and who had become close friends.

"Do you have any feelings you'd like to talk about?" I asked, when I would carry in his breakfast tray. "You'll feel a lot better, if you talk about what you're thinking about, lying here in bed." I tried to encourage him.

"Oh, I'm okay. I just have this lousy cold. All I need is lots of water and some sleep and vitamin C, and I'll be over this in no time."

So much for my trying to help! I was hurt and angry that he would not share his feelings. I knew he must have a thousand thoughts about us, the Community, and my being here all summer. Well, if he wouldn't talk to me, maybe he would say something to the Elmers or Father Lane. But it was no use–Dan just continued to blow his nose, drink pitchers of cold drinks, and read his book.

When he had finally recovered, we decided to take a day off. And once again, I made up my mind to make this day happy and pleasant. And so we spent one marvelous day touring Cape Cod, from Chatham to Provincetown. We started our adventure in Chatham, where we went into an art gallery. We spent an hour admiring the many oils and watercolors of typical Cape scenes. Should we buy one? No, it's crazy! "Why don't we buy an oil to go over our mantel in the living room?"

"Let's think about it," said Dan, always the cautious one.

We got back into our car and went on with our tour.

We had packed a picnic basket filled with thick sandwiches, chocolate chip cookies, cans of Coke and bags of Fritos. There is nothing like fresh salt air to whet the appetite. We headed now for the wild, windswept dunes of Truro and Wellfleet. Scrubby pine and bayberry bushes were all that could be seen on either side of the deeply rutted, sandy road leading to the National Seashore. The beach itself stretched for miles, as far as the eye could see. And there was the ocean, a vast expanse of indigo and turquoise spread out before us like fine Indian silk waiting for the dressmaker's shears. I could hardly bear to leave this awesome sight, but we had many places yet to visit.

When we finally reached Provincetown, we took a walk down narrow Commercial Street, eating ice cream cones and poking our heads into the tiny, unique stores. Oh, what a day! I was as happy as I'd been out in Hawaii. And Dan was happy, too; he suggested late that afternoon that we drive back to Chatham to have another look at those oil paintings. We did and found one that pleased us both—a seascape of Nauset Beach, dunes and the deep blue sea—so we bought it.

Dan finally had to go back to his office, and I was surprised at how much I missed him. Having had several weeks away to think about our marriage and our life together, I realized that I simply could not go on hating Dan, just because he was not my idea of the perfect mate. I realized that I was punishing him continually for not being the man of my dreams, and that there was no man on earth who could give me all the attention I wanted. Taking care of a large group of teenage girls for the summer had shown me that I had to put Jesus first in my life; and having to go to Him in prayer constantly helped me to keep my head on my shoulders. I saw that it was an absolute necessity for me to get off the throne, where I wanted to be treated like a queen, and to turn to Jesus in the many times of stress and strain. I did not have the answers for these young girls, and I certainly couldn't cope with all their problems in myself. There just wasn't time to think much about myself that summer, as I prepared three meals a day for my hungry gang. The girls were helpful and did much of the work, but someone had to keep everything organized–with tables to set, clothes to iron, laundry to be folded, two dogs to walk, rooms to be dusted and vacuumed, and a garden to be weeded.

During that summer I met another woman my age, Sunny Hale. She had come up to the Community on a retreat, and decided to stay on for a few days to live in. And since Dan had returned to Cleveland, there was room for Sunny in our bedroom.

My first impression of Sunny when she arrived was that she was super-thin and quite nervous. I sat on my bed and watched her getting ready for breakfast. She spent a long time fixing her hair and make-up. She combed her hair over and over again, trying to get it just so. While she combed her hair and put on lipstick, she confessed that she missed her three children who were 5, 9 and 12. She had left them at her sister's home, and she was worried about them. Would they be all right this long without her? I assured her they would be fine, and suggested she hurry up. Obviously, she had no idea about the pace of our life in Community. We had an early breakfast before our Holy Communion service at 7:20 A.M. There were many who shared the same bathroom, so we had to move quickly! I tried to gently hint to her that she'd have to be quicker about getting ready, or we'd have to leave her behind. She was so preoccupied with herself I had to laugh, because I realized that that was exactly the way I was, when I had first come.

Sunny was, without a doubt, the skinniest girl I'd seen in years. I was struck by the thinness of her arms and legs and the hollowness of her face. She was a pretty woman, but the acute gauntness of her cheeks and neck took away from her beauty. Had I looked like that, before I had stopped smoking? I was sure that I had when I had gotten down to 110, for I was four inches taller than she. We spent the next three or four days together, sharing a bedroom and getting to know each other, before she went on retreat. At the end of the second weekend, she returned to Texas. I wondered what her reunion with her family would be like. She certainly was a dramatically different gal on Sunday than she had been the preceding Monday! She seemed amazingly less nervous and tense at the end of the week.

Looking back, it was as if God had placed a full-length mirror in my room at Damascus, so that I could see myself in Sunny. I could tell from our many conversations that she and her husband Bud had many of the same communication problems that Dan and I had. How much of our strung-out emotions were tied in with our physical appearance? Sunny and I were so similiar in our tense, nervous and controlling behavior–did it have anything to do with excessive thinness? I think so! We both had quantities of deep feelings of inadequacy pushed way down, that needed to come out into the light. To cover up those feelings, we tried very hard to be perfect and that included being the thinnest person around. We were determined to be on top, and it was intolerable to be wrong! I could see that Sunny was someone who was used to being in charge; she was capable, very intelligent, and seemed to know exactly what she was doing. But underneath that cool facade was a girl exactly like me who really could not make decisions, was in constant fear of being wrong, and worried continually–about what other people thought of her.

Well, I knew all about those fears and that determination to succeed. I had spent quite a few years pursuing the goal of ultimate thinness, and therefore, in my mind, perfection. I wanted everyone to admire my great stamina and self-control. What I had never understood was their horror at how thin and gaunt I really was. I was so intent on gaining approval and respect, it never occurred to me that I was punishing my body–and my family–by being so full of pride and willful stubbornness.

As we sat around the Damascus dining room table that summer, I began to enjoy the bountiful meals. For the first time in years, I relaxed and freely ate good, nutritious food, not the kind of junk stuff that I would secretly binge on. There were all kinds of fresh vegetables from the Community gardens, homemade breads, cakes, and cookies, and many new recipes to try. It seemed that everyone who came to visit brought a favorite way to make oatmeal bread or banana muffins. But my bondage to the scale remained. Each day I weighed myself to make sure that all those tempting goodies I ate did not push the dial on the scale over 125 pounds. I was still very much in charge of my weight and had no intention of changing in that department.

It was interesting to see the different weight problems I encountered with my teenage charges. The girls I lived with came in all shapes and sizes and with various appetites, too. Some ate to assuage their unhappiness, while others refused to eat anything if they were upset or angry. Over and over again, I saw myself in these girls who had so many of the same problems growing up as I had. The hurt feelings, angers, insecurities, and jealousies with brothers and sisters were there, just as they had been in my own family life. Food had become a tool, or weapon in some cases, and a comfort for others. The thin girls pushed their food around the plate and barely nibbled a bite, while the overweight teens were slipping into the kitchen and snacking day and night. Unable to have their own way all day long, at least they could have what they wanted to eat. We would discover that boxes of crackers and jars of peanut butter disappeared from the pantry shelves. Raisins and nuts would be found under beds when we vacuumed. Their graham crackers and potato chips eaten late at night reminded me of my doughnuts gobbled up at snack time at summer camp in Maine, or my gorging bouts in the closet at boarding school!

The summer of 1974 came to an end with Labor Day weekend and my birthday celebration. When Dan returned to the Cape to drive us back to Cleveland, the children and I were very glad to see him, and to think of going home again. But when it came time to leave, it was surprising how hard it was to say good-bye to all our friends. Our suitcases were full of memories of those happy summer days.

"Well," I said, as we settled in the car, ready to go, "We'll have lots to do at home in Cleveland; won't it be fun to see the house again?" The agreement from the back seat was somewhat less than wholehearted. And so, with our station wagon full, we headed for the Mid-Cape Highway to the bridge, turning back for one last look at our waving friends. I didn't feel as confident and happy as my words to the children sounded. Actually, I now dreaded my usual fall schedule that was about to start up again with the beginning of the school term. What could I do to break out of the mold? And to be honest, did I really want to give up the frenzied pace? If I did, what would I do to pass the time? Would Dan and I get along better after a summer of separation? I surely hoped so, but I was filled with doubts and fears as we left the Cape.

September, October, November–the months rushed by, and soon it was Christmas again. The season was frantic as always, but we got through it, and then in February, Cay and Judy had promised to return again to Cleveland for another week of teaching and counseling. Anne and her husband Don were as enthusiastic as we were whenever Cay and Judy were coming to visit. Anne was very real with me, so I always knew how she felt about things. She didn't hesitate to tell me if she was angry or upset, and she shared her joys as well as her fears and sorrows. We talked daily on the phone and spent hours together each week, either at her house or mine or in prayer group in Bible study. As we both struggled to be obedient, we needed encouragement as well as reminders where we had strayed off course. God had given me Anne to be a help to me, and I hoped I was able to be the same to her. She spoke up, if she thought I was angry or controlling or willful, especially when we worked on a project like getting ready for Cay and Judy to come and lead a retreat.

I had a strong tendency to take charge and start giving orders, instead of working side by side with Anne. It had always been so much easier just to do everything myself, my way. Now I was trying to learn how to give up my struggle to be on top and to work *with* someone like Anne. By the time Cay and Judy were due to arrive we had filled their days with a very busy schedule from morning until night.

One night, when Cay and Judy and Dan and I were settled in our library for one of our special late night talks after all the guests had gone, they asked about my summer at Damascus the year before. I told them how peaceful and fulfilling I had found that time to be, even though there were many moments when I felt I could not cope with all those teenage girls another minute. But there was no question that the fruit of living in obedience to the will of God was peace in my heart—the same peace that I had so longed for at that first retreat in Brookwoods, New Hampshire. What did it mean to live in obedience? For me, it simply meant being faithful to the schedule of the day, serving breakfast on time, leaving for church on time, observing a quiet time after lunch for resting or reading, being on time for my daily prayer vigil hour, and being honest and speaking my feelings, whether I wanted to or not. For any group of people to be able to live together in harmony, there had to be honesty, and that meant that sometimes there would be conflict which needed to be resolved. We always seemed to get stuck in our own hurt and anger, and chose not to be open and honest or needy with one another. I had too much pride and would not show my neediness to Dan. To my friend, Anne, yes, but to Dan? *No!*

After spending several days with us, Cay and Judy suggested that it might take more than just one summer to get the help we both needed. Had Dan ever considered taking half a year or maybe even a year off from work, to come to the Community for further time for healing? No, Dan said, he had never once considered the possibility of taking a leave of absence from his company—responsible presidents did not just take off and leave for six months—let alone a year! So much for that idea!

Cay and Judy also suggested that we might pray and see if God would want our family to come to the Community for the very special time of Passiontide, the two weeks prior to Easter. Well, now it was my turn to say no, I didn't think so! How could we not go to Florida for Spring vacation? We had *always* gone to Florida, since I was thirteen years old, and this year, at long last, we were first in line for that deluxe three-bedroom villa! Oh, God, please don't tell me You think we should go to Cape Cod, instead of Florida!

But we did promise to pray about it. And after four days of trying to avoid the issue, I knew God was trying to say something to me. And I also knew what it was: We were supposed to go to the Cape. The travel agent was speechless, when I said to cancel our plane and hotel reservations for the five of us. But in my heart I knew we had taken another step forward in our walk with Jesus.

Shortly before they left we were again sitting in our library with Cay and Judy. They had noticed how tired I seemed. I didn't know what I could do about that; I was locked into a round of club meetings, hospital meetings, bridge group, et cetera, that had me going from 8:00 A.M. until 5:30 P.M. every day of the week but Sunday. I was worn to a frazzle, simply because I did not know how to say "no." I did not dare say "no," for fear that I would be disapproved of by my friends, my mother, or anyone who asked me to do a job. All those jobs represented places that I thought needed me. And I desperately needed to be needed; then I was worth something to someone.

But now, thinking about all the things I'd seen while they were here, I found I had a new perspective on my priorities. I seemed to be able to see them as God might arrange them, instead of me. And I felt emboldened to go over my list and divide up most of my responsibilities into two groups: B.L. and B.J. The former meant resign before Lent, the latter stood for resign by June. Resign? From everything? How could I possibly do that? Little did I know, but God knew, that by June I would once again be loading up the family wagon with suitcases, children and our new puppy, Lucy.

The final decision to take a leave of absence from Cleveland came in March, while we were in the middle of one of our intensely competitive, weekend tennis matches with an aunt and uncle. Ever since Cay and Judy had offered the suggestion about taking a year off, I had been in conflict. Should we go or not? But it was really up to Dan to make the choice, because of his business commitments. There were days when I was ready to pack and take the next plane, and other days when I did not see how I could possibly say good-bye to anyone in Cleveland. I was afraid my old friends would forget me too soon.

Well, on this particular day, Dan and I were in the middle of a cold war battle, but this Sunday was going to have a different ending. Suddenly, without any warning, Dan turned to me on his way back to receive the serve and said, "I think we should move to the Cape for a year. I'll take a year off." I repeated it to myself slowly, shaking my head in amazement. "Yes, take a year and go live at the Community," Dan replied quietly as he positioned himself inside the baseline. I was so shocked, I just stood there, my back to our opponents, staring at him. "Come on," he said, smiling, "we're playing tennis." I turned and looked over at my aunt and uncle, to see if they had heard anything. Apparently not, because my aunt was waiting to serve the ball. "What's going on over there?" she called out. "Are we playing tennis, or what?"

"Oh, we're ready. Go ahead and serve." I managed to smile as I took my place at net.

For the next couple of weeks, I felt as if I was in a daze, as we prepared to go to the Community for Easter.

Now all of a sudden the tables were turned, and Dan was calling the shots. I was relieved on the one hand that something was finally happening to him, but now I was jealous that suddenly he was in charge.

During the two weeks of Passiontide, we made all the necessary arrangements for our year at the Community. The Lord truly blessed us, those cold, blustery March days. I was introduced to a book during that Lent, *My Imitation of Christ*, by Thomas à Kempis—a little book that I could tuck into my pocket, but it fed my heart, instead of my fantasies and daydreams. My days were spent in the kitchen at the Ark, learning how to bake special Easter breads, instead of by the swimming pool in the Florida sun. I had never before paid much attention to this sacred time of year; Passion Sunday, Palm Sunday, and Holy Week were usually spent on the beaches. But now, in the sunny kitchen of the rectory, as I kneaded dough, I came to see how little I knew or understood about what the Passion of Jesus really meant. The final Easter Sunday Service brought tears to my eyes, with all its beauty in song, prayer, flowers, and the stately, but joyful service of Holy Communion in the Episcopal *Book of Common Prayer.*

We returned to Cleveland with the task of telling our parents we would be leaving for a year. We planned to rent our Cleveland house "as is," and just take our clothes and our dog. I felt very comfortable with this arrangement, but was extremely anxious about sharing our plans with our families because I knew they were going to be most upset. They were. We invited my parents out for dinner, to break the news to them first.

"How can you just up and leave? How can you walk out on all your responsibilities? What about the children?" they asked. No one in the family had ever done such a radical thing as we were proposing to do, just pack up and leave. They shook their heads in disbelief. "Why on earth would you do such a thing? It's just crazy thinking!"

We tried to explain, but it was no use. They were too hurt and angry to understand. Things went just as badly with Dan's parents. Never mind that Dan was forty-one and I was thirty-six; they saw us throwing our lives away on some fanciful whim, some terribly immature decision. Nor was there any reconciliation from that point on. Nothing we could say or do would change the awful strain on our now broken relationships. Dan and I knew in our hearts that God was trying to cut us from our past and our unbelievable dependency on our parents, so that we would both be free to be husband and wife with each other–and the son and daughter–that God had created us to be.

The months of April, May and June were spent getting ready to go. We found a business executive who wanted to rent our house furnished and keep our cleaning lady, Lula, who came in twice a week to look after things and water the plants. I felt very relieved and grateful to God that everything would be well cared for during our year away. I packed trunks and boxes and sent them ahead. And as planned, I resigned from my clubs, boards, and volunteer job, and said my good-byes to all my friends in bridge group, prayer group and Bible Study. Saying good-bye to Anne and Don was the hardest of all, but they also visited the Community often now, so I knew I would see them again.

My parents had sold the big, beautiful house we had grown up in and had built a handsome, small country home with terraced gardens, a swimming pool and a pond complete with fish and a row boat. They were especially sad that the grandchildren would not be there to swim in the pool or fish in the pond. All the time the house was being built, Mother had been looking ahead to the enjoyment of having her grandchildren around her, and now we had spoiled that. But Dan and I now saw clearly that for our marriage to survive we had to get away. As long as I remained in Cleveland, I would always be Cornelia Manuel, David and Anne Manuel's daughter, or Mrs. Daniel B. Ford, Jr.–young Dan's wife. Not that that was bad; it was just that I did not know how to function as an individual person in my own right. I did not know who *I* was.

Both my brothers had gone away to college, served in the Navy, and then married and found jobs in other parts of the country. They had formed new lives with their new families. Dan and I had married and stayed where we were born. I just stepped right into the same shoes and walked the same path as my mother had before me. Our social calendars were almost identical as we traveled through our days. I even worried about what the newspapers would say about me when I died. The grand old ladies of Cleveland society all had paragraphs about their civic contributions. In the back of my mind, I wanted to accomplish many things so that there would be good deeds listed after my name, almost like senior entries in a yearbook. That seems pathetic now, but that was my life and my last will and testament. And that really would have been my epitaph–but God had more, much more, for me to learn about goals in life, about what really counted. Up to this point, I had been pressing towards the wrong mark.

16

A Spiritual Hospital

I leaned my forehead against the small window of the twin-engined plane and watched the gray waves all too close below. The plane dipped alarmingly, but I didn't really feel afraid. Normally I was terrified flying over water, but today everything seemed so unreal. It was hard to believe that I was flying to Cape Cod all alone–Sunny, who had never wanted to drive sixty miles without her husband, was now going all the way to the East Coast from Texas, and didn't even care.

"God surely hasn't brought me all this way just to drop me in the Bay," I mused.

The children had accompanied me as far as Indiana, where they would be spending a few days with my sister's family. I had been relieved that in their excitement over the flight and the prospect of visiting cousins, they had seemed unaware of the tension between Bud and me. It had been hard saying good-bye to Bud at the airport, not knowing what the future would hold for our marriage, but knowing that the situation was desperate. Far from being able to patch things up, if anything I had made them worse; in fact, I couldn't even help myself.

I was a physical, emotional and spiritual wreck. Our marriage was in a shambles, I was unable to function as a mother, and I could not eat and looked thinner every day. Family and friends wondered what was wrong, but I had too much pride to confide in anyone I knew. Somehow I had to get some answers; I had to have some help in putting my life back together, and finding out where to go from here.

The idea of Cape Cod had first come to me on that terrible Fourth of July afternoon. After Bud had left, in the back on my mind I remembered something Peter Marshall had said–a passing remark he had made at dinner about a place on Cape Cod, where people could go who needed help. "That's for me," I thought. "God knows how much I need help." I kept thinking about it, and finally I called Peter to ask him for the number of the Community of Jesus–over the protest of one of my best friends.

"I think the whole idea is ridiculous," Marge had told me. "Why are you even considering going so far away? Jesus is right here in Lamesa, too."

But the idea persisted, and one day, feeling a little foolish and not really knowing what I would say, I dialed the Community's number. A pleasant voice answered the phone, but I found it very hard to explain what I wanted. "I, uh, just need to get some help," I kept repeating over and over like an idiot, and finally two very kind women were on the line.

Through a flood of tears I was telling them the whole story, and then Judy answered, "Cay and I feel that it is right for you to come, and it just happens that we have a women's retreat next week, followed by another one on the weekend. Since you are coming such a long distance, why don't you plan to stay over for both?"

The idea of two retreats sounded a little repetitious, but Bud thought I should try it, and I was so needy that I was ready for anything. I still had no idea what the Community of Jesus was all about. Was it a rustic retreat center of some kind, cabins on the beach? Would I need a bedroll? What kind of clothes should I take? And what sort of people would want to live together in a community anyway? But all the unknowns seemed unimportant, if I could just get help.

Peter had said that the directors of the Community, Cay Andersen and Judy Sorensen, were unusually gifted by God in counsel and discernment, and I wanted to meet them and talk to them and see if they or someone else could help me answer the questions that kept going round and round in my head.

The little commuter airplane finally got all three wheels down on the runway, and eventually taxied to a stop in front of the little Hyannis terminal. I came down the steps, shading my eyes against the bright July sun. They had said that someone would meet me, and sure enough a nice-looking blonde woman waved from the side and seemed to be looking right at me. "Sunny Hale? Hi, I'm Betsy Catlin. Can I help you with your bags?"

"Oh, yes, thanks very much! They're pretty heavy. To tell you the truth, I didn't how what to bring, so I just brought a little of everything." The four pieces of luggage suddenly seemed a bit much for a week's visit.

During the half-hour drive to Orleans, I kept up a steady barrage of questions, "Are we far from the water? What kind of trees are those along the road?" Most of all, I was anxious to find out what sort of a place I had come to, and what the people were like. "Where were you from before, Betsy? When did you move to the Community? How many children do you have?" It was impossible to imagine whole families willing to give up their own homes and jobs to come together because they felt God calling, but as I watched Betsy out of the corner of my eye, she seemed reassuringly normal, in fact, very much like my friends at home.

"Here we are; this is the Community of Jesus." Betsy slowed the car, and I caught my breath in astonishment. I certainly had not expected anything like the expansive white colonial building, stretching gracefully above the green lawns and bright flower beds, with a spectacular view of Cape Cod Bay. It was a far cry from the little cabins that I had envisioned, and to think I had almost brought my bedroll!

Inside Bethany, as the retreat house was called, beautiful antique furniture gleamed from frequent polishings. Everything looked lovingly cared for, and there were fresh flowers in abundance. After I had registered in the front hall, a Sister showed me to a comfortable dormitory room to unpack, and then there was just time to hurry to the chapel for the traditional Monday night meeting.

Red carpeting, lovely hangings, oak pews—so far everything had been surprisingly like our church at home, but as the first hymn was announced, I began to feel ill at ease. The hymns were very different from any that I had ever sung before. I had never used an Episcopal hymnbook, and I didn't like it. Everything seemed strange and unfamiliar. I didn't like the way the man was directing the music, and in my opinion we sang far too many songs. I had seen two women who I was sure must be Cay and Judy, and I was impatient to hear them speak.

When the teaching did begin, the dark-haired lady, Judy, read from a text in Romans, but I was so busy looking around that I was soon lost. "Whatever are they talking about?" I wondered. "And how can they speak, first one and then the other, and never use any notes at all?" I had never seen anything quite like it, but I was too wrapped up in myself to concentrate on what they were saying. My mind kept going back to the way that our youngest, Kathy, had cried when I had left her that morning, and how much I already missed the children. They were only twelve, nine, and five–much too young to be away from their mother for a whole week. Maybe this had been a crazy idea after all; I should have listened to my friend Marge. I would call the airline in the morning and change my reservation and go straight home. Bud and I just needed a little time together; it had been a terrible idea to leave him right now. We should be together. Maybe things were not as bad as I had thought.

When the meeting was over, and the last hymn was finally sung, I sighed with relief. "Now if I can just find a phone somewhere."

A friendly lady next to me smiled. "I'm here from Virginia; wasn't that a wonderful teaching?"

"What? Oh, yes, wonderful," I murmured, hoping that she wouldn't realize that I hadn't paid attention. "If you'll excuse me, I have to make an important call."

One. . .two. . .three rings. Why isn't Bud answering the phone? What if he's not home? When at last he finally answered, I began to cry. "Oh, Bud, this is not the place for me. This was a terrible idea; I don't know why I ever came. I want to come home tomorrow. We can pick up the children and all go somewhere for a few days. We just need a little vacation; that's all. I miss you all so much, and I want to come home!"

Instead of consolation, there was silence on the other end of the phone. Then Bud finally spoke. "Sunny, look: You've traveled all that distance, now stay at least a few days and give it a chance. I'm packing now to go fishing tomorrow with Tom, and I'll call you when we get back. Now just try to relax and have a good time. Good night."

"But *Bud!*" I cried in a whisper, only to hear the click of his receiver. I put the phone down, trying to hide my tears from the Sisters, who were busily going here and there in the front hall of the retreat house. "Is something wrong?" one of them asked, offering me a tissue, and before I knew it, Cay and Judy appeared. Had someone told them about the retreatant who was crying on the telephone?

"Oh, I'm sorry, I didn't mean to bother you," I blurted, "but I'm so upset. I just called my husband, and–and he didn't want to talk to me, and he doesn't care if I ever come home again or not–" and I dissolved in waves of self-pity. "I just want to go home!" I wailed.

But somehow just the presence of the two women was calming. They didn't offer me sympathy at all, but I sensed their compassion. When they spoke, I dried my eyes and listened. "Why don't you let Jesus take care of your husband," Cay was saying, "and let the Holy Spirit do in you what He wants to do. Someday you may look back on this as the best thing that ever happened to you! Now I think you should go to bed and get a good night's sleep." What she said seemed to make a lot of sense, and with a sigh and a teary smile, I decided that I would do exactly that.

The next morning, I opened my eyes to music. For a moment, I wondered if I was hearing angels singing, but the beautiful harmony was being sung by Community Sisters who were waking the retreatants. "This day, this day, will be a diamond day. If you will listen and obey, a golding diamond day." I stretched out on the comfortable bunk bed and listened. Somehow the gloom and panic of the night before had lifted, and I actually felt more rested than I had in weeks—and even a little bit hopeful. "A golding diamond day!" I didn't know exactly what that meant, but somehow I felt it was going to happen to me.

I joined the other women on the retreat—about twenty in all—in Bethany's beautiful dining room for breakfast. Looking out the tall windows, I saw a wide sweep of sparkling blue water, broken only by the massive glacial boulder for which Rock Harbor was named. "What a view!" I exclaimed. Then my attention turned inward, for the Sisters were serving heaping platters of scrambled eggs, sausage, and hot sticky buns. "Oh, I never eat much breakfast, but maybe I will have just one roll. They look so good." I could already tell that it was going to take all my will power not to gain weight on this trip.

Soon Cay and Judy joined us, and the conversation began at once. As they talked informally, this time I listened—and began to hear some things that really made sense to me. Today I had no trouble focusing; in fact, it sounded as if they were talking to me and me alone. Everything they said described me perfectly, yet all the other women seemed to be listening as intently as I. Cay and Judy talked about how often we try to be God and control our own lives, and the destruction that that brings to relationships and to families. They talked about idolatry, which they explained as putting any person or thing before God. They talked about selfishness and self-love, about jealousy and the way it strangles and stifles the life in those around us, and about the demands we put on others to love, worship, and adore us. They might have been reading my life history! And then they talked about Jesus, Who came for sinners just like me and Who alone could help me to live in Him, instead of myself. The meal was over much too quickly; I wanted to hear more. There was no question about it now; I was definitely going to stay for both retreats. I was hearing something that I had never heard before; or perhaps I had heard it in the Gospels, but it had never seemed so relevant to my life as it did now.

The retreat flew by. There were times of teaching and times of quiet, but much of the retreat took place around the mahogany table at meal times. This made me a little uncomfortable. The food looked so delicious, was so beautifully prepared and appetizingly served, that it was almost impossible to resist. "You know, I feel very guilty eating this dessert," I confessed to one of the Sisters serving the dinner.

"You shouldn't feel guilty. You should enjoy it as a gift from God." That was certainly a different way of looking at eating!

The first retreat ended on Wednesday, and the second retreat would start on Friday night. I asked if I might visit in one of the Community houses in between, and Cay and Judy arranged for me to go to the house called Damascus.

Walking over with Community member Belle Elmer, I looked around at the attractive Cape Cod houses scattered throughout the neighborhood. "Everyone certainly keeps a beautiful yard here," I remarked. The truth was, I was a little apprehensive. I had grown to know and appreciate Cay and Judy and the Sisters, but what would the Community families be like?

"I'm sorry that you won't have a bedroom to yourself," Belle was saying, "but it's mid-summer, and all the houses have many live-ins right now. We've put up a cot in the bedroom with Camie Ford and Dee Tingley, and I think you'll like it there."

I did like the lovely room with its cheery furnishings. It was kept with the same care that I had noticed in the retreat house, and there was a flower on the pillow of my cot. Unpacking, I stopped to read again the card that had been on my bed the first night of the retreat:

There isn't anything in your life that won't eventually and ultimately be touched by the Holy Spirit.

Um. . . I wondered what that might mean, but I had the feeling that it was going to prove true.

With sixteen people assigned to the house, meals at Damascus were lively, but I enjoyed the hustle and bustle. The Elmers made me feel very much at home, and everyone was gracious and friendly. The first thing I noticed about my roommate Camie Ford was that she was very thin and very attractive. As we chatted before turning out the light that night, we seemed to have a lot of things in common. She was about my age, we had both been married in the same year, and we both had three children, and so on. But in other ways we seemed as different as night and day. She was very much the person that I had always wanted to be–well-to-do, self-confident, poised. "I'll bet she has never had the problems I've had," I thought.

One afternoon I made an appointment to meet Father Lane, the Community priest and chaplain, in the chapel. Cay and Judy had talked about the spiritual benefit of having a life confession, and I certainly wanted to experience every possible blessing before it was time to go. At first I felt a little awkward and self-conscious, sitting there in one of the pews near the front, talking to a man I had never seen before about my sins; wasn't the whole thing going to be a little embarrassing?

But Father Lane soon put me at ease. "Now just relax; you don't have to be so prim and proper. Why, you act like you're wearing spotless white gloves. The truth is, you're a sinner like everyone else, and you need to accept that about yourself." We talked about the things that I had heard on the retreat, and whenever I wanted to talk about Bud and what he had done, Father Lane gently steered me back to the subject at hand. "You need to keep your eyes on yourself and where *you* are wrong," he reminded me. I did have a lot of things to confess to the Lord and ask His forgiveness for, but somehow I felt very unemotional and detached, almost like I was reciting a list that had nothing to do with me. When I had finished, Father Lane nodded, "Your sins are many." I felt a twinge; why did he have to say that? But as he made the sign of the cross on my forehead and prayed the prayer of absolution, I did feel lighter and freer. "Be sure to keep praying for the gift of repentance," Father Lane told me, as he hugged me good-bye.

All too soon Sunday arrived and it was time to leave for Boston to catch my flight back to Dallas. Once again I stood in Bethany's front hall, and once again I was crying. But this time it was because I wanted to stay, not leave. Here everything made sense, and I had found hope by beginning to face my wrongness. Here I had gone to God in confession and had been assured of His forgiveness and His grace. And here I had been accepted in spite of my weakness and my imperfection and my need–or maybe because of them.

"God builds out of ruins," I had been assured. But what if the damage to our marriage was so lasting that even God couldn't help? "Trust Jesus," I was told, and so I went on my way, asking Him to take charge of the life that I had so badly managed. I had set out to build a kingdom, where I could be the princess, and it had brought me pain and despair. Now it was time to let God show me His plan and His purpose, and to ask Him to make me into the person that He had created me to be. I had not liked Sunny Barrow Hale, and had set out in my own way to remake her into a person that would be acceptable. Well, I had failed. It was time to let God try.

Cay and Judy had cautioned the retreatants not to go back and try to express in words what had happened, but rather try to live out the truth that had been heard. And above all, not to go home and tell everyone else where they were wrong, but to stay in Jesus and continue to look at where I myself fall short. That was the hardest part. As I walked down the airport tunnel from the plane I could feel the Texas heat and I could see Bud waiting up ahead, standing taller than most of the crowd. I waved to him, but when he caught my eye, I knew that things were not good. He asked a few questions about the trip, but when I started to go into detail, I could tell that he had lost interest. Although he had been willing for me to get help, he himself had wanted no part of it. I had to bite my tongue to keep from telling him all that I had heard. If I could just get Bud to the Community, all our problems would be solved. No, that's not what I am supposed to be doing, I caught myself. I am supposed to keep looking at *my* sin, not at Bud's.

"Lord Jesus Christ, Son of God, have mercy on me, a sinner," I prayed over and over again in the next few weeks, as I tried to keep looking at my wrongness and tried to be obedient at home to what I had learned. Mother Cay had said, "If you're sorry, you'll change." If I was really sorry about how selfish and unloving I had been toward Bud, then I needed to start doing loving things. "Lord, You're going to have to help me, because I don't even know where to begin!"

He did. One obvious way came to mind at once: I'll get up and fix his breakfast! For the fifteen years of our marriage, I had prepared hardly any breakfasts for my husband. Bud, the farmer, was up before the sun, and I loved to sleep late. Most mornings he had breakfast down at Turner's Cafe, while the children and I grabbed a quick bite, just in time to get them to school.

But now I knew that was wrong. The only problem was waking up. I set the alarm and got out of bed at 5:45, but couldn't keep my eyes open. Maybe a cold shower would help. So I went straight from the bedroom to the bathroom and turned on the cold water full blast. That did it! When the meal was finally on the table, we sat there together, and I tried to think of something to say. What interested him? What would he want to talk about? Conversation was hard; there was still a great gulf between us.

Almost every night I called the Community for help. "Belle," I would cry, "I don't know what's going to happen. Things seem to be getting worse, not better." She was always patient and willing to take time to help me, even when I called at the most inopportune times and got her out of bed.

"Sunny," she told me, "you have to put Jesus first in your life. Maybe Bud is going to stay, or maybe he will choose to leave. You can't control that. I wish I could tell you that you're never going to suffer, but I can't. You're going to have to trust the Lord to give you the grace you need, whether your marriage is healed or not."

But God *has* to heal our marriage! What's the point of my trying to change, if God isn't going to heal our marriage? The idea that I might have to be willing to let Bud go was completely unacceptable to me. She doesn't realize that I can't have any sort of life without him. She just doesn't know how I feel. Of course Bud will stay! Of course God is going to make everything turn out all right!

There were so many areas in which I needed to change; it was time to take an interest in the things that Bud liked to do. At the Community, when I had complained that Bud watched television, someone had suggested, "Have you ever thought of watching it with him?" No, I had not. So on Monday night I resisted the desire to retire to the bedroom with a good book, and instead sat down to watch Monday Night Football with Bud. To my surprise, it actually wasn't too bad. And on Sunday afternoon, when Bud started out of the house to drive around the fields to check on the cotton, I put aside my usual nap and asked if I might come along, too.

Just from visiting the Community and observing the life there, I had been convicted about how lazy and self-indulgent my own daily routine was. I knew that it wasn't right to take a little morning nap after the children went off to school. And it wasn't God's will for me to go shopping every day, just to buy anything that happened to appeal to me. I knew that we should visit Bud's family more. In one area after another, it was now blatantly apparent how totally selfish I had been for so many years. My life had centered around me: my weight, my opinions, my desires–me, me, me! But now that I could see all the places I had been wrong, surely Bud would see that I was changing, and everything would be all right between us. What I didn't realize was that it wasn't just the things I did that drove Bud away; it was who I *was*, and that this change would have to go much deeper.

One August morning, about three weeks after I had come back from the Community, I fixed Bud's favorite breakfast of scrambled eggs and biscuits. "Aren't you hungry?" I asked, noticing that his plate had scarcely been touched.

Maybe he doesn't feel well, I thought; he has been very quiet for the last few days. Later, washing the dishes, I remembered that I hadn't heard the pick-up start. That's funny; it's very late for him to still be home. And where was he, anyway? Walking into the living room, my heart sank as I saw Bud standing in front of the large windows, staring out into the bright morning sunlight. Even before he turned toward me, I knew what he was going to say.

"When are you going?" I asked.

"This afternoon," he said wearily. There was a terrible note of finality in his voice. He wasn't angry; he wasn't upset; he was just going. And we both knew that he meant it. "I'm sorry, Sunny, but we both know it's not working. I'm going crazy, and I have to go. You'll be okay. You're strong."

I'll be okay! He has the nerve to tell me that I'll be okay! I bit my lip so hard that it almost bled, and I clenched my fists until my nails dug into my palms. I can't fly off the handle. I can't lose control. I've got to be reasonable. "But, Bud, I don't want you to go! You can't go! Things will be better; I'm going to change–"

He shook his head slowly. "Sunny, you don't have any idea. . . ." He stopped for a moment, then went on. "I'm sorry, but I just can't believe things are going to get better."

Then I began to feel the rage start deep inside–a cold, hard fury. Here I am, practically on my hands and knees, begging him to stay, and he says that I'm strong, that I don't know what he's talking about, and that he doesn't believe me! How can he be so cruel? I have tried so hard to please him, to show that I am sorry and want to change, and he doesn't believe me! It hadn't worked; it hadn't made any difference. I had tried to trust God, and now look what was happening! Well, I would show Bud how wrong he was! I would show him that I was not strong, that I needed him–that I didn't want to live without him. I could not–I *would not*–let him go!

With cold calculation, I made a choice. "I'll be back in just a minute," I said. "Stay with the children, will you?" There was no way that I would be able to cope with three children by myself. There was no way that I could face a future without Bud. I ran into our bathroom, opened the medicine cabinet, and then ran on to the car. I knew that pleading, arguing, even trying harder would be useless; his mind was made up. But I had to make him see that he had to stay; I would get the message across to him somehow. I couldn't let him do this to me. Of course, I wasn't really going to hurt myself; I loved myself far too much for that.

I stopped the car a few blocks from the house in an empty church parking lot. It was a bright sunshiny summer morning. In all the comfortable brick ranchhouses of Park Terrace, mothers were fixing breakfast, children were laughing, fathers were getting ready to go to work. How could my world be falling apart on such a beautiful day?

I opened the large bottle of aspirin and shook out a

handful. The first one tasted bitter, and I made a face as I washed it down with a sip from a can of soda I'd brought with me. After a while, they began to stick in my throat; the aspirins were much larger than I had realized. Somewhere I had read that aspirin couldn't really be fatal, so I kept swallowing them, one after another until the bottle was empty. Then I opened the prescription bottle of pills that I had found in the cabinet and swallowed some of them; I had no idea what they were. At first I was very careful to just take a few; I didn't want to hurt myself, just frighten Bud. But as I went on, I began not to care anymore and to lose count. Maybe it would be simpler just to stop feeling. Did I really want to go on living in a world that I couldn't control? But finally I started the car and drove home. I didn't want to frighten the children, so I called Bud into another room and told him what I had done.

As we drove to the hospital emergency room, a very different feeling came over me. I just didn't care anymore. I had done all I could do, and it was no use. Even if Bud did decide to stay, it would not be right. I would know that I had forced him to stay, out of pity. There was no way that I could control my life, or his, any longer. I felt dazed, resigned, hopeless. Just tired of striving any longer.

And could this really be me, lying on a metal cart in the emergency room of the same hospital where all three of our children had been born, where I had worked in the Ladies' Auxiliary, where I knew everyone and everyone knew me? Here I was, having my stomach pumped out. My God, what had I come to? What kind of a monster was I? What was I doing to our children?

I didn't respond when Dr. Perkins came in, or when he kindly tried to talk to me about what had happened.

I just shut my eyes and wanted him to go away. I shook my head, "It's no use, it's all over, and I don't care any more." I didn't even want to see Bud. If he wanted to go, then I would let him go. Part of the lethargy was the drugs, part was exhaustion, but also there was a real sense of surrender, of just letting go. I was at the bottom; I had done the most selfish, vindictive thing of all. I can't hold on any longer; I can't run my life anymore. I am too tired, and it's all too much.

I give up.

I don't remember too much of what happened in the next few days. Bud took me home from the hospital, and we began to resume the motions of our lives. As much as I tried to push it away, the picture of that awful, hopeless afternoon in the hospital filled my mind. It brought me face to face with the humiliating truth of what I had done, and all pretence and self-deception were stripped away. I saw myself as I really was–and I was ashamed. What a terrible price my children nearly had to pay for my sin, and how easily I had nearly sacrificed all our lives out of my vindictiveness and rage. The worst of it was that I had known better. I had had help; I could have turned to Jesus.

Bud and I didn't talk much. What was left to say? He had every right to hate me. I had willfully destroyed the last threads of our marriage, I had pulled that life down around us, and there was nothing left at all. I had played my last trick. I had no idea what he was thinking anymore, no idea what he would do. We tried to act normal for the sake of the children, but the house was filled with emptiness and fear.

Again and again throughout my life, God had reached down His hand to me at the point of my greatest need. When things were hopeless, when there was nowhere to turn, when I got to the end of myself, God in His unfathomable love had been there. Through no merit of mine and in spite of my repeated ingratitude, He continued to show mercy. In this situation, nothing short of a miracle could help us. And God incredibly did one.

I wasn't expecting it. In fact, I didn't even believe my ears at first. Bud had come in from the farm that evening in late August, and was leaning against the kitchen counter, as I put the last minute touches on dinner. His face was lined, and he looked thin and worried. This summer for the first time he had started to look his thirty-eight years. He looked like a man who had been through hell.

"Something has got to happen," he was saying. "I don't know what to do next. I need help . . . you need help. Maybe we should talk to somebody together. Do you think they would let us both come to that Community in Massachusetts?"

In three days, we were on our way. Coming in for a landing low over Boston Harbor, I could see the sunlight glinting off the glass of the John Hancock Tower; and as the plane lined up on final approach, the narrow two-storied buildings crowding the waterfront were unmistakably New England. I had to pinch myself to believe that it was really true, that Bud and I were here together, that we were actually in Boston. We had decided to rent a car and drive the ninety miles down to Orleans, located at the inner elbow of the Cape. It was a beautiful drive, and there was a lot to see, but I felt uptight and nervous. My mind was racing far ahead. What if Bud didn't like the Community? What if no one could help us? And how could I ever tell them what I had done, especially after all the help they had given me? Even if we both wanted a new start, would we ever be able to forget the past? With all that had happened, nothing could ever be the same for us again. And how in the world do you start out to build a new life?

We drove into the Rock Harbor parking lot just as the last glow of the sunset was reflected in the shimmering, iridescent water of the Bay. At Bethany's front door, we were greeted by Sister Irene, "It's nice to have you back so soon, Sunny!" We climbed the winding stairs and were shown to one of the beautiful guest rooms on the second floor. "You can have breakfast whenever you wish," we were told. "Get a good night's sleep. Father Lane is expecting to see you in the morning." The vase of fresh-cut flowers on the bureau, the basket of summer fruit, and the little welcome card brought tears to my eyes. God's love was everywhere.

"It's so quiet and peaceful here," Bud remarked. We opened the window wide, and the white curtains billowed out with the ocean breeze. Within minutes Bud was sound asleep in the comfortable bed. I hadn't seen him that relaxed in a long, long time.

The next morning we sat contentedly outdoors in the circle behind Bethany, a little grassy area edged with impatiens and lilies-of-the-valley. As we enjoyed a leisurely breakfast, we watched the life of the Community pass back and forth. People moved about purposefully, but never rushing, and everyone took time to smile or nod in our direction. Just as we were finishing our last cup of coffee, I saw a familiar figure in black clerical attire, approaching. "Oh, here you are," called Father Lane. "It's such a beautiful day; I thought I might find you here."

As we counseled with Father Lane in the library that morning, he didn't seem shocked or even particularly surprised by the things we told him about ourselves. He spoke to us lovingly but very directly about who we are and the reasons for the problems that we now had. "Sunny, you are control in a velvet glove," he told me. "No man could live with you; you have literally driven Bud away. Nothing ever satisfied you. You always demanded more. And Bud, you should have spoken up a long time ago. You have to repent for your passivity. You both made the mistake of never being honest with each other and never confronting one another. Your marriage has been built on idolatry, and the end of idolatry is always hatred." Then he told us about himself and the need for Jesus in his own life. We never felt condemned or judged; we knew that Father Lane accepted us because he knew himself and he loved us.

As he talked about the forgiveness and the love of Jesus, I could see the light begin to come back into Bud's eyes. "We can only forgive one another when we know how much Jesus has forgiven us," he said. When I told him about the pills I had taken, he shook his head in sorrow. "Suicide is the ultimate in control," he said, and I knew that was the truth. At the end of our time together, Father Lane led us in a prayer asking for the forgiveness and the bloodwashing of Jesus, and then we accepted the forgiveness that He gave by His death on the Cross.

Later that day we strolled around the Community grounds, and wandered down to the beach in back of Gennesaret. It was good just to walk along together, not saying anything, but having a real sense of God's presence with us. The strain between us was at last beginning to lessen, and for the first time in years we felt close. We stood for a few minutes on the sand, watching the waves gently moving toward the shore. Bud reached over and took my hand, and tears came to my eyes—good tears. We stood together quietly for a long time, watching the water and thinking how good God had been to us, to bring us all this way to find healing and reconciliation and new life in Him.

Arm in arm, we walked back to the retreat house, and just as we were going in the back door, out came Cay and Judy. We knew that they had been leading a retreat for a group of ladies from Alabama, and I had been afraid that we might not see them at all. But as busy as they were, they stopped on the steps to meet Bud and to talk with us for a few minutes. They smiled at me, and I knew that they knew that God was giving us a real miracle. Out of the ruins of a dead marriage, He was bringing forth new life!

That night, for the first time in a long time, Bud and I began to talk about how we really felt about things. I asked his forgiveness for all the hurts of so many years, and especially for all that I had done that summer. There was a growing openness between us, as we tried to do what Father Lane had said and be honest about all of our feelings. It was not always going to be easy, but we believed that God had called us together in marriage, and we wanted to go on together in Him. We made a new commitment to each other and to Jesus. No, things would never be the same for us again, and thank God for that! We didn't want the old life back; God had something much better in store.

In the morning there was time for one more meeting with Father Lane who hugged us both and reminded us that our hope was in Jesus. We lingered as long as we could before driving back to Boston to make our plane connections. Not only had God given us a brand-new marriage, but He gave us a second honeymoon as well; only much better than the first! It was our first visit to New York and Washington–a wonderful week. We rode the ferry over to the Statue of Liberty and took the bus tour through Manhattan, marveling at our first sight of its skyscrapers and hearing the roar of the city, but most of all just enjoying being together, so grateful for God's incredible goodness.

When we got back to Lamesa, we wanted to share what had happened with everyone. One by one, we paid our Christian friends a visit. I had to smile as I listened to Bud describing the Community. "I guess it's the most beautiful place I've seen." He paused and thought for a moment. "One afternoon I sat in the main retreat house living room and watched one of the Sisters clean a chandelier. I couldn't get over the way she did it, really caring about every facet, every piece of it–and singing while she worked." He shook his head. "You know, it was all done for the glory of God, and to please Him. She didn't even know I was watching." Bud's enthusiasm was contagious and that fall of '74 twelve of us went to a Community retreat in Bermuda. After that we started meeting regularly once a week in order to help one another to talk about our needs and our desire to have Jesus in every area of our lives.

One evening the following spring in one of our meetings I mentioned an area of my life that had continued to bother me. "You know, I've been thinking about weight, and the way that I worry about it so much. It's not right, and I know it, but I don't know what to do about it. I can't seem to get rid of the compulsion that I feel about it. My happiness depends too much on what the scale says, rather than on Jesus."

One of the men in the group chuckled. "Then why don't you throw away your scale? If you'll do that outward action, I believe God would heal you on the inside."

Throw away my scale! The idea was frightening. And yet I really did want to be free of the obsession with weight. "Okay," I agreed, at length. "It scares me, but I'll throw the scale away!" If I was going to give up control of my life, it would have to include this area, too.

It was a beginning. There was a great deal more healing still to come.

❧ Camie ❧

17

Time to Grow Up

There was no looking back when our red station wagon pulled out of the driveway to head East, on that hot, sunny July 2nd. Five Fords, one black dog, and piles of suitcases were jammed in together for the long drive as we started off for Cape Cod to begin our year at the Community of Jesus. I was excited but apprehensive, too; this year would be the longest time ever spent away from Cleveland family and friends. Summer camp, boarding school, and college required no more than ten weeks at the most before I returned to home and security. My parents had always been no more than a phone call or a fifteen-minute drive away.

I was grateful for all my live-in experiences of the previous two summers; they had prepared me somewhat for the year ahead. But as usual I had many questions: Who would we live with? Would our dog be happy in her new surroundings? Would the children like their coed schools, come fall? Would they miss their old friends a lot? There were no answers to these questions. "Well, I'm going to have to trust God every day, that He will take care of our family," I thought. "And what about my scale?

I'm going to have to keep my scale handy. They eat such good food all the time." As the numbers of miles to New York on the road signs lowered, I tried to quiet my squirrel-cage mind. The children asked dozens of questions, too, but I kept saying over and over, "We'll just have to wait and see! We'll find out everything when we get there."

They knew that Dan and I had been having problems getting along, because I had made my feelings clear on many occasions. One in particular came back to me as I glanced at my needlepoint bag on the floor beside my feet. I loved to needlepoint and had been doing pillows, tennis racket covers, footstools and other items for years. My mother had taught me the basic stitches and then I studied books on needlepoint, went to lectures, and loved to browse through shops that displayed the latest methods, designs and finished works. I always took needlepoint along with me wherever I went, so I could keep busy and not snack. This was especially true after I'd stopped smoking. If I had to go anywhere where I might have to wait I'd bring my needlepoint along and work on that, instead of having a cigarette.

One evening, we had taken the children out to dinner at Howard Johnson's. We often went out on Friday evenings if I didn't feel like cooking. This particular evening I was not even interested in eating dinner, let alone cooking it, because I had been out to lunch with friends, so I sat with a cup of black coffee and my newest needlepoint creation, a cover for a footstool for our bedroom. I had spent hours on the piece and was pleased with the way it was turning out. I had taken a sample of our bedspread to a friend who had designed the cover to go with our material. It was going to be very elegant when I finished. The waitress brought hamburgers and

French fries for Dan and the children, and a fresh cup of coffee for me. Dan reached for the catsup bottle and knocked over my coffee cup, spilling coffee all over the needlepoint.

"Oh, you *stupid jerk!*" I cried, jumping up from my seat and grabbing the wool canvas away from the dripping table top. "Look what you've done! You've ruined my canvas–oh, I hate you! I could just kill you!" I sobbed, not paying any attention to the stares from the surrounding tables. The girls and Danny just sat there numb, with tears in their eyes. I was so furious I was shaking and could hardly find words to say after my first outburst.

"It's okay, Mommy, we'll fix it," said Liza, trying to calm me down. "We'll wash it out when we get home."

"I'm sorry, Camie, I really am," Dan said, not knowing how to cope with this crazy woman. "I'll call someone to see how to get the coffee out." He was trying so hard to be helpful.

"Oh, don't bother–you'll never get coffee out of this mess!" I grabbed the wet canvas, walked over to a trash can, and threw it away, then stalked out of the restaurant and went to the car. Liza and Lexa went to the trash barrel and took the needlepoint out, wrapped it up and brought it with them. I refused to speak to anyone, went to my room, and slammed the door shut. At that moment, I hated Dan with every fiber in my body. I lay in bed that night as far away from him as I could get and hardly closed my eyes all night, I was filled with such anger.

The next morning, I decided I would have to call the Community and get some help. I could not go one more hour with all these feelings, and besides, I ought to tell someone what had happened. How soon could I call? I dialed the number of the Ark as soon as I thought they would be up. Betty Pugsley answered.

"Oh, Betty, you don't know what Dan has done!" I sobbed into the phone. "He has ruined that special needlepoint I was working on for our bedroom. He spilled coffee all over it, and–"

"Whoa, slow down," Betty said, soothingly. "Start over, and tell me what happened." I told her all about it, trying not to cry, so that she could understand my words. When I finished, instead of consoling me, she calmly asked, "Why were you not eating? Why did you skip dinner?" I explained that I had been out to lunch and didn't want to gain weight.

"You know, Camie, you were rude and hurtful to just sit there, when your family was trying to have fun, eating out. You know it hurts Dan and the kids when you refuse to eat with them. If you had left your needlepoint at home, this would never have happened. It's not Dan's fault the canvas is ruined. Do you see that?" she asked, as I gulped and sniffled and blew my nose.

Suddenly, I did see it. "Oh, dear, that's awful!" I exclaimed, and started crying all over again. "The children have told me that they wished I would eat with them and not just sit there. Oh, dear, it really is my fault, not Dan's." Now, the memory of my anger returned, as I recalled the terrible scene of the night before. Oh, what a fool I was! No wonder the children were scared of me this morning! No one had dared speak a word. "Betty, I am dead wrong. I'll have to apologize for my behavior, quick! Oh, I'm so sorry!"

When I hung up the phone, I went in search of Dan. The children were huddled together in the library, watching Saturday morning cartoons, and they tensed when I came in, not knowing what I was going to say this time.

"Where's Daddy?" I asked, sitting down with them on the sofa. They looked at each other before Liza replied.

"He's gone out to the needlepoint store, to see if there is anything that can be done to save your needlepoint."

"Oh, kids, I am so sorry about last night! That was a terrible thing I did. It was not Daddy's fault; I should never have brought the needlepoint into the restaurant." I gave them a kiss and a hug and waited for Dan to return, so that I could tell *him* how sorry I was. I felt wretched. I could see very clearly that my crazy behavior had a devastating effect on the children and on my husband. And now I could also see that I still needed help and we were going to where I could get it. The kids seemed to know this, too. They knew that life at home was usually happier and brighter for the first couple of weeks after my return from visits to the Community. As for themselves, the girls had made close friends there and were excited about seeing them again. Dan, at age eight, was bewildered by the whole idea of changing houses and schools. But he had grown up quite a bit the year he repeated first grade, and we felt comfortable with his starting second grade in a new school situation. Dan and I expected to find more healing in our marriage than ever before as we lived together with whatever family God would put us. Certainly that had been our experience the summer before. We had learned a lot about ourselves in those two weeks the two of us had had together. I knew God was dealing with me, showing me more and more about my self-centeredness, my strong opinions and my willfulness. Well, now He had a year to reveal to us, through conflicts and resolutions, how our marriage could work happily. And that was something to be excited about!

The Ford family was the first family to come to the Community to live for a whole year as "live-ins." Most visitors and live-ins came for much shorter periods of time–often for a week or two, as I had done in the past. We were greeted with warm "hellos," hugs, and many helping hands to unload our travel-grubby station wagon. That afternoon many of our friends stopped by Damascus, our assigned house, to welcome us.

We would be into the summer routine before we knew it! The very next day was the Fourth of July, which meant a colorful parade in the morning, followed by a sumptuous hamburger, potato salad, and ice cream bar picnic. To this day, I look forward to the Orleans Fourth of July parade, complete with imaginative floats, marching bands, and fire engines blowing their sirens!

A few weeks after our arrival, Mother Cay and Mother Judy suggested to us that it might be good for Dan and me to live together in our home, without the distractions of the summer-full houses. We needed time alone together, to get to know each other in a much deeper way. I had always escaped any kind of relationship with Dan through my countless activities or personal interests. Well, now it was time for Dan and me to get to know each other without any children, jobs, or social friends to hide behind. For the rest of the summer I would work around our house and garden while Dan joined the Community work crew, and our children would be with the other Community children their own age, Liza and Lexa with 12-to-14 year old girls; Danny with his friends, Rick and Paul. I would be with them every day at coffee hour, and of course whenever they had a problem that needed me there. In the meantime, Dan and I would have ample opportunity to get to know each other–for the first time in our married lives.

Dan would return for lunch out on our sun deck and a time of reviewing the events of the morning. We spent a lot of time working in our yard together; always before we had had a gardener and yard crew to do the work. Now every evening after supper we went out into the warm evening to weed, cut grass, trim hedges and try to work together as a team. But this "radical therapy" of the two of us being alone together was not always easy, and there were many times that we had to go next door to our friends at the Ark for counseling help. It was hard for two totally independent people to come to agreement on where to work and how long and did we want to water plants here or there. But we were beginning to learn to make decisions together and that made it all worthwhile.

As we had first lunch and then dinner together, just the two of us sitting on our sun deck with the view of Cape Cod Bay in the distance, we were ill at ease, and without any children to talk to or any other adults we had little to say. But if we didn't want to eat in total silence we had to make an effort to have conversations. I had never realized how much talking we did with and to the children at meal times or any other time for that matter. We had lost—or rather, put aside—the ability to care for one another. We had avoided outright conflict by leading very separate lives, coming together only when necessary. But now I was learning to say: "You hurt my feelings when you didn't say anything about the loaf of bread I baked today." Or Dan would say: "You hurt me, when you didn't want to share the hymnal in church." It was not easy to be open. I discovered that I did not know how to be honest. I thought I was saying what I felt, but I discovered that I really didn't know my true feelings, and I needed others to help me to see just what they were.

One feeling I did know I had was anger at being out of control. It made me furious to never know what Dan was going to do or say. I was so used to doing my own thing and who cared what he did or where he went? Now we had to discuss and plan our work and our day together. But as time went by a funny thing happened: The more real and honest I found I could be, the more acceptable I felt. People seemed to be friendlier, or else as I opened up I let the walls around me down, and my new friends were able to come closer. I knew that in Cleveland I would never dream of saying how I really felt, because I was so afraid of what people would think.

At times, I really hated being at home; I was so used to being busy and out with my friends. To stay home just cooking and cleaning and doing laundry was boring to me. I had never learned how to just relax, because I'd been so busy trying to accomplish something important, and vacuuming the living room and scrubbing the kitchen floor did not satisfy my need to be somebody doing great things. Well, the Lord had other plans in mind for me that involved "healing me from the inside out." God was trying to help me to see just who I was–a thin, tense woman compulsively driven to achieve success. He wanted to teach me how to just "be," without having to be a "somebody." For sixteen years of marriage, except when I was at the beach on vacation, or by the club pool, I had never sat down long enough to enjoy the day or the houses we had or the children or my husband–I was so busy running here and there. Now I had nowhere to run to; no parties to dress up for, no bridge lunches to prepare for, no board meetings to attend. I walked around our house with dust rag in hand, wiping off a table, straightening a picture, or smoothing a pillow, and all the while raging inside: Dear God, please let me do *something!* I can't stand all this stupid housework!

While God was working on my inside emotions, He also spoke to me about my weight. I may have been out of control about my housework and my daily activities, but I was certainly in control about my weight! Never a day went by that I did not step on the scale to make sure I *did not* go over 127 or 128 pounds, and 130 was my absolute top weight! If I weighed in a pound or two heavy, I cut back on my food, ate more salads and skipped the bread and desserts that Dan always enjoyed. If I was going to change how I communicated with Dan and others in my attempt to live for Jesus and not for myself, then I would have to learn to give my weight over to the Lord, too.

My counseling friends had talked with me about how nervous and tense I was. Did obsession with thinness and my opinions about weight have anything to do with this? Well, yes, I had to admit that I knew my disposition was directly related to how much I had eaten and how much I weighed. "Don't you think God can help with *all* the areas of your life?" they asked. And, of course, I knew He *could,* but I wasn't sure yet if I wanted Him to or not. In spite of everything I wanted to be in charge of what I ate. Well, once again, the Lord had other plans for me.

About the middle of September, one warm, hazy afternoon, I received a phone call to come over to the Ark. That was not too unusual, as Dan and I went over there almost daily to talk with Father Lane and Betty Pugsley, who had been very patient and helpful over the past few weeks. Betty sat down with me in Father Lane's study and told me that Mother Cay and Mother Judy were concerned about how thin I was. Right away I tensed up. I knew what was coming. Betty paid no attention to the anger that flashed across my face and said, "They think it might be very helpful for you to gain some weight."

"Oh—really?" I asked icily. "How much?" My heart started to pound and I was shaking, I was so angry.

"About twenty or twenty-five pounds," Betty replied, ignoring my rising hysterics.

"Twenty-five pounds!" I cried out and burst into tears. "You've got to be kidding! I am *not* going to gain twenty-five pounds! That is too much! It's not good for my varicose veins to gain weight. Carrying that much extra weight will just add to my leg problems. None of my clothes will fit!" I was sobbing at this point. Betty didn't say anything. She just sat and waited. "No! Absolutely not, Lord! You are asking too much!" I jumped up from the sofa and stormed around the room like a caged tiger. I did not know what to do or say next.

But after I ranted and raved with Jesus, that still, small voice inside that I had come to recognize as God spoke to me: *If you are ever going to grow up and become the woman I want you to be, you must give up your opinions about weight, food and appearance.* Opinions I had plenty of—the first one being that I could never be thin enough if I was going to be a success! Rich people are thin. People who ate too much lacked self-discipline. I was superior because I could refuse food. Food was not important; looking good was. To look good, I had to be thin. It was as simple, and as complex, as that. Furthermore, I knew then and there that I would not take one step forward in my Christian walk if I was not obedient to what I heard God saying to me. I stalked out of the Ark, down the walk to Nineveh and threw open the back door. "This is the end!" I shouted at Dan, who knew nothing of what had just happened. "This is the end!" I repeated even louder. "I have to gain twenty-five pounds, and that's too much." All I had to do was say "gain weight," and I was crying again. I don't think I've ever been so furious in my whole life as I was that day. Yet I knew I had to do what I was encouraged to do–put on weight!

Gaining twenty-five pounds was the hardest task in the world for me, and I didn't do it overnight. I had to learn to eat frequently and in small amounts since my shrunken stomach would accept only so much food. I started out by having toast with my bowl of cold cereal or my egg. Gradually I added two pieces of buttered toast to my breakfast menu, and then another piece of toast with jam at mid-morning, or a doughnut. I loved bread even then, and to this day I can eat that anytime. I began to have sandwiches for lunch instead of salads and cottage cheese. And funny thing: as I increased my food intake I began to enjoy my meal times more. Dinner was the hardest meal for me to eat because dinner was the meal I had skipped the most often in Cleveland. Looking at all that food on my plate made me angry and my stomach would shut down. "I just can't eat all that," I would wail at Dan.

"You've got to try," he said, with little sympathy.

All went well until one day I stepped on the scale. I had been advised not to weigh myself at all, and I had been obedient until this day. Up went the dial, past 130 to 136 pounds! 136! I burst into tears and cried and cried. 136! The last time I weighed that much was after Liza was born fourteen years ago! I was devastated–Dear God, please help me to get through this situation which was like torture to me. I was in a new state of panic. I knew it! I had told Dan this would happen. I knew if I ate all those doughnuts and rolls, there would be no end to this. I was going to blow up like a balloon! Every doubt and fear came roaring back into my head, as I stood there, staring at the scale. 25 pounds! I'll look like a blimp and all my years of effort will have been wasted.

I really had a battle on my hands that night, as I told Dan what had happened and the panic I felt. He calmed me down and helped me to see how utterly ridiculous my fears were. I had to plead with Jesus to give me the grace to go through with this. Jesus! Help me to trust *You* in this!

The weeks went by that fall, and the needle continued to creep upward. Once again, I stepped on the scale, and this time the dial registered 141! Was there no end in sight? To make matters worse, my dear friend Anne and her husband Don were coming for a visit. Would they notice any change? The day they arrived, I ran to give them a hello hug. "How do I look?" I asked Anne, and before she could answer, I quickly said, "I've gained twelve pounds, can you tell?"

"You look great," she assured me. But I was sure she had said that to be polite. I'll bet they're really shocked, I thought. It was still very difficult for me to believe Dan or anyone when they assured me I looked fine! How could I believe them when I saw a pudgy-looking person in the mirror? My distorted thinking was still there.

Those twelve pounds represented sheer agony to me. I do not mean to imply in any way that it was a breeze to eat my way through three, four or five meals a day. Quite the contrary! There were many times when I was consumed with guilt. How could I give in to my self-love, to my greed and lust for food, after all these years? Matters were no longer in my own hands–I had given up; become weak. The power struggle for ultimate control was lost. It was a terrible struggle to drink a coffee milkshake. Each sip screamed: *calories, calories!* I could not eat a piece of cake or a slice of pie without automatically tabulating every calorie it contained. I still could not bring myself to drink a Coke, after years of only Tab or Diet Pepsi or, better yet, black coffee. The only way I could finish a meal was to have Dan or a friend sit with me and encourage me.

But after those first twelve pounds, eating did become easier for me. My fears gradually subsided as I received many more compliments about my new figure. Whenever panic set in and I went down into the pit of despair, my friends were very patient and loving.

The next plateau on the scale came at 147 pounds. Even *I* had trouble remembering now what I looked like twenty pounds thinner. I had slowly bought new skirts and dresses only one or two sizes up, which was encouraging for me. Being tall gave me extra inches for the distribution of those pounds. By the end of spring, about nine months after I started my new regime, I had gained five more pounds, bringing my final weight to 152 pounds. Well, in spite of all the tantrums, trauma, fears and anxieties, I was still alive, felt wonderful, and ate everything served, at any time.

That is until one day late in May when we had gone to Nauset Beach for one of those wonderful, warm spring days, when the sky is so blue that you know that summer is just around the corner. A group of us had set off down the beach for a walk. I was dressed in my usual outfit of blouse and wrap-around skirt. Coming towards us on the beach, I thought I recognized some people—very unusual to see old friends out here in the middle of Nauset Beach. Sure enough, oh dear, I did know this group that was fast approaching.

"Camie? Dan Ford? Is that you?" They had seen us now, too!

"Hello! Hello!" We laughed with hugs and kisses for old friends from our days with the Society of Industrial Realtors. Joan and her friend were two ladies I had spent many an hour with at reception after reception. "What are *you* doing here?"

"We live here on the Cape," I replied, feeling *very* self-conscious. These two girls were sharp-looking, dressed in the latest bathing suits, and I felt fat and frumpy.

"You've changed. Have you put on weight?" they inquired with raised eyebrows. Oh, brother, have I put on weight! My face froze in a tight smile. I wished the sand would open up and swallow me right then and there. Oh, dear, how on earth would I ever be able to go back to Cleveland in just a few weeks, looking like I thought I did?

I could see very clearly that I still cared much too much about what other people thought of me. Not only did I want to be center stage, but also I wanted to be highly approved of. I thought I was accustomed to the extra inches around my hips and waist, but meeting these old acquaintances set me back. Dan and Father Lane once again came to my aid and strongly told me to stop worrying, give up my pride, get my eyes back on Jesus, and see that I had so much to be grateful for. My bondage to self-starvation had been broken, and no idle comments were going to take away the healing God had done in me over these last nine months. Just to be free to eat was a miracle I would never have dreamed possible only a few short months ago.

Many more changes took place in my life during this traumatic year, in addition to my figure's new shape. I had a lot to learn about what it meant to be a Christian, to go deeper into this new life with God in His Son, Jesus

Christ. The most important lesson for me was to learn to take myself off the throne, from where I had ruled my life, and let Jesus be first! I did not know the first thing about coming down from my fairy princess throne. How should I deny myself?

Well, I could start by letting my opinions die–I had so many, about everything; how to clean a house, how to bake, how to decorate a room–I was always ready with my opinion whether it was asked for or not. I had all the answers and would let people know just what I thought–Miss Know-it-all. I had also learned that it was very difficult for me to be wrong. I absolutely *had* to be right–I couldn't let Dan win; somehow that would mean my brothers had won over me. If I were ever wrong, then that made Dan right, and that fact was intolerable. We would disagree about the silliest things, such as what time to set the alarm for in the morning; he liked to get up early in the morning to work out, while I wanted to sleep until the last possible moment. He liked to go to bed early, and I liked to stay up late, reading. He liked the window wide open and no blankets in the summer; I liked a blanket and not so much fresh air. I liked to watch TV; Dan didn't, and wanted me to turn it off. In Cleveland, we had gone our own separate ways, and done exactly as we pleased. But not so anymore.

The fastest way to find out just how wrong you can be is to live with two other women. In October of that year our three months alone together had come to an end when other Community members joined our household. Now there were three women working in our cozy, little kitchen–three women, each of whom had hitherto managed her own home, raised her children, and had strong opinions about how things should be done. We each had to learn the lesson of doing our work according to God's will, not our own. So many decisions would come up each day–how long to boil eggs for soft-boiled; how often to do the laundry; when did the plants need watering; do you pull the drapes at night.

One of the hardest things was having to eat a lot, when others around you were dieting. Carole Roberts was always careful about calories and ate lots of salads, fruit, and cottage cheese. I was jealous of her light lunches, while I stuffed down my sandwiches. That was the crazy thinking that I did. I saw Carole as getting ahead of me in approval and acceptance as she tried to lose weight while I was getting heavier. In the past my friends were envious of me, because I was so thin. No one was envious of me now, as I put on pound after pound. I wanted people to be jealous of me; it made me feel important, worthy of notice.

In spite of all our differences of opinions, Carole, Dana Smith and I had fun together, too. I learned that three does not have to be a crowd. Two months earlier, I had been complaining to Dan about how lonely I was, and now God had given me two new friends to talk with, work with, laugh with, and yes, cry with, too. I hated it when Carole would tell me how controlling and bossy I was, and I had to tell her every time that she made me angry. But just telling her made me swallow my pride. And Carole helped me by doing my hair, and Dana would help me with sewing and knitting. I knitted a wool ski hat for Carole for Christmas to match her new parka. We all had a good laugh when she tried it on.

When the New Year had begun Dan and I moved to another house, Nazareth, where we would live for the next few months. Once again we learned how much we relied on our opinions and our knowledge, and not Jesus, to guide our lives. We lived with Betty and Paul

Mitman, a couple who had been in the Community since it was first incorporated in 1970. They were older than we were and certainly knew more than we did about Community life. But instead of learning from them, we fought against them. In my mind, Betty became my mother, and I found it very difficult to listen to her. I was in rebellion about gaining weight, and I did not want to listen to another woman's ideas and suggestions. From the time I left home to get married, I was determined to be my own boss, and no one was going to tell me what to do, especially around the house. So now I liked to think that I was right in each situation that arose which was ridiculous because Betty had much more experience as a housewife and mother.

Time after time we would sit down to plan a week's menu, and Betty would remind me of what I needed to eat, or what her family enjoyed. I had my own ideas of how I was going to gain my weight, but now I was living at Nazareth, Betty's house, and she had her own schedule, which I did not want to go along with. Until that winter I had no idea how rebellious I was or how much I hated being told what to do. My reactions to these situations were no different than they had been back in Cleveland–really what I wanted, plain and simple, was to have my own way and do my own thing, forever.

Lent that spring was an especially difficult time for me. We had undertaken several personal disciplines for Lent, which included special prayer times in the Community chapel, extra time for reading Lenten books, and very simple meals, all of which cut directly across my will and showed me my tremendous self-love. My rebellion increased weekly. I was fighting others instead of fighting myself–I did not want to choose to hear what God was saying to me, through my husband or anyone we were living with. By the time of Passiontide, the last two weeks of Lent, I was already spending a lot of time thinking about going back to Cleveland in July.

At that point I knew I had hardened my heart against the Lord. I did not want to follow Jesus if it was going to cost this much. I wanted my own way, but inside, way down deep, I was miserable. I did not like that hard pit of anger in my stomach. My spoiled brat behavior was constantly manifesting itself; I was ashamed on the one hand, yet tenaciously holding on to my will on the other.

During Holy Week, the last week before Easter, we individually spent a couple of hours a day reading the Bible. I remember so well the cold, windy afternoon when I lay on the bed with that familiar, empty feeling inside, as I picked up the Bible and turned to Jeremiah. I felt in total despair as I read with tears in my eyes the assigned reading for that day. In the 17th chapter, the Lord says: "Cursed is the man who puts his trust in mortal men and turns his heart away from God. He is like a stunted shrub in the desert, with no hope for the future; he lives on the salt-encrusted plains in the bitter wilderness; good times pass him by forever. But blessed is the man who trusts in the Lord and has made the Lord his hope and confidence. He is like a tree planted along a river bank, with its roots reaching deep into the water . . . a tree not bothered by the heat, nor worried by long months of drought." I wanted to be like that man, and I felt as if I had just walked for weeks in the desert. I was lifeless and dry, all shriveled up inside.

I sat up on the bed and continued to read on in the 30th chapter, where the words seemed to leap out from the page: "So don't be afraid, O Jacob, my servant; don't be dismayed, O Israel; for I will bring you home again from distant lands, and your children from their exile.

For I am with you, and I will save you, says the Lord. Even if I utterly destroy the nations where I scatter you, I will not exterminate you; I will punish you, yes . . . you will not go unpunished. Why do you protest your punishment? Your sin is so scandalous that your sorrow should never end! But, I will give you back your health again and heal your wounds."

These passages seemed to be speaking directly to me. God was telling me that He would look after me, in spite of my disobedience, my willfulness and my choosing myself before Jesus. I was crazy where food was concerned. For sixteen years I had gone through various stages of self-starvation, and here God was saying He would restore my health, in spite of the fact that I had turned my back on Him. Between tears that poured down my cheeks, I read and reread those chapters of Jeremiah.

"Jesus, I'm sorry," I whispered. "Please forgive me for being so stubborn, so self-righteous, and so very willful! I want to go on with You, dear Lord; I can't go on by myself. These past few months have been hell for me. Oh, God, I'm sorry for being so stupid!"

By the time Easter Sunday arrived, I knew there was a resurrection life for me in giving up my way and doing the will of God, as best as I was able. I had taken control of my life away from God and had turned my back on Him, gradually deadening myself to that still, small voice inside. During Holy Week, I had finally come to the end of my rope and even *I* could no longer stand myself. The answer lay in my trusting Jesus, for He alone could give the peace that passed all understanding. I had lost that peace some months ago, but now, this Easter, I had found the answer–Jesus.

My conversion experience was only the beginning of

a long journey, not an end in itself. I understood now how Christian felt in John Bunyan's classic story *Pilgrim's Progress.* I, too, would find many a detour off my chosen path, and many "a mire of despair" to fall into; but nothing could stop me from my quest to know more about and live more in Jesus. I had done a pretty poor job of it, living in Camie, and had certainly made a total mess of my life. The day I first walked around the Community, I knew God was real, and that He wanted me and had His hand on me. God had chosen me and called me to leave my worldly ways and live a life dedicated to following Him, and not the whims of society. I was to serve Him, not myself and all my selfish desires and vanities.

That Easter Sunday the sun came out in my heart as well as in the brilliant blue sky overhead. Forsythia was in bloom everywhere, reflecting the warm golden light. I have a picture in my photo album of our three children and me taken on that Easter morning. We were smiling and happy, inside and out. There were many hurdles to come during the turbulent times in the ensuing weeks. But our friends patiently helped me to see that I had lived for years in my private fantasy world of dreams, and that my expectation of the marriage relationship was total unreality. I was demanding that Dan give to me, be to me–everything. And only one person could do that–Jesus. Moreover, I wanted to have God's place in his life. But Jesus *could* come in and change my heart if I truly wanted Him to, and I did. "Jesus, help me to clean this bathroom"–it sounded so simple, and yet I had spent months turning away from Him.

We continued to make our plans to return to Cleveland even though, as I look back now, I can see that we had nudges from the Lord to stay. But we were adamant; we had said "one year" to our families and that's what it was going to be. When I think back about that time now, I realize just how willful I still was. My ears were closed to hearing the Lord say anything other than "go home." I missed our beautiful house back in Gates Mills, the rose garden, and, most of all, having the bath all to myself. As our departure day approached I found myself thinking more and more about my Cleveland friends, lunches out, movies, all the "fun things" I used to do. I couldn't wait to shop to my heart's content, although I would now be looking at clothes a size larger.

We made more decisions: to drive home alone and let the children spend the last two months of summer in the Community. They were not at all excited about going back to Cleveland because they loved the fun, fellowship, and good times enjoyed by all the young people. But Dan had joined me wholeheartedly in the decision to return. A year was long enough for the president of a firm to be away. The company needed him!

The July 4th weekend arrived. Was it really only a year ago that we pulled into the driveway at Damascus? It seemed like five years, I thought, as I began to pack the suitcases. Once again the sun was shining brightly on the locust grove behind the chapel. Hamburgers and hot dogs sizzled on the outdoor grill, while long tables were laden with huge bowls of potato salad, three-bean salad and fresh fruit salad. Later in the evening the whole Community gathered out on the front lawn of Bethany to watch the fireworks display in Rock Harbor. Only one more day before we left–I felt a mixture of sadness about saying good-bye to those who had been so patient and kind. But I was also excited about what was in store for us at home.

And so on July 5th, with the red station wagon packed to the brim with trunks, suitcases, boxes and plants, we were ready for the long drive back to Ohio. Most of the trip I let my mind wander over good times with old friends, tennis and iced tea on the clubhouse terrace, lunch out with the girls, dinner at Mother and Daddy's, the feeling of being needed when I went to a committee meeting or board meeting. In a year's time I had completely forgotten how *bad* the bad times had been, and basically wanted to continue living "my wonderful life," which hopefully had been patched up enough so that the good times would last.

Our parents greeted us with cautious enthusiasm. The apron strings had been severed with a painful cut, and undoubtedly they wondered what was next. Were we serious about our plans to redecorate the house? We were talking about new carpet, new wallpapers, new curtains–all sorts of extensive and expensive changes in our already beautiful home. Yes, we assured them, we were here to stay!

The time Dan and I had together while the children were still on the Cape was a time of adjustment. We still did not feel comfortable being alone together so the first few weeks we ate out a lot with friends and saw every new movie in town. We were definitely an item of gossip and speculation on the cocktail circuit. Our friends didn't really understand what, why and where we had been for one whole year. We had literally dropped out of sight. We tried to explain to a few people whom we felt close to, but soon realized that no one, not even our parents, understood how close to shipwreck our marriage had come, and therefore, how necessary it had been to get away.

About three weeks after our arrival home our country club was having a dinner dance to welcome new members. We were invited to join a group of our friends for cocktails before dinner. I was not particularly anxious to go because I didn't think I had a long dress that would fit, yet I recognized that it would be the perfect opportunity to let everyone know that we were back. But when I looked in my closet my anxiety escalated: just as I had suspected–nothing to fit my enlarged shape. I would have to swallow my pride and go out and buy a larger dress. Did I really want to go to this party? After some searching through the shops, I finally bought an evening dress that would do and off to the party we went.

I don't think I have ever been as nervous as I was that night, driving up to the club. What would everyone say? How would they greet us? Do I look okay? Will anyone notice my weight? I was certain that all the girls would look at me–which they did not–and I was all set to have a miserable time. But to my surprise we were warmly greeted by everyone. In fact, one old friend came up to me and as he put out his hand to shake mine he exclaimed, "I don't know where you've been this past year, but you look absolutely wonderful!"

I didn't know whether to laugh or cry, as I realized how loving of God it was to let me hear that spontaneous compliment. All those years that I had struggled with my diet and willed myself to obtain the thinness that I considered perfection had been for nothing! I had thrown away *twelve years!* I had been so proud of my clothes, so vain about how I looked, and here I was at the club wearing a nondescript dress and weighing 25 more pounds than I had before I left and I looked "absolutely wonderful." Twelve years when the children were growing up, and our marriage should have been growing, too, instead of falling apart. Well, by God's grace, it wasn't too late;

we would start now, with a new beginning.

In late August we headed the wagon east once again to bring the children home. I had missed them and wondered how their time at the Community had been. But I had not realized how much I missed *all* our friends there, as well as the children, until we saw their happy, smiling faces. All at once, I was very teary and choked up but I quickly suppressed those reactions and smiled back. Sensing that the children might be reluctant to leave, we planned a stop at Hershey Park on our way home to stay overnight at the grand old Hershey Hotel, and I made sure we left as quickly as possible. I hoped the children would sense a new depth of love and understanding between Dan and me. Things were not perfect by any means, but they weren't as bad as they had been. Hopefully I would be able to give the children my full attention when we talked together–I would sit at the table and actually eat breakfast, lunch and dinner. That, in itself, was a miracle.

Once again after school started I was faced with making choices about how to spend my time from 8:00 to 4:00 every day. Would I go back to my old frantic routine? I hoped not! I had learned a few lessons in the last year, and was determined not to wear myself out as I had done before we went away. And indeed, I found my disposition had greatly improved as I continued to eat three normal meals on a regular schedule. My weight began to drop slowly after our return to Cleveland. I don't really know why, because I was certainly eating. It could have been the tennis I was playing, or all the gardening, or just the housework in a much larger house, or simply that I had given up eating between meals. Whatever the reason, all together I lost about twelve pounds over the next four months, and then my weight seemed to stabilize of its own accord, and I have weighed the same, give or take a few pounds, for the past seven years. In the meantime I have learned a great deal about proper nutrition and what I need to eat in order to feel good, look good, and maintain a well-balanced diet. The freedom I now experience to eat whatever appeals to me, to eat out in restaurants and to enjoy dinners with the family, is worth all it took for me to finally give up my dreadful obsession with losing weight.

One interesting occurrence began to take place: One after another, friends began to call and ask me out for lunch, just the two of us. The pattern was always the same: We would start off with idle chitchat while we waited for our food, then questions would be asked about our year away, and then my friends would begin to share their troubles, seemingly insoluble problems with their marriage or children or family relationships. They seemed to need to talk to someone and sensed that I was the right one. I must have spent part of each day listening to one friend or another and, where possible, telling them very gently, very low-key, about some of the similar problems that Dan and I had had, and the One whom we had found who had the answer—who *was* the answer. But very few were ready for such a drastic solution, it appeared, and so in most cases I would simply add their names to my growing prayer list.

My friend Anne was certainly glad to have us home again, and with her I picked up right where we had left off a year before. Once again, we spent hours together, sitting by her swimming pool, or on her porch, talking about our lives as Christians, our children, the pressures on young people today. Anne and Don were raising three children, too, and that wasn't easy, with all the temptations of alcohol, sex and drugs that faced them every day in the schools, on TV, and at the movies. We found we were continually saying "no" and were constantly busy trying to find out about and provide wholesome, clean fun for the kids to enjoy.

Those weeks of September, October, and November seemed to fly by. All the interior decorating of our house was finally completed, much to our liking. And I did manage to slow the pace of my schedule, and keep it slow. But I was worried about young Dan. He seemed withdrawn and standoffish. His teacher and I had a long talk; she promised to keep a close watch, and assured me that seven- and eight-year-olds sometimes had trouble moving in and out of schools.

Before we knew it, it was time to be thinking about Christmas and making plans. David had called on the phone: "Hey, are you guys coming east for Christmas?" Well, we had been thinking that way, but we were torn apart with our decision. What should we do? Should we stay in Cleveland for Christmas, and fly up for New Year's Eve? Or should we leave December 24th, to be with our Community family on Christmas Day? I didn't know what to do, for I knew how disappointed our parents would be if we left early. My parents decided they would go to Houston to see my brother Bill and his family. We talked it over, Dan and I, trying to come to a decision. It was so hard trying to please everyone, which was what I had spent my life doing!

Finally, we decided to go to the Community for Christmas. I called the airlines and made reservations for December 24th, for the five of us, then called my brother on the phone. "We're coming, we're coming! We'll fly to Boston and rent a car to drive down to the Cape. We're on our way! We'll be there on Christmas Eve for dinner and for the Midnight Service!"

"Great!" he replied. "Barbara will be thrilled!" But now we had to break the news to our families. My parents came over for dinner on December 22nd, and we exchanged gifts that night before they left for Houston. Dan's parents came to dinner the following night, and we celebrated Christmas together with them. Both evenings felt a bit awkward and strained for me, and I was relieved to arrive at the Cape the following afternoon–more than relieved; as the front door of my brother's house opened, I burst into tears. I seemed to be making a habit of doing that, every time we arrived at the Community. Then I didn't know whether to laugh or cry, as we gave everyone a big hug and a kiss.

Now that we were here, I was so glad that we would be able to be a part of the Midnight Service, when the celebration of Christ's birth was shown in such a magnificent and moving way, with candles flickering, the chapel all decorated, the white poinsettias at the altar surrounding the Baby Jesus' cradle, and the choir singing "Glory to God in the Highest." We and our children all felt so happy to be back among our friends, who all seemed very glad to see us. We spent the evening chattering away like magpies, trying to catch up on all that had been going on since last summer. The months we had been away seemed like years, and now it felt so good to be sitting in David and Barbara's living room, listening to one story after another and jumping up to hug each person who came by to say hello. "We made the right choice, coming here for Christmas," I whispered to Dan, as we walked home from the chapel after the very special service, and he gave my hand a squeeze.

This vacation, Dan and I spent most of our time with David and Barbara and in between all the excitement there was quiet time to think. Dan was just as involved with his business as ever. I still called him "Mr. Downtown Cleveland," because he spent all his time working with companies who were either moving into or out of one downtown office building or another. I thought he felt he had to work twice as hard now, to make up for the year he took off.

As for my own life, I was not satisfied at all. I should have been thrilled to be in our beautiful, redecorated house, free to come and go as I pleased. But the truth was I felt just as insecure and lonely as I had years before. I missed the security and deep friendship I felt whenever I was with the women of the Community. Dan had his business life that kept him busy morning, noon and night. But when I came home from a luncheon I was faced once again with my empty, meaningless life. And the truth was, I was tired of playing taxi driver every afternoon. It was my own fault; no one else was to blame. But that did not stop me from feeling trapped. What was the great purpose? Did the children really care? Or was I doing all this out of some subconscious, second-generation compulsion to make sure that every talent was utilized to the maximum?

One day, at the lunch table on the Cape, I nearly choked on my Reuben sandwich, when David suggested that perhaps God had other plans for us besides living in Cleveland for the rest of our life.

"Hey, Cam, did you ever think you might be called to move here permanently? You know, become resident Community members?"

"You've got to be kidding!" I exclaimed, gulping down some coffee. "We just finished decorating our house."

"Well, don't put it aside too quickly," he replied. "You

wouldn't want to miss God, if that idea just happened to come from Him." Dear David, trying to organize our life and upset our apple cart–no thanks!

And that was what we told him at the beginning of the week. But as New Year's Eve approached, I began to think more and more about what he had said. Could I really give up that dream house in that dream location? If we did move to the Cape, we would certainly need a house bigger than Nineveh. Nineveh was little more than a Cape cottage–what would we do with all our belongings? What about the children–would they want to go to public school again? What would Dan do for a living? It was one thing to take off for a year, when he knew his position as president was being held for him, but what could he do on the Cape? Besides, he loved what he was doing and was enormously successful at it–he would never give all that up.

"David, you've got to be crazy! We cannot pack up and leave when we've just gotten home! You find Dan a job, and then maybe we'll think about it!" I hated my life being out of control, and now here my brother had thrown me into a complete tizzy with his preposterous suggestion just when everything had all settled back into a convenient, working routine. I could overcome my life's loneliness and emptiness in time; I just wasn't busy enough yet. Besides, what would our parents say if we packed up and left again–this time forever? I didn't think I could handle telling them that piece of news.

On December 30th, I went off to the hairdresser to get my hair done for the New Year's Eve buffet dinner celebration, and when I returned, the house was empty. Where was everybody? I learned that Dan was with David and Barbara and several other of our friends, over at Damascus.

"What's going on?" I asked, as I took off my coat and scarf and looked around the cozy living room, where the group had gathered. They were talking with Mary Ann and Bob Jamison, another couple spending Christmas at the Community. Bob was a senior executive at Dictaphone in Connecticut, and like us they had been associated with the Community for a number of years. Now it appeared that they, too, were considering moving to the Cape with their children. Well, that's interesting, I thought; God has brought two families together with the same decision to make. I listened carefully to Bob and Mary Ann, who seemed to have the same questions I had. How would we be able to move when there were jobs to be found, houses to sell, children to switch schools?

But as I sat and listened and talked myself, I became more and more excited and more sure that the Community was where we belonged. I was able to help Mary Ann, and she helped me, to see that arrangements *could* be made, problems could be solved. We talked all afternoon, right on through dinner, and into the wee hours of the morning. When we finally tumbled into bed Dan and I were in complete agreement with our decision.

Once again, I was laughing and crying all at once. I had that same sense of excitement and anticipation that I had experienced at my conversion. What did God have in store for us now?

18

I'll Take the Reins Now

"You're going to *what?*" My mother couldn't have been more shocked, if I had told her that we were planning to rob a bank. "You can't be serious! Cape Cod is two thousand miles away! How can Bud possibly take a year off from his business? Who will harvest the cotton crop? Surely you don't plan to change the children's school? And what about your beautiful house?"

As she spoke I could understand how she felt, because I had had all the exact same feelings myself when the idea had first occurred to Bud and me. Were we really hearing God? Could it really be His will for our family to rent our house and spend a year at the Community of Jesus on Cape Cod, with Bud trying to run his business and the farming via the long distance telephone? Practically speaking it did not seem to make any sense at all, but Bud and I both had the unshakeable conviction that that was exactly what God did want us to do, and we were going way out on a limb of faith to do it.

It had all started with a perfectly reasonable short visit to the Cape that August, just as we had done the summer before. We were going to take the children again for a two-week stay as part of the Community's living-in program, which meant that we would live in one of the Community homes, sharing their daily life, work, and fun, actually being part of their family and learning more about ourselves in the bargain. Last year's experience had been tremendously helpful, and we were looking forward to another good visit this year.

Bud had been a little worried, however, about being gone for two full weeks. "I hate to leave the crop that long," he had told me. "We need a rain, and there'll be a lot to do if we should get a shower while we're away. Someone would have to run the sandfighter, and I have hoe hands to look after, too." But in the end he had put his objections aside, and we were on our way.

"Oh, I'm so glad that we're going to be at the Ark again this year!" I rattled on to Bud, as we arrived at the door of the two storied shingled rectory. We had stayed there last year and had grown to love Father Lane and his wife Lenny, and Rick and Betty Pugsley, who were the music directors of the Community. "Isn't it nice that we can relax, because they already know all about us, and besides they have such a good time as a family." One thing that had struck me the year before was how much Community people seemed to enjoy life, and everyone was free to laugh and joke about himself. I took myself much too seriously to be able to do that, but I liked the joy and humor and honesty of the households, and I looked forward to two weeks in such a lively atmosphere. Bud would probably be helping in the gardens, I would be working in the Ark kitchen and around the house, and the children would be involved in the busy summer schedule with friends they had met the year before.

From the very beginning, however, it had seemed

like a different kind of visit from the previous summer, as we felt a special awareness of God's presence. Both Bud and I remarked how much coming to the Community felt like coming home, even though we really hadn't been there that long before.

Our bedroom at the Ark was upstairs at the end of the hall, and one night as I lay in bed moonlight streamed in the open windows. Unable to sleep, I could hear the nocturnal serenade of peepers and crickets down below as I tossed and turned. Why was I so wakeful? The bed was comfortable, and I had had a busy day and was pleasantly tired, but my eyes were wide open. "Lord, are you trying to say something to me?"

In the morning I mentioned my wakeful night at the breakfast table, and the feeling I had that I should be listening, that God was trying to speak to me. "I know what you mean," Bud agreed. "I know that God is telling me that He wants to be first in my life–before job or farming or anything else, but I don't know exactly how to do that." Both of us wanted God's will for our lives, but we also wanted to be financially secure, independent, and in control. What if God was calling us to a deeper commitment than we were prepared to make? What then? The idea was more than a little scary.

That night, right after dinner, Bud slipped out of the house and went down to the chapel to pray. As he knelt in the semi-darkness, he asked God to help him get his priorities in the right order: God first, then business, and self and ambition last. It was a time of soul-searching and inner struggle, but as he looked at the Cross he was aware of the tremendous love of Jesus, and of the price that love had paid. Finally, the time had come. "Lord, I want to give my life completely to You," he prayed, and when he arose he was a different man. When he returned to the Ark, he was committed to putting God's will first, no matter what the cost.

"I don't know what it will all mean, Sunny," he told me later that night, "but I do know that we have to put Jesus first in our lives." I had a queasy feeling in the pit of my stomach when he talked like that, but I knew that he was right. Jesus did have to come first, yet I still hoped that it didn't mean that I was going to have to give up too much.

A few days later we talked with Mother Cay and Mother Judy, as the Community members now called them, about what had been happening. "I wonder if maybe we shouldn't try to stay for longer than two weeks," I heard Bud saying, to my surprise. "I don't know how we could work it out, but I know we need a lot of help in our marriage and with our children. People have stayed here for several months or even longer–what do you think?"

When their response came, it was in the form of a question: "Had you ever thought of staying for a year?" The moment they asked, we knew in our hearts that that was exactly what we should do. But a *year!* How could we ever work out all the details? It seemed impossble; God would have to show us how to do it.

Sure enough, one by one the problems were solved, one step at a time. Things fell into place in an amazing, unbelievable way. Within two weeks, Bud and I had flown back to Texas, told our parents, packed our things, and rented our house to a nice couple who were willing to look after Rebel, our Shetland sheep dog. Bud made some temporary business arrangements, we picked up the children's school records and, before we knew it, we were on our way back to the Cape.

I marveled at God's timing. "I know this had to be

You, Lord. I don't know what You have in store for us, but I know that it's going to be a memorable year." That was a slight understatement I was later to find.

Right away, I was out of control. The Ark household often had as many as fifteen people assigned to it, with Father and Lenny, Grandma Lane, Rick and Betty and their two children, five Hales, and usually three or four people who had come to "live in" for shorter periods of time, though they didn't sleep there, plus an occasional Bethany guest or two. With so many people to care for, with the large house to keep, and with laundry for fifteen, life had to be much more organized than I had ever experienced before. My first real problem was with the bathrooms.

"Sunny, would you please do the downstairs bathroom this morning? I'll take care of the ones upstairs," Lenny asked one day.

"But I just spent a whole hour on it yesterday! Surely it doesn't need cleaning again already? At home I only cleaned our bathrooms twice a week!" (Actually the truth was that Lucy, our cleaning lady, had cleaned them; I hated to clean bathrooms and avoided it altogether.)

"With so many people in and out, they really do have to have daily attention," Lenny explained patiently. "Look, I'll go over it with you today and show you some timesaving methods. You should be able to do a thorough, loving job in fifteen minutes."

I was grateful for the lesson, although I privately thought it ridiculous to talk about doing bathrooms "lovingly." I did a little mental arithmetic. "Let's see, three bathrooms in the house times six days a week equals eighteen bathrooms a week! I wish Lucy was here!"

The next big hurdle was the grocery store. I had

been at the Ark only a few days when Betty asked me to help her make out the marketing list. "It will help you to get some idea of what to buy tomorrow when you do the shopping," she said casually.

"When I do *what?* You don't mean I'm going to buy a week's groceries for this house of fifteen people by myself? I can't do that!"

Betty smiled. "Now don't panic! It's not all that difficult, and besides, there's really not anyone else to do it. I have to be in the music room all morning, and Lenny will be away. We're going to work on the menus for the week right now and then do the list together."

"But, Betty, I don't know the brands you all like here. I don't know how much of anything fifteen people will eat; I'm used to just five! And what if I spend more money than we have?" I could foresee all kinds of disasters.

"This will be a wonderful opportunity for you to pray and lean on Jesus," Betty replied cheerily, "and besides, there will be other Community women shopping from other houses. Everybody goes on Wednesday. If you really get stuck, you can ask one of them."

The next morning I stood indecisively inside the glass doors of the Stop & Shop supermarket, wondering what to do first. "I should probably get a cart," I thought, just as I spotted Mary Jackson who lived down the street from the Ark. She was happily pushing two carts pyramided with rolls of paper towels, boxes of cereal, and countless loaves of bread. As I watched, fascinated, she parked her carts in the checkout line and went back to get two more, equally bulging. *Four* grocery carts! "Hi, Sunny!" she waved. "There's a good special on hamburg today!"

"Thanks," I murmured. "Where is the meat

counter?" Hamburg–she must mean hamburger. They don't even call the meats by the same names up here! I found that to be even more of a problem at the meat counter. Beef roast was on the menu for Sunday night's dinner, but I couldn't find anything labeled rump roast or even a sirloin tip, which was what I had always bought in Texas. Poking among the neatly arranged, cellophane-wrapped packages, I debated, "I wonder if this one has to be cooked in liquid, or if it can be oven-roasted." Just as I was giving up in total confusion, I heard someone call my name.

"Hi, Sunny, what are you getting?" It was Helen Helms, one of the Community women whom I had seen a few times.

"I wish I knew! I'm looking for a roast for Sunday night, and I can't find anything I ever heard of!"

"We like this bottom round, and it's on special today."

"Oh, thanks, Helen," and I grabbed the biggest one I saw, with a quick look at my watch. I had noticed that Helen's basket was full, and she seemed to be almost ready to leave, and I was just getting started.

Up and down the aisles I went, studying my list and carefully reading the labels on every jar and can. I wanted to be sure to get exactly the right thing and the most for the household's money.

Finally I was in the check-out line with my three carts of food. How much was it all going to cost? Now we would find out if I had enough money to pay the bill, or if I would have to put half my items back. I held my breath while the checker rang up the ticket. She pushed the total button, and I heaved a sigh of relief. I had just made it! Feeling quite proud of myself, I parked in front of the Ark and hurried inside to tell everyone about my exciting morning. The house was curiously silent. Where could everyone be? Someone certainly must be here; it was lunch time–lunch time! Oh, no, I had forgotten all about the 11:45 chapel service. I tore out the door and up the path through the trees toward the chapel, but I was too late. The service was over, and I met Betty and Lenny hurrying home to get lunch on the table.

"Oh, there you are! We thought maybe you had car trouble."

"Oh, no, everything went well, but I just finished. I bought everything on the list, and I even had money left over!"

"That's great, Sunny, but four hours is a long time to spend grocery shopping. Did you remember to pray?"

Pray? I hadn't thought of it once. I had been so busy trying to be right and figure everything out for myself; I had left Jesus out of my whole morning. No wonder it had taken so long!

Seeing my chagrin, Betty smiled kindly. "Now don't go down the drain! You'll have plenty of opportunities to try again, and next time, let Jesus help you."

Mealtimes at the Ark were in some ways the best and worst part of the whole day. I liked sitting with the whole family at the big round maple table in the warm, informal kitchen, and this was the time to talk with other members of the household about the day and also to get help with any feelings or problems. That part was good and I liked listening to other people talk about their experiences and watching them just be themselves. They were honest about their failures and shortcomings and didn't pretend to always be perfect. I didn't care to be too honest myself, but I liked being around people who were willing to be real and who were willing to listen.

The part about meal times I *didn't* like was the food.

Oh, I don't mean the way it tasted–it was delicious. That was the trouble–how was I going to be around three good meals a day and not gain weight? It had been one thing to come and eat for two weeks last summer; I had gone on a diet as soon as I got home to lose the extra pounds, but now I was here for a year!

One morning at breakfast I refused the pancakes that were being passed around the table. "Could I have just a half grapefruit, instead? I'm not very hungry," I said. Nobody said anything or even seemed to notice, so at lunch time I was emboldened to turn down the tuna fish sandwiches that Lenny had made. "If there's any extra tuna, I'd prefer to have it plain on some lettuce. I really don't like to eat bread at lunch." And that worked, too! But dinner would be the most difficult time of all because the plates were served by whoever was sitting at the head of the table. "Just a small helping of roast pork, please, Father Lane," I requested, "and no noodles at all. I'll just have a large helping of salad, instead."

This time Father Lane looked up. "You know, Sunny, you've come here for a year of healing. Part of that healing comes by first being obedient to the Lord in all areas of your life, even in small things like eating. Are you willing to give up your control in the area of food and just eat whatever the other people in the house are eating, and not have to be special? If you are, I believe that God will bless you. I have a feeling that this could be a very important area in your life right now."

I sat there for a moment in stunned silence, fighting to keep my anger from showing. I couldn't very well make a big scene and say that I was never going to eat noodles–what would everyone think of me? No, I would smile and agree to eat whatever was served, but I had no intention of giving up control of my food. They might put noodles on my plate, but that didn't mean that I would finish them. What difference did it make to God what I ate for dinner? The whole idea was ridiculous! "Oh, sure, Father, I'll be happy to have the noodles," I said, smiling sweetly.

But it was getting harder and harder to keep up my good behavior, and after Nelda arrived in the house, it was impossible. Nelda and her husband had come to live at the Ark for three months, and she and I would be working together in the kitchen and around the house. "But I've been here longer," I thought. "It's not fair for her to get to do everything that I do. She's brand-new." That particular afternoon was going to be devoted to pie baking. Of course Nelda turned out to be an expert, and in no time at all three beautiful lemon meringue pies sat cooling on the counter, while I was still struggling to roll out my pie dough.

"Let me help you," Nelda offered.

"No! I can do it myself, and besides it's time to go down for coffee hour now." It was a relief to leave the whole sticky mess and go down to the front lawn of Bethany, for the mild October afternoon was pleasant and sunny, and coffee hour was still outside. A big circle of chairs was arranged on the lawn, and two of the Community ladies were serving tea and coffee and snacks from the long brick porch. Some of the people worked on needlepoint or knitting projects, but I was content just to sit and bask in the sun.

"Oh, hi, Darlene," I greeted another live-in who sat down beside me. "Listen," I added in a conspiratorial tone, leaning toward her, "am I glad to see you and get away from that perfect Nelda for an hour. She's a real goody-two-shoes, and she's driving me crazy!" The hour's respite passed all too quickly, and soon it was time to go back to the Ark to start dinner preparations.

When I walked in the front door, Nelda was nowhere in sight, and I was surprised to see Betty in the living room. "Oh, I thought you were down at Bell Choir rehearsal," I began, and then I saw the serious expression on Betty's face and my heart sank. What was the matter?

"Sunny, I think you should know how much you have hurt Nelda by your remarks down at coffee hour today."

So that was it! I should have known it would have something to do with Nelda! She must have come up behind our chairs. "I don't see why she was so upset," I defended myself angrily, "and how was I to know that she was listening? Anyway, I was just teasing!"

"Were you? I don't think you know yourself at all, Sunny, or how much pain you can cause other people by your sharp tongue. When you are angry or jealous, you lash out, and what you say really cuts. This is what Bud has lived with for years, and you are still doing it to all those around you. But you don't have to go on this way—you know Jesus!"

She continued to talk, but I was no longer listening. I refused to believe all those terrible things about myself. I wasn't really like that. Maybe I did get a little jealous; who wouldn't, with another person in the kitchen? But I would never intentionally hurt anyone. It was just a misunderstanding. Tears rolled down my face, but they were tears of self-pity, not sorrow at what I'd done. Betty had held up the mirror, but I had refused to face the reality of what was reflected there; I preferred to see the fantasy of my own creation. I hardened my heart against the truth and turned away from the mirror, and from Jesus.

Bud and I had our first big fight in the Community a few weeks later on a November evening as we walked home from the Monday night teaching meeting. "I've been talking to Dad on the phone," he said. "They've had a frost, and it's almost time to start stripping cotton. I think I should go back to Lamesa for a few weeks to be sure that things are going well, and to take care of the fertilizer business, too. I want to talk about it at the Ark and see what seems best, but I really need to go by the end of the week. What do you think?"

"What do you care what I think? Your mind is obviously already made up! Do whatever you want to!" I snapped nastily, as I flounced into the house and up the stairs. "I'm going to bed!"

"Sunny, come back here, and let's talk to someone. You can't go off angry like that."

Ignoring him completely, I went straight to bed and turned off all the lights, lying stiffly with my face toward the wall. Why did Bud get to fly off on a plane, leaving me here? Maybe I would like to go, too! Besides, I didn't want him to go; I wanted him here with me.

I could hear footsteps coming firmly up the stairs, and Bud's determined voice called to me through the door. "Sunny, get up and come downstairs. Let's talk to Father Lane."

"Go away! I'm asleep!" The footsteps faded, and I smiled to myself in the darkness. He could go get help with his feelings, but I would stay right here.

Then I heard *two* sets of footsteps approaching–he had brought reinforcements! Then Father Lane's no-nonsense tone, "Sunny, you get up and come downstairs right now. There is no excuse for this behavior."

"Oh, all right!" I cried and put on my robe and slippers and went downstairs, feeling more than a little foolish. Why was I acting like such a baby? Why was I so unwilling to listen to Bud? When I had thought our marriage was breaking up, I had been willing to look at where I was wrong. But the minute the pain stopped, I was "all right" and right again. I had come here to get our marriage fixed up, but was I myself willing to change? "I'm sorry, Father Lane, I've been acting like a spoiled brat. I'm sorry, Bud; I don't know what was wrong with me."

Father Lane had a pretty good idea. "Sunny, pray about your jealousy of Bud. I think your tantrum tonight was simply jealousy."

Jealousy of Bud? Impossible! "Why would I be jealous of Bud? We are a married couple. He's my husband. I'm not jealous of him!"

Father Lane shook his head. "I still think you should pray about it. Bud has been a real blessing ever since you all have come here, while you've had a lot of ups and downs. I think you are jealous of his success and his ability to get along easily with so many people. I think you are very lonely, but you need to see that you put up plastic walls to keep people away. Bud is willing to give of himself, and you're not. And one more thing: Do you see how much you've hurt Bud by refusing to talk with him or support him in his business or whatever he chooses to do? When are you going to stop hurting him?"

Once again, I quickly turned away from the mirror. I could see that it was wrong to have a fit and go to bed, but all this jealousy business was too much. I am not that bad! I may have a few faults, but I'm not all that bad! Father Lane has helped me a lot, but this time he's wrong. I *know* I'm not jealous of Bud!

So I quickly put the whole scene out of mind as during the next weeks my attention turned more and more to the question of our future. Bud and I had been talking about it a lot, even though our year was barely one-third over. Somehow we were beginning to feel that God had brought us to the Community for more than just one year–that in fact He might be calling us to make this our permanent home. That would mean giving up our source of income, because obviously Bud couldn't go on forever commuting back and forth to Texas. "It would be very hard to give up farming," Bud admitted, "and I can't think of anything that I could do on Cape Cod. They certainly don't have much agriculture here. But I know that if it is God's will for us to come He knows that we'll need to make a living, and He has the perfect solution."

Well, if He did then I wished that He would tell me what it was. Bud's faith was stronger than mine; in fact, mine was very shaky. I, too, felt that we were supposed to move here, but what would we do without a job? Where would we live? And how could I ever give up my beautiful house in Texas? And this was the most difficult question of all, for we had already found a buyer. How could I leave the house of my dreams, the one that I had always wanted and had worked so hard to make perfect? How could I give up that beautiful wallpaper in the kitchen? And I had spent weeks choosing just the right carpet for the living room. To me the house was almost like another child and the idea of selling it was intolerable.

One day, soon after New Year's, Bud and I went to talk with Mother Cay and Mother Judy about the feelings we were having and the questions that were on our minds. We sat down with them in the beautiful living room of Bethany, and I remembered so well the first time that I had seen this room, just two short years before. So much had happened in our lives since I had arrived as a needy, desperate retreatant. Jesus had been faithful to put the pieces of our shattered marriage back together. Was I still as grateful as I had been then? Or did I forget about my need for Jesus when things seemed better?

Mother Cay and Mother Judy sat together on the little sofa near the big picture window in Bethany, and Bud and I sat on the larger sofa nearby them. "It's good to see you both," Mother Judy smiled. "How have things been for you?"

They listened patiently as we blurted out all that had been happening during the past few months. Sometimes we interrupted each other as we talked about our uncertainty about the future, about Bud's love for the cotton farm, and about the buyer for our house in Texas. What was God's will for our family? Were we mistaken, or was He really calling us to leave West Texas far behind and make Cape Cod our permanent home? How could we know for sure?

When we had finished we looked at them expectantly, hoping that somehow they could have the answer that would settle every question and solve every problem. But that was not the way God worked. Mother Cay and Mother Judy looked at each other for a moment, and then Mother Cay spoke. "Of course, you know that we cannot tell you what God's will is for your lives; that is something that He, and only He, can tell the two of you. It may be that you are hearing God's call, but you need to pray about it until you are both at peace. Then you'll find that all the details will fall into place. Whether you are called here to the Community or called to live the rest of your lives in Texas, the most important thing is to be in the center of His will. That is more important than job or house or anything else, for it is the only place you will ever truly be fulfilled."

I looked at Bud, and he nodded. Of course God

would tell us. All we had to do was be willing to hear, and He would make His will known to us.

Then Mother Judy turned to me. "Sunny, how are you? I've been concerned about you."

Suddenly I was in tears, telling them about the trouble I was having getting along with the other live-ins, and how much I loved the house in Texas and how hard it would be to give it up, and how worried I was about the children, and on and on I talked, scarcely pausing for a breath. When I was finally through, Mother Cay handed me a box of tissues, and Mother Judy went on thoughtfully.

"You know, I wonder if a lot of your problem doesn't have to do with your weight. You are very thin, and I think that makes you nervous and anxious. If you will gain ten pounds, I think you will be much happier and calmer, and more able to hear God in your daily life. I think it is important for you physically, and just as important for you emotionally and spiritually."

I froze. *Ten pounds!* I couldn't gain ten more pounds; that would make *twenty!* "But you don't understand; I've already gained almost ten pounds since I came here, just eating three meals a day. I weigh more than I have in years; already my clothes are getting tight. Ten more pounds, and I'll be a blimp!"

But my logical objections didn't seem to persuade anyone. "You are still thin," Mother Judy said. "Have you ever heard of anorexia nervosa? Sometimes people who think of themselves as fat are really very thin."

"Oh, we've heard of that," Bud agreed. "Sunny, isn't that anorexia the same thing the doctor in Dallas told you about that time?"

"I think so," I said vaguely. Why did he have to open his big mouth? I didn't want to talk about anorexia.

There was nothing wrong with me, and I didn't need to gain any weight, and if we didn't get out of here in a hurry I was going to fall totally apart. Aloud, I promised to think about gaining weight, but inside I was seething. If anyone thinks that I am going to ruin my life by gaining twenty pounds of fat, they are wrong. No way!

I managed to control myself until we reached the privacy of our bedroom at the Ark, and then I let my real feelings fly. Bud stood amazed, as I raged and cried hysterically. "You don't understand! I'd rather be dead than fat! My life will be over if I gain weight! Everything I have worked for and planned for will be gone. That's too much to ask of me. I don't think Mother Cay and Mother Judy really meant it. I can't do it; I won't do it! Why should I care what anyone else thinks; *it's my life!*"

And then I turned on Bud. "I hate you! If you really loved me, you would have never mentioned that doctor in Dallas! Why did you ever have to say that? Now they'll think I am *really* crazy. I don't have anorexia, and I never have. There is nothing wrong with me!" And I fell across the bed, sobbing wildly.

At first Bud tried to talk to me, but it was no use. "I don't know how to help you," he said, "but you've got to have some help."

Hurrying out into the hall, he ran into Rick. "Come quick! I don't know what's the matter with Sunny!"

I liked Rick, but I didn't want to see him or anyone else; I just wanted to be left alone. "Go away; I feel awful! I'm going to bed." I didn't even try to act nice.

"Sunny, you can't go to bed; it's four o'clock in the afternoon. And you can't lie there and cry forever, either. You need to talk and get through this. We want to help you. It's time to face your fears; it's time to let God heal you in these painful areas. Jesus wants you to be completely whole, but you are going to have to do your part."

I sat upright, and my voice was beginning to rise again with anger. "There's nothing wrong with me! I don't need to be healed!" Furious now, I screamed at Rick, "You all want me to be fat! You're just jealous! I am not going to gain any weight, and I am *not* sick! I weigh lots more than I used to. Maybe I was a little thin when I weighed 100 pounds, but that was years ago. All I've done since I came here is eat, eat, eat! And now I weigh almost 120! That's already too fat! How can I gain any more? Now go away and leave me alone!"

"Okay, Sunny, the choice is yours," Bud answered. "But you had better look at this tantrum and find out why you are acting like a crazy person. You have let your weight rule our lives for fifteen years! And you had better decide what you are going to do about it." They went out and closed the door, and I was alone at last.

I paced back and forth to the window, to the bed, and back again. I won't do it! I can't do it! Why should I do it! But now I was arguing with myself. In the back of my mind a nagging question was beginning to form: What if they were right? What if that doctor in Dallas years ago was right, when he told me to gain weight? I know I have an obsession with weight–*but 130 pounds!* I *can't* weigh that much!

Downstairs, I could hear the sounds of dinner in progress: water running, the refrigerator door shutting, and people talking and laughing. It must be almost six o'clock by now. What was I going to do? Should I stay up here in my room and refuse to come down? Somehow I didn't think that would be such a good idea. And what was it that Bud had said? Something about my weight ruling our lives–that was the truth. I knew that *was* the truth. *But 130 pounds!* What was it that Mother Cay had said, long ago at that first retreat? "God never asks us to do anything that He doesn't also give us the grace to do it."

"Okay, Lord, I'm putting this whole thing in Your hands. I don't want to do it. I'm not even convinced that I need to do it. But I'm willing to do it–provided You give me the grace. I know that all my life I've been terrified of getting fat, and now I'm going to deliberately choose to gain weight. It doesn't make sense, but I want to be free of the fear and the power that this thing has in my life. Bud's right–it has ruled my life–our lives–for fifteen years, and it's time it stopped." The tears were gone now, and the rage was gone, and I just felt very, very tired. I combed my hair and went down to dinner.

"Okay," I said later that evening, as the dishes were being cleared. "I've decided to do it–I'm not even sure why, but somehow I feel that God does want me to gain ten more pounds. I want to be honest about it: It's the last thing in the world that I want to do, and I think 130 pounds will be a catastrophe! But I'm going to choose by an act of my will to do it, and I am going to need a lot of help."

"We'll be here," Betty smiled. "But nobody is going to force you to eat; it has to be your own choice. We'll always be around to talk and to encourage you and help you with your feelings, but the real battle will be yours. And this is the time that you will really learn who Jesus is. It's in our weakness and our need that we turn to Him. This will probably be the hardest thing that you ever do, but God will give you the grace to walk through it."

The next weeks and months were dreadful. Just facing every day was a struggle. When the alarm went off, I wanted nothing more than to pull the covers up over my head and pretend that none of this was really happening. Yet wasn't that the way that I had lived my life, always refusing to face reality? Preferring to live in a make-believe world rather than face anything unpleasant or difficult? That had brought disaster; it was time to grow up and learn to live in the real world. "Jesus, please help me," and I put my feet on the floor.

At breakfast, I had to pray again. It was my least favorite meal of the day, and I had always tried to eat as little as possible. Well, if I am going to gain ten pounds, I might as well get it over with, I thought. So now I sat down to an early morning meal of eggs, bacon and toast with jam, or perhaps a big bowl of hot oatmeal with cream and brown sugar. I felt stuffed. "Jesus, please help me get these eggs down!" I ate and prayed, ate and prayed, all day long, at every meal and at snack time. "Jesus help me!"

Just as important as the eating was the talking. I found that eating triggered a multitude of feelings, and as I talked about how I felt, I began to understand myself more, and to see a little bit more of who I was, and why I had become anorexic. It was like a ball of string unraveling. . . .

"I feel so out of control!" I stormed one day after a lunch of peanut butter sandwiches. "I know that I am going to start gaining weight and never stop until I look like the fat lady in the circus! I'm afraid to give up control of what I eat! I'm the only one who knows what is right for me!"

"But where is God in your life?" Father Lane reminded me. "You have to give up control, so that He can take charge." I looked at him, surprised. "It's funny you should be talking about that. I had a dream about that very thing. Bud and the kids and I were going along in a covered wagon, and everything was just fine, until I got worried and reached over and took the reins in my own hands. Then the wagon swerved, and we went into the ditch and almost turned over. You know, it's foolish for me to trust in myself. If I'm in charge, we really are in trouble!" And for awhile, everything seemed clear again.

One afternoon in early spring I stood in my bedroom, crying, when Betty walked by the door. She poked her head inside. "What's up? You look like you lost your best friend."

"It's worse than that," I wailed, pointing at the clothes thrown on the floor and draped across the bed. "I've been trying on last summer's clothes, and I can't wear a thing!" Catching a glimpse of myself in the mirror, I cried even louder. "Just look at me in this skirt; I look horrible. I am so ugly! How can I ever go out in public again?"

"You can't really trust the way you see things right now," Betty told me calmly. "You've been looking at things distortedly for so long that you really don't see yourself clearly at all. After a while you will begin to get your perspective back. Right now you will just have to believe other people who are telling you that you look much better than you have looked in years."

"Amen!" Bud chimed in heartily, but I was not convinced.

"And what is my mother going to think the next time she sees me?" I went on. One of the hardest parts of spending a year on the Cape had been leaving my mother.

"She will be glad to see you looking so much better," Bud assured me.

"Oh, no, you don't understand! She is small, my sister is petite, and all my Davis aunts are tiny. I know Mother is going to think I'm too fat."

"Well, maybe it's time you stopped demanding

approval from your mother; after all, you are thirty-eight years old!"

The raw, blustery winds of March blew straight across Cape Cod Bay, and sometimes it seemed that spring would never come. During Lent, I kept right on eating my seconds and ice cream desserts, while the others in the house were fasting. "This doesn't seem very religious," I complained.

"Lent is a time of sacrifice–and for you, it's much more of a sacrifice to eat!"

But I was getting tired of eating, I was getting tired of watching the scale go up and up, and I was getting tired of housework and daily church services and being honest about my feelings. Some days I forgot to pray altogether. Often I let my mind wander back to the way "it used to be" back in Texas, conveniently forgetting all the bad parts and remembering only the good.

"Wouldn't it be wonderful to sleep late every morning?" I asked myself. And when Lucy had been around to do the housework I had more time to read, or shop, or talk on the phone for hours. I wanted to be the only woman in the kitchen again–then I could do things my way! I'm tired of having to work with other people and consider other people and live with other people! I'd like to have just my own little family around me in my own house again. Bud and I were getting along much better now; maybe we'd had all the help we needed. Perhaps we were a little hasty to think about staying here permanently; even a year might be too long. We've been here almost eight months now; maybe that's long enough. And yesterday the Ark scale had registered 127–three more pounds to go, and I felt like I should have "Goodyear" printed on my side! If I went on a diet right away, I could still get rid of those extra pounds! The rebellion grew and grew, as I continued to live in unreality in my mind.

The opportunity I had been waiting for came suddenly during Passiontide, when Bud came back from work crew on Wednesday to talk about a trip to Texas. "It's going to be planting time soon, and I need to fly down for a couple of weeks to get things started. I'm thinking of going the week after Easter."

"Bud, why can't I go, too? It's been eight months since I was there, and I'd like to see my mother. I want to go with you."

"But, Sunny, we're right in the middle of our year here; I don't know if that would be a good idea."

I started to get angry, but I knew I had to keep control of my temper if I was going to get what I wanted so I continued slowly, thoughtfully. "Why do we even have to stay to finish the year? I'm not at all sure we're called to live here. Maybe we are, but maybe we're not. Before we decide anything, I think we should all go back for a while, to really be sure before we make any sort of permanent commitment. You know, if we decide to sell the *land* that is very final!" I knew that Bud had been having his own struggle with the idea of selling the land.

It worked! "Well, I don't know," he wavered. "Maybe it would be a good idea to go back and really make sure that we are doing the right thing before we burn our bridges. But what about the children?"

"We can take them with us!" I said, unable to contain my enthusiasm. "Let's go now–this week! This is Wednesday; if we start packing right away, we can leave by Friday!"

"But do you think it's right to go so suddenly? Before Easter? What about the people in the Ark, who have spent so much time helping us; aren't they going to be hurt? And where will we live when we get there? The renters are still in our house until June 1, and then the buyer will take possession."

I had already thought of that. "We can stay with my mother, until we find something else. I think we should take the children out of school and go now!" I knew that if we hesitated and Bud had any chance to think about it, we were likely not to go at all. But now that I had momentarily convinced Bud, I began having trouble with my own conscience. That same inner voice that always argued with me had started up again. Was this really God's will–to yank the children out of school and leave like thieves in the night? And why was I running? Wasn't it simply so that I could control my weight again? Or maybe I thought I could somehow undo the sale of our house if I was there in person. Was I still hoping to find peace by leaving a difficult situation and looking for an easier way? Or maybe I was just plain mad and jealous and having another temper tantrum.

I shut out the voice. My will was set; I hardened my heart against the disquiet within, and within two days we were packed and pulling out of the Ark driveway.

The April day was bright and shining, as we drove down Defiance Lane and turned onto Rock Harbor Road. Spring's arrival was cheerily heralded in every yard with clumps of yellow daffodils, and forsythia was bursting into bloom. But I hardly noticed; I was trying to ignore the sound of sniffling in the back seat. "Don't cry!" I pleaded with the girls. "We're going to have a fun trip home! We're going to drive to New York City and Washington, and you can see the Empire State Building and the White House and lots of exciting things like that. Then we'll fly home to Texas, and be there in time for Easter."

"But I wanted to be *here* for Easter," said Leigh, refusing to be consoled. "I wanted to sing with the Children's Choir and go to Easter dinner. I don't want to leave, and I didn't even have time to tell everybody good-bye."

"And now we're going to miss Jill and David's wedding!" Kathy joined in, and at that they both cried even harder. Michael was very quiet, looking out the window, lost in his own thoughts. No one seemed at all enthusiastic about seeing the Empire State Building.

Well, they'll feel better in a day or so, I told myself. They have to have time to get used to the idea. Once we get back to Texas, and they see their grandparents and their old friends there, it'll be fine. Children adjust quickly.

But why did I feel so sad? I really am perverse! Now I am actually on my way back to Texas, where I can make my own schedule, do as much or as little as I please, eat what I want or nothing at all if I feel like it, and yet I don't feel a bit happy. I just have this terrible dread in the pit of my stomach. We're just at Brewster; it's still not too late to turn back. I know they would understand and forgive me, if I just said that I had made a mistake, and that I really don't want to go after all.

But I can't keep changing my mind. Bud has to go to plant the cotton, and I don't want him going without me. It drives him crazy when I can't make up my mind. I'll feel better once we get off the Cape. Making my voice sound as cheerful as possible, I turned to the back seat again. "Now, kids, maybe the hotel will have an indoor swimming pool!" And I chattered on to cover up the terrible feeling that we were driving out of God's will, by my own willful choice. I had set it all in motion, and now I would have to go through with it.

It sure didn't seem like Good Friday as we drove into

Lamesa for the first time in eight months. It seemed more like eight years that we had been away. I felt as if I was revisiting a world that I had lived in a long time ago, when I was another person. There were the same billboards, the same flat fields, bare and brown this time of year as they waited for the planting rains. Over there was the Piggly Wiggly grocery store, and the station where I had always filled up the car with gas. We turned up the winding street into Park Terrace on the way to my mother's house. I hope we don't go by Hillside Drive; I'm not ready for that yet. It should feel like we're coming home, but instead I feel like a visitor.

The feeling increased as the days went on. It's just because we're not in our own home but staying with Mother, I told myself. Yet even after we had moved into a rented house, the feeling persisted. "Do you know what I mean, Bud? It's a little like coming back as a ghost. I used to live here, and I can remember the person I was then, and the way I used to live, but it's impossible to be that person again or even to pick up the pieces. It's as if that life is over, and there's no going back."

Bud tried to listen, but he had plunged right into the busiest season of farming and the fertilizer business, and he was under tremendous pressure from morning to night. The children were soon back in school, and now I was finally free to do just exactly what I pleased. But I couldn't seem to remember what it was that I had so badly wanted to do. I didn't seem to have the energy to make out menus, and puttering around all by myself in the kitchen wasn't as much fun as I remembered. I could do whatever I wanted–but I didn't want to do anything. Our friends called on the phone, but I didn't really want to make plans to have them over or to go out. It was all just too much trouble.

I didn't even care whether or not I lost any weight. It didn't seem to matter that much any more. And besides, I had gotten used to eating again, and now I liked to eat. I didn't even want to go on a diet. The only thing that I wanted to do was read. I went down to the public library and checked out a stack of Agatha Christie's. They were easy to follow, and they occupied my mind. I read one after another, day and night. I was having trouble sleeping, so I read into the wee hours of the morning. Lucy came to clean the house, I did a little laundry, but mostly I sat in the house and read. And church was even worse. The first Sunday I broke down during the hymns and had to leave, and after that I tried not to listen.

It was almost as if the clock had been turned back. I was right back where I had been, only this time it was worse. This time I knew what I should be doing, and I knew that I had willfully refused to do it. God had shown me the way to wholeness and I had demanded my own way instead. I had brought this pain and apathy on myself; I deserved every bit of the hell that I was now living in. I had thought that gaining the weight and standing against myself had been difficult, but it was nothing like this! For before, God had been there in that tight spot to call upon and to turn to, and now it was as if the grace had lifted and God had given me up to my own way.

And I had to watch the effect that my willfulness had had on those around me. Changing schools so suddenly, right at the end of the year, was not easy for the children, and I was so wrapped up in myself that I didn't want to take the time to discipline them and care for them. They had been growing in Christ, and now I saw them forgetting everything that they had learned, and demanding to have their own way—like their mother. They were a mess, and unhappy, and it was my fault.

And why had I ever thought that Bud and I were getting along better? Within three weeks, we were barely speaking to each other, and I was again taking out all my anger and guilt on Bud. We were back in our cold war of silence, and leading two separate lives.

Finally, Bud could stand it no longer. "Sunny, I don't know what it is you want! What is it going to take to make you happy? Is it a house? We'll buy a lot and build a house. You can build it any way you want."

"I don't want to build a house! I want my old house back."

"You know that you can't have that house back. We both agreed to sell it, and it has been signed and finalized. There is no way you can have it back. Maybe we can go and look at the Jefferson house. I heard that Mrs. Jefferson might be willing to sell it, and it's right across the street from where we lived." In his desperation, Bud was willing to buy one of the most expensive houses in town, even though it was way over our budget. Anything to try to get a little peace. The children liked the idea of a backyard swimming pool, but as much as I was tempted, I knew that we weren't supposed to have that house. I knew it wouldn't change the terrible feeling I had inside. No, the Jefferson house wasn't the answer.

"Okay, then, let's get a membership in the country club, and you and the children can go swimming every day, and we'll have lunch there on Sundays. You need to get involved again." So we spent the long afternoons of June and July at the pool, and the children learned to do the backstroke and to dive, and I sat by the side of the pool and worked on my tan, and tried not to think.

I don't remember what the argument was that brought everything to a head. It was early August, and very hot and dry, and it was dinnertime. Something happened at the table, and suddenly Bud and I were both very angry. Since we tried never to fight in front of the children, we went into the bedroom and shut the door before I exploded.

"It's *awful* here! We never should have come back! I hate it here, and I hate this rented house. I knew we shouldn't have sold our house, and I knew we shouldn't have left the Community!"

"Sunny, you were the one who was pushing to leave, and now you haven't tried one bit to make it work!" Bud shouted back. "All you want to do is punish me, and you've decided never to be happy, just to get even with me. It was our decision to sell the house, and we *both* decided to leave. When are you going to stop blaming me for everything that goes wrong in our lives?" And he turned and went out of the room, slamming the door, and drove away in his pick-up.

We're right back where we started, I told myself. Three years of healing have gone down the drain because of my willfulness, and our marriage has lost all of the ground that it had gained.

I remembered, then, what Mother Cay and Mother Judy had said on that spring afternoon when we had told them of our decision to leave the next day: "Of course you must do whatever you both feel that God wants you to do, but we want to tell you of our concern for your marriage. God has begun the work of healing, but there is still much to be done. Sunny, there is so much still operating in your life that can be destructive to your relationship with Bud. You haven't really seen and faced your jealousy of him, and you really don't know yourself at all." I had refused to listen, but they had been right! And then they had given us both a hug and said, "We want you to know that we love you very much, and the door is always open."

Just thinking of their love now made me start to cry. How well they knew me, and yet they still loved me. They had been able to see just exactly who I was, and *still* they loved me. Was it possible that God still loved me, too? Oh, God, I wouldn't blame You if You never helped me again. I am so willful, and so stubborn, and every time I get in charge, the wagon goes right into the ditch again. You tried to warn me, and I wouldn't listen. I turn to You when I am hurting, and when there isn't any other way out and then, when things get better, I forget everything You have shown me and go right back to my old ways. You have given me so many good things, and I have been ungrateful and turned my back on You and accused You. Lord, I don't even know what it means to be grateful or to love You. I've just wanted to use You. I've been a big phony. I said I wanted to commit myself to You and follow You, but in my heart I have only served myself. I don't know anything about repentance. I don't even know who I am.

But, please, could I have one more chance?

19

Just Plain Me

It's funny how, when you take a major step toward God's will for you, all the seemingly impossible obstacles and logistical problems seem to melt away before you. Enrolling the children in the Nauset public school system was a breeze, and young Dan even got the same teacher he'd had before, who had been transferred to the third grade, and of whom he was very fond. And as for that beautiful home of ours—but that's getting ahead of the story. There was one hard part that was not going to get any easier: telling our parents that we were leaving Cleveland for good. But much as I would have liked to put it off, I knew that we had to tell them right away, before they heard from anyone else.

We told Dan's parents first, and then mine, and neither the Fords nor the Manuels really understood. Nor did there seem to be anything we could say that would help. We had tried to explain before, when we had gone for the year, but had been unable to and were even less able to explain this move. Both families felt that we were throwing away our lives, especially Dan, with all that he had worked so hard to achieve. To spend almost twenty years with a company, and then turn his back on it, just when it was at the height of its success. . . .

We tried to tell them how close we had come to divorce, how empty our lives had been before we had begun to discover what it meant to live for Christ—but they refused to believe us. We had done too good a job of selling our image as the with-it, got-it-all-together couple. And as for trying to explain what it meant to answer a call of God—we might as well have been speaking Greek.

The hardest part for me was with Mother. She was grieving, and because of that my father in his way was grieving, too. He explained that one of her fondest dreams when they had built their new country house in Gates Mills was to have had the grandchildren out to spend hours swimming in the pool and fishing in the pond. Mother had been extremely fond of her own grandmother, and had named me Cornelia after her, because she had spent her growing years surrounded by cousins who all congregated at her grandmother's estate on Long Island Sound. Any hope that she might have similarly enjoyed her own grandchildren's growing up years had now been shattered.

I felt absolutely terrible. I knew we were doing what God wanted us to, that any hope of attaining peace and fulfillment in our own lives depended upon our answering His call. And I knew that He would honor our obedience and in time would heal the hurt that Mother and Daddy were feeling. But that did not make the present pain any less.

The only way to get through the next two months was to turn to Jesus every hour of the day and to pray for grace. The only two people in Cleveland who really understood why we were leaving were our dear friends

Anne and Don. I talked to Anne daily, as we went through our preparations for packing. Fears and doubts were always close at hand if I allowed myself to fall into self-pity over my parents' reaction to our move.

Our next task was to sell the home that we loved so much, with its five acres of wooded land and the best view in the valley. There was no question that it was one of the most desirable pieces of property in all of Gates Mills or Hunting Valley. But try to sell a house of that size in January! No one bought a home in January. Yet in two weeks, we had sold the house–to the very gentleman who had rented it from us the year we were away. Truly another miracle, we agreed. There was much grace on us, because only after the bill of sale was signed did I realize how much that house meant to me. It was a home I was proud of and could entertain in, gracious and warm, but elegant, too. That was the way I wanted people to picture me. Dan had his company, and I had my house. In fact, the last large party we had was his company's Christmas party. Everything was at its sparkling best, all decorated for the holidays, and I hoped I was the perfect president's wife and hostess. Now, just a few weeks later, the decorations were packed away along with all my china and crystal.

The remaining weeks before we moved were spent in packing carton after carton with our personal belongings. We had the backbreaking job of going through all the books, records, clothes, toys and games and the junk that accumulated during our eighteen years of marriage, and our separate lives before that.

Each morning I would wake up with thoughts of the day's packing spinning through my head. There were moments when I thought, I just can't get out of this bed. I can't face another box, make another decision. I must call the church and see if they want all the clothes I won't be needing. Those ski pants that don't fit can go, and so can all those slack outfits. I won't be wearing those cocktail dresses or evening pajamas. Where will I store the old nursery furniture? I know, I'll give it to my hairdresser who's having a baby. Jesus, help me, please, to know what to take and what to give away or throw out.

I truly felt the presence of Jesus and the grace of God, as we went through each room, discarding or packing our "treasures." We gave away boxes and boxes of items to our church for its Spring Rummage Sale, and books to the local library, and friends were invited to take what they wanted as they helped me pack. It was a time of mixed emotions–on the one hand, I wanted to keep each item I picked up as a reminder of our past, and on the other hand, I was ready to throw everything away and have a completely fresh start. There were so many memories as I went through the children's books, records and toys. I could easily have spent a whole afternoon just remembering. But, no, I knew I had to keep moving; too much to do.

Where would I store everything? Over and over again I had to decide what to put into long-term storage, what to put away for immediate use at Nineveh, and what to give away. It was exhausting physically, as well as draining mentally. When we finally finished we filled *two* huge moving vans for the trip to the Cape. Everything on the vans would be put into storage until such time as we either bought or built a bigger home than the one we now owned at the Community.

The weight that I had slowly lost during the summer months stayed off during the Christmas holidays and these final weeks in Cleveland. It didn't seem to matter what I ate, my weight never went over 135-136 pounds. I was so busy every day, I seldom thought about food and just ate whenever I was hungry. Friends often called for lunch and dinner dates. What a wonderful feeling, to never have to worry about calories! I could and did eat anything on the menu that tempted me; in fact, I now enjoyed studying the menus and deciding what looked good. In the past, I would have skipped breakfast and would always order a chef salad or fruit plate with black coffee or a Tab, hardly glancing at the grilled sandwiches, fried onion rings, French fries or cheeseburgers with bacon. I was totally relaxed about eating–when I felt full, I stopped eating. No longer did I stuff myself with the idea that I would soon starve myself. I ate regularly–no more missing meals so that I could gorge at a later time. Sometimes, if I thought about it, I would stop and marvel at how God had healed me in the area of eating, where I had been so sick with my obsessions. To be free to eat whatever I pleased, whenever I was hungry–a miracle!

We spent our last night in Cleveland at my parents' house. It was not an easy time. I felt sad at dinner, sitting around the table, much as we had so many years before, and I was also sad because I knew how they felt about our leaving. My father had little to say and retired to his bedroom early. Mother and I watched TV together for a while, chatting about nothing in particular; then she, too, said a hasty good-night and went to bed. I could hardly swallow the lump in my throat. We said our good-byes quickly the next morning, both sides fearing tears, and got an early start on our drive east.

One good-bye on that last day I will always remember. The movers had rolled up the rugs and were carrying out the furniture, when our friend and minister, Bill Shively, arrived at the door. Of all people in Cleveland, he understood best why we were leaving. He knew that we had found peace and contentment at the Community and just wanted to wish us the very best. We had always been honest with Bill and had shared our innermost struggles with him. He had encouraged us, guided us and listened to us throughout all the hard times. It seemed like forever, and yet it had been only a few short years since I first sat in Bill's office. Bill shook hands with us and said he hoped all would go well in our new life ahead. I felt his love and care for us at that time and I had to swallow quickly to keep the tears from coming. I was going to miss all my friends at St. Christopher's. Over the years of Bible studies, rummage sales, social outings and vestry meetings, we had made many friends and had developed some very close relationships with several families.

As the miles sped by on the thruway, the anticipation of us all being together at the Community soon outweighed any sadness I felt about leaving Cleveland. We had put our hand to God's plow, and I can honestly say that there was little looking back. I couldn't wait to unpack and settle down, once and for all. It had been a long time since we had lived in our little house, Nineveh, across the street from David and Barbara. There were now pictures to be hung and my china to put away in the kitchen cupboards. I had brought along my best looking plants, and a few boxes filled with some of my favorite knick-knacks to put in the living room and bedrooms. Nineveh had always looked attractive, but somehow impersonal. At last we would be surrounded by our own furnishings, our bedspread on the bed, and our towels in the bath. Dan didn't know why that was so important, but I told him that any woman would understand.

We arrived at the Community tired but happy to be greeted with hugs and kisses from all our Community family. It was a very warm welcome home for us. The children were laughing and talking all at once, as each one tried to tell us everything that had happened since we left in early January. They were as delighted as I was to see our old familiar furniture moved in and in use once again. There was my mahogany desk with its cubby holes, now in my bedroom. The chest of drawers was in place along with favorite lamps, and pictures were hung throughout the house.

"Hey, it's beginning to feel like home!" I exclaimed as I reached down into a huge carton to lift out my wooden salad bowl and the pretty green luncheon plates I liked to use.

"Where shall we hang this gold mirror?" Dan asked, as he attached new picture wire to the back. "How about here in the hallway?" The children helped to unpack and we put away as much as we could that first day.

Winter snows, rain and sleet gave way to the brilliant blue skies of a Cape Cod spring. These months of April, May and June were a time for Dan to prepare for a new business venture. One of the biggest hurdles to face was what Dan would do for a living. Many a night in Cleveland he had lain sleepless in bed, as he struggled with this question. There was no industry on Cape Cod to speak of, so that meant no office buildings or plants to lease, buy or sell. Real estate on the Cape was strictly residential or small business, not forty-story office buildings or huge warehouses for mammoth corporations. What could he do? Should he commute to Boston every day? But that did not appeal at all.

Photography had always been a real love of Dan's. We had albums of his photographs, both black-and-white, and color. There was no question he had talent in this field, especially for landscapes. God had given Dan a gift of seeing a picture in an old barn, a wind-swept dune, a broken split-rail fence against blue sky. Why not enlarge these pictures, mat them with complementary colored mats, and frame them for hanging in homes or offices? We talked and talked about the possibilities of a photography business, and Mother Cay and Mother Judy were very encouraging, so plans began to take shape. Dan found office space in Orleans and a place to set up his necessary equipment. One thing led to another as the idea took off. And as things fell amazingly into place, I was thrilled to see him happier than I'd ever known him. He spent days traveling from one end of the Cape to the other, photographing fog, mist, boats, seagulls, old barns, stone fences, beaches and dunes, until he had a large collection of pictures. Dan had asked David and Barbara, Dean Smith and John Sorensen as well as me to serve as his Board of Directors and critical eyes. We all selected our favorite photos and helped Dan to organize the business which became known as The Ford Collection. Before we knew it, he was selling his pictures to corporations all over New England for their executive offices. We were so grateful to God for showing us the way to get this venture started, as Dan was able to use his two great gifts–for taking photographs and then selling them! In four years, he has sold more than two thousand.

That summer was particularly busy for us. Dan and I were looking after a full house of live-ins, from June to September. As the months went by it became apparent that Nineveh was just too small. Yet there was nothing for sale, so we decided to buy land and build. As it happened, just the right piece of property *was* for sale–a piece overlooking Cape Cod Bay, about five minutes' walk from the chapel, with a high enough elevation that we would never have to worry about high tides or sand washed up all over our backyard. We talked about it and prayed about it, trying to find out what was God's will. Neither of us liked the idea of building, recalling the traumas that my parents had had building their dream home, and so it was with some anxiety and trepidation that we bought the land. Once again we were in a quandary: What kind of house did we want to build? The shape and size of the house would be decided by the size of the property, which was a long and narrow piece with a beautiful view. In Cleveland, we had overlooked the Chagrin River and its surrounding valley. Here, we had the ever-changing bay with its foamy whitecaps one day and mirror calmness the next. We wanted our kitchen and dining room to face the water so we could see the tide coming in or going out. I also wanted a fireplace in our bedroom for evening fires in the winter, when the fierce northwest winds blew.

Bill Andersen, Mother Cay's husband and an excellent contractor, was to be our builder. Together we spent many an hour discussing the plans that we had prayed about, asking the Lord to help us with every decision. We trusted Bill's judgment from his years of experience working on Cape Cod, and we certainly knew nothing about building a house. We drove all around our area of the Cape, looking at windows, roofs, doors and shutters, paint colors, shingles, trying to get ideas before we finally settled on the traditional white-cedar shingle that turns a soft gray with age, black shutters and white trim.

"Bill, when you get to the kitchen, I want it to be very practical, but unusual, too–you know, special. I expect to spend a lot of time in the kitchen, now that I love to eat and cook for everyone, too." I smiled happily at the thought of a kitchen made to order. Maybe building the house would be fun after all. "Let's make it yellow, blue and white, with a huge red-brick fireplace. I want space for a table for eating, a sofa for sitting down by the fireplace and lots of cabinets for china, and a food pantry and–" I could hardly talk fast enough as the ideas came pouring out.

The first week in April, 1978, a bulldozer, looking like a gigantic yellow Tonka Toy, came to dig our foundation, nicknamed the Ford Foundation by one and all. What we had feared would be a nightmare turned out to be loads of fun and a very happy experience for us, as the house took shape and grew in size.

In September of that year many of us in the Community were busy making plans and getting ready for a trip to Europe. We were going on a four-week "Roots of Faith" tour of England, Scotland, France and Italy, during which we would visit ancient cathedrals, churches, monasteries and convents. We would visit places of historical and religious importance, from Canterbury Cathedral to Iona and Lindisfarne, to the Cathedral in Turin, Italy, where the famous Shroud of Christ was on display for the public for a brief time of viewing, and finally to St. Peter's in Rome, where we had an audience with the Pope, the next to last one for John Paul I.

These four weeks were a most special time for us all, as we had the opportunity to travel with Mother Cay and Mother Judy, who taught us much about our need for Jesus in our daily lives as we toured from one saint-hallowed church to another. But as much as we learned of our spiritual heritage, thanks to our directors we learned even more about ourselves, as our trip became almost a rolling retreat.

I felt deeply moved to be sitting in the congregation at some of these magnificent cathedrals and listen to our own choir sing for several of the services. One of the high points of the trip was to learn Gregorian chant from the French nuns at Argentan and the monks at Solesmes who sing today the ancient services of the Church, just as they have been sung for centuries. The visit to Turin to see the Shroud of Christ was an unforgettable experience. I could hardly believe I was actually in Italy, in a slow-moving line, approaching the high altar and the Shroud. (For the first time in forty years, it was on display for just a few weeks, and scientists from around the world would shortly be studying this incredible piece of cloth.) I can see it in my mind today as clearly as I did that hot, summer afternoon, and being overwhelmed by the suffering Jesus had undergone.

Upon our return from Europe at the end of September, we went right over to our new house to see what progress had been made. Jill Elmer and Betsy Sorensen, two of our close friends, had arranged a welcome home coffee at the house in the bright new kitchen. The girls brought fragile tea cups, delicious coffee cakes and sweet rolls and lots of steaming hot coffee for all the workmen, Dan and me. I was in tears at the thoughtfulness and love that was shown to us that morning. We were so excited to be home again, and to see our new home being built right on schedule. The decorating was completed on time, too, with no delays and no problems. Everything was completed very much to our satisfaction, so that we were ready to move in Thanksgiving week. We certainly had a great deal to give thanks and praise to God for!

It was a traumatic day for me when the two moving vans finally came from the storage warehouse. Bill

Andersen and I stood in the garage to watch the men unload the vans piece by piece. I had not seen most of our furniture since moving day in Cleveland, and now here I was in Orleans, standing in the middle of the garage of our new five-bedroom home. As each piece was carried into the house, I told Bill where it had been or what we had used it for. The memories of all those years in Cleveland came flooding over me, and I just stood there with tears once again streaming down my face, as I remembered both the good and the bad from my past. To this day, when I look at Dan's favorite leather chair, I can see him in our old library with the girls sitting in his lap, each one holding one of our cats.

They were getting to the end of the load now; the smaller things were coming in. There was the telephone table, much like my mother's, which used to be in our library, too, as hers was in hers, and which had become the symbol of my old way of life. Was I down or bored or perhaps fearful or anxious? Mother or a friend was only a phone call away. Schedules, carpools, parties, plane reservations–so much of my routine had been centered around that phone and its table. There was a little drawer in the table, in which I kept our Christmas card address book, which also had everyone's up-to-date phone number in it. Recalling that little red book brought to mind that at one point we were sending out as many as three hundred cards a year. That number has dwindled down to about fifty now, and seems to have leveled off. In the meantime, we have nearly double that number of close friends here, with whom we have, needless to say, a great deal in common. In fact our Community friends are really more like family than friends–family, in terms of close relatives of whom we are particularly fond. And that's only natural, considering how much of our lives we share, beginning with the call that brought us here.

Do we miss our Cleveland friends? Sure–when we remember some of the good times we shared, which now seem so long ago. If someone from Cleveland is in the area, we're delighted if they can come by for a visit. "Come and see," we say, and they are invariably surprised at what they find. "This isn't at all what I expected!" they say, and we laugh. But we feel no desire to go back for a visit, except occasionally to see our parents or for a family wedding, because God has planted us here, and we have a new life to live–a life that for us has so far been more challenging, rewarding and fulfilling than we could possibly have imagined. And best of all, we have both found the peace that eluded us all our lives. It's not always easy, and certainly no bed of roses, but the peace is worth it–it really does pass all understanding.

We had moved into our house by Thanksgiving, as planned, but we still had much work to do around the front and back yards. The house looked very bare and unfinished until grass started to grow and lilacs, azaleas, hydrangeas and rhododendrons flowered around the windows and doors. We had a name already chosen for our home. We had been sitting in church one morning, listening to the New Testament lesson being read. It was the story of Paul and Barnabas going out to teach. They came to the city of Antioch, where the followers of Jesus Christ were first called Christians. Dan and I both turned and looked at each other, as we heard the Scripture being read.

"That's it!" I whispered, "That's the perfect name for our house."

"Yes, I think so, too," agreed Dan with a smile. It was

settled, then; Antioch would be the name for our house on the hill, overlooking the bay.

The Lord is so good and loving to us, and He provides for our every need. In the spring of 1980, Bud and Sunny Hale and their three children came to share our home. Our paths had crossed back and forth as we had returned to Cleveland, and they to Texas. Now, I thought, "how interesting that God has put two super-controlling women in the same kitchen." Here we were, two women who had each suffered from anorexia and had each gained 20 pounds in the healing process. We both had such strong opinions about food and also came from two very different geographical locations. Sunny loved Mexican food. I couldn't stand even the smell of chili, let alone eating a taco or an enchilada. My favorite meal was roast lamb and potatoes with gravy. But, if you are from Texas beef country you just don't eat lamb! Well, God must have smiled at that; He knew how much we had to learn about Community living, and how, in each other, we would almost be looking in the mirror.

In addition to working together in the kitchen, we had to learn to help each other with all aspects of our daily life, including disciplining our children. Sunny, knowing full well my problems with diet, would occasionally say to me, "You're looking a bit gaunt in the face; have you been eating enough? What's going on inside that you're not talking about?" For an anorexic, even though recovered, can easily slip back into the old pattern of skipping meals, losing weight and then liking the results and the feelings that come when the needle on the scale goes down, down, down. We knew the importance of keeping our weight up to the level that we had found to be the right place physically, psychologically and emotionally for each of us. If my weight dropped five pounds because of stress or change in diet, it showed up immediately in my emotional well-being. And now I have discovered that what I eat is as important as how much I eat, for a sound, physically healthy body. For I have discovered, thanks to Cytotoxic Testing, that I am allergic to a number of common foods that I had eaten all my life. By avoiding them, and rotating foods (i.e., not having the same thing more than once in a four-day period), I've found that I can maintain my ideal weight without dieting at all, now that the Lord has changed my eating habits. But all that is another story. . . .

Sunny was terrific with young Dan, who could be the most obnoxious teenager on earth when he really set his mind to it. She had no trouble speaking up to him and correcting him if he left the bathroom messy, did not pick up his clothes, or claim his clean laundry. I, on the other hand, was able to speak with more authority to her daughters about the neatness of their closets and bureau drawers. It is so much easier to deal with another child than with your own. Somehow our own children often don't seem to hear us; they tune us out. But Dan surely responded when Sunny spoke to him!

I had always found it much easier to work alone in the house, but here we were together, both of us perfectionists, set on doing things our way. I wanted to be in charge, make all the decisions, and be the top boss. But that was not the way of Community life. There were four of us to decide how things should be done now, and in spite of what I thought it was a relief to be able to discuss a project or an idea with someone else. In the past Dan and I had often ended up in our worst fights on those rare occasions when I couldn't get him to do something I wanted. Now the Hales and Fords talked and prayed together and reached a joint decision.

There was a temptation, of course, each day for either Sunny or me to "go into the woodwork," and let the other one make the decisions. To work beside another woman with exactly the same nature was a great will-crosser, and since we both wanted to avoid conflict at all costs, we would smile sweetly and tiptoe around. But that didn't last very long, because we had learned, over the previous years in the Community, that the only way we could live in any kind of real harmony was to be open and honest with all our feelings. So there was conflict from time to time, but we found that once we had worked it through and gotten it resolved, we had each grown and matured some in Christ.

We had been sharing Antioch with the Hales for a year when God began to lead me in new direction. The time had come for me to start traveling with Carol Showalter and Mary Haig, co-directors of a Christian group diet program called 3D, and Lorie Jack, the associate director and dietitian. Carol, Mary, and Lorie are invited to speak all over the United States about a diet that is Christ-centered, follows a sensible diet plan, provides a daily Bible study and devotional and involves meeting weekly with a small group of women or men who share similar problems. But the main thing it teaches is how to really care in Christ for others. There are active 3D groups in all fifty states with more than 80,000 graduates of the program. A lot of these women have asked questions about anorexia nervosa and the related binge-purge disorder, bulimia.

When I am on a trip with Carol and Mary, I can give firsthand information about how I recovered from this psychological eating disorder. Talking about my experiences in front of a group of women is still painful for me. I do not like looking back over my life, and I do not want to recall those terrible memories of self-starvation. Yet the more I talk, the more I see about myself and realize that this public speaking is also part of the healing process.

It was on one recent 3D trip that I saw more clearly than ever the dreadful, hurtful way I had behaved towards Dan over the years. Yes, he had loved the real estate business, and spent a great deal of time at his office, but what did he have to come home to? A starvingly hungry, angry wife who was consumed with herself. I was either on cloud nine or in the depths of depression, ready to ignore husband and children in an endless pursuit of thinness.

I can picture the motel room in Grand Rapids, where the girls and I were resting one evening after a 3D meeting. Mary's son was about to become engaged, and we were talking about marriage. "I would love to start all over," I sighed. "I made so many mistakes and behaved so terribly. I wasted a lot of years with my crazy thinking. I feel just awful about what I have done to Dan and the kids, and there's no way I can ever say I'm sorry."

"Sure you can," they agreed together. "Why don't you call him on the phone and tell him what you've just told us?"

"Oh, he'll think I'm being silly and foolish."

"No, call him up. He'll be happy to hear from you." So I did. And he *was* glad to hear from me! I told him how sorry I was for being such an awful wife, and burst into tears. He forgave me, and we both laughed and cried over the phone. So it's never too late to say: "I love you, and I am sorry."

Twenty years ago, I was trying desperately to be perfect; a perfect wife, mother and responsible young member of society. I did not know that perfection is found only in Jesus, never in self. I wanted so much to be recognized, respected, envied and admired that I was at the point of sacrificing my children, my marriage, my health and everything I had going for me.

Now here I am, a forty-three-year-old woman faced with choices to make again. But this time, I am a Christian who is trying to follow Jesus–who knows that to *keep* that peace which passes all understanding, I must be obedient to the truth I know in my heart. I must speak out what I think and feel, and then be willing to see where I am wrong; where my opinions have taken over again, and I have taken control.

Dan and I still have our problems, but they are resolved much, much faster than ten years ago. As I write this story, I am appalled at my past behavior as a wife. But I'm glad to have written it, for it shows me so clearly who I was before Jesus came into my life–and who I still am, whenever I turn my back on Him. Father Lane, our chaplain, once said to me in one of our many counseling sessions, "Well, Camie, you may not think Dan is any Prince Charming, but remember, you're no Cinderella, either."

I laugh every time I recall that conversation. I am certainly not Cinderella, even if I thought at one time I was a "Fair Lady." Thank You, Jesus, that those days are over and done with, and I don't have to be anyone but just plain me.

20

In the Mirror

I was in hell—a hell of my own choosing. And now that I could *see* that, I wanted out. The only thing to do was to go back to where I had gotten off the track, and start from there. Only pride stood in the way.

I knew that I would have to call the Ark and just tell them how totally wrong I had been—and how through my willfulness I had dragged all the people I cared about down into the pit with me. I reached for the phone—and hesitated. How could I tell them? It was so humiliating! But I recognized where that thought was coming from—I had gained a bit of discernment about hell recently—and resolutely took the phone in hand and dialed.

"Hello?" I recognized Betty's voice, and I plunged right in, talking a mile a minute, telling her what I had seen, and how sorry I was that I had forced us to leave, and now Bud and I were a mess, and I didn't know what to do next, and—

I paused for breath, and she was able to get a word in. "Sunny, that's great that you are seeing these things, but where is Bud in all this? How does he feel about it? And what does he think you should do?"

"Oh, he's involved in his farming again, and he doesn't believe me, when I say that I want to go back to the Cape and really get through the thing this time. He says he can't go running back and forth across the country every six months, and he doesn't think that I'll ever stick with anything," and I started to cry.

Betty was compassionate but not consoling. "Can you blame him? Have you really thought about what it does to Bud and the children, when you keep changing your mind? You know, Bud was ready last year to take a big step. He was excited about it, even though it meant giving up the one thing in the world that he most loved to do, and then you did a nose dive and got very negative and wanted to leave, and then within days you were sorry about that decision. He doesn't know what you might decide tomorrow, and Sunny," she paused, "neither do you. You are as changeable as a weather vane, and I can see why he would be very reluctant to trust you."

"But, Betty," I sobbed, "how can I stay here? I'm so unhappy!"

She was unmoved. "For once in your life, why don't you stop worrying about yourself, and think about the rest of your family? What does God want you to do? You need to pray about it and talk to Bud about it, but you have to be willing to stay in Lamesa. You can't escape just because the circumstances are difficult. Sometimes we have to suffer out the consequences of our sin for quite a while, so that we really will want to give it up and change. I have no idea what God wants you to do, but I think that you are going to have to start by listening to Bud!"

Bud and I did talk about it, when he came back. We prayed about it for several days, and the decision that we reached was not an easy one. He knew how much I wanted to go back to the Community to try again, but would I really stay? What would I do the next time my will was sharply crossed? He could see that I was far from healed; mentally and emotionally I was just as anorexic as I had ever been, regardless of the fact that I had gained weight.

"I am willing for you and the children to go back without me when school starts," he said finally, "while I stay here to take care of the business and harvest the crop. I'll come up for Thanksgiving, and then we'll think about what to do next."

Go without Bud? I didn't want to do that! But–I needed to prove that I wanted to change. So we called the Community to ask if the children and I could come, and although it was their busiest time of year, they said that they would find beds somewhere, and we were very welcome.

God had been merciful and kind to give me one more chance; Bud, too, wanted me to be healed, and incredibly the Community once more welcomed me with open arms–and hearts. Now it was up to me. Would I be willing this time to pay the price of wholeness? Would I be willing to look in the mirror and face the reality of who I was, without turning away? Time would tell.

What a relief it was to get back! The Community was just as beautiful as I had remembered it, and September was always the best season of all at the Cape, with crystal-clear days and uncrowded beaches. The Community flower beds were still a riot of summer color, with geraniums spilling gaily over the window boxes of the houses, and the "Fish Garden" in front of Bethany was still in full bloom. Driving up Uncle Ben's Way, I could see the

Ark just ahead, and it looked like home. "I'd be glad to clean every bathroom in the house!" I thought. And once again Father Lane, Lenny, Rick and Betty hugged us and welcomed us back as part of their family. "How can they do it?" I wondered. "I have acted like a real Judas, and they just keep on loving me and trying to help me. I don't understand it." One day I talked to Father Lane about it.

"Yes, we were hurt when you left so abruptly," he told me. "You and Bud were very much like a son and daughter, and it was hard to see you go in such rebellion, knowing that there was so much more that God wanted to do in your lives. But I can forgive that hurt, because I know how much Jesus has forgiven me. And that's what you need to learn, Sunny: how much Jesus has forgiven you. Pray that God will show you who you really are, but don't forget to pray for the grace to be able to accept it." I did pray that way, and when God began to answer that prayer in months ahead, I could see why Father Lane had reminded me to pray for grace.

But for now the golden days of autumn stretched out before me and there was a real sense of relief in getting back into the disciplined routine of Community life. And what a blessing it was to be busy—too busy to spend all my time thinking about myself. It was good to know that there would be order in the day, and a real sense of accomplishment at night when I looked back at the ironing done, and the dinner that had been prepared, or maybe the pantry neatly arranged. For a time, even the little will-crossers, like 6:30 breakfast or going out to Compline on a rainy evening, didn't seem to matter too much, because I was so grateful just to be back. Almost every day, I was jealous of someone or something, but it didn't bother me too much. I did try to give it up, but at the same time I didn't see that much wrong with it. Besides, I thought, that's just the way I am. The children settled back into school and picked up their schedule of trombone, violin, and flute lessons, and as the weeks passed, it began to seem as if we had never been away.

One morning I tore the October page off the kitchen calendar and stood looking at the next month in amazement. Could it really be November *already?* I shook my head. But the days were definitely getting shorter, and there couldn't be much more Indian Summer weather left. Coffee hour on Bethany's front lawn would be moving inside any day now. It was hard to believe that two whole months had gone by since Bud and I had last been together. With the fast pace of Community life, there hadn't been that much time to dwell on it, but I knew that I missed Bud very much.

"It won't be long until he's here for Thanksgiving," I told my friends at the Ark. "It's been hard to be apart for this long, but it's been a growing time for me. With this distance between us, I can see how much I have used Bud, and how much I have depended on being part of a couple. It isn't possible now to hide behind him. I'm beginning to have to look at myself as a person, and realize that Bud is a person, too, not just my husband. Also, I can see that I demanded that life be a certain way, and when it didn't happen I punished Bud. I can't wait to see him again, but I'm nervous about it. Last summer was terrible. I don't know if our marriage is able to survive what I've done to it, and we've been apart for a long time. I just don't know how it's going to be."

In those days, every so often on Wednesday evenings the Community would show a rented movie in the Fellowship Hall, when all the resident members, live-ins, and children would gather to enjoy the latest Walt

Disney entertainment with plenty of popcorn and lemonade. The film was on, and the big room was almost completely dark; but when the kitchen door opened, I caught a glimpse of a tall silhouette. It was Bud! He was here! Eagerly I climbed over the knees of the people sitting near me, and stepped on a few children in the aisle, as I made my way hurriedly toward the back. Throwing my arms around Bud, I ignored the audience around us. "I'm so glad you're here!" I whispered. "I've missed you so much! And Bud, oh Bud, I'm so sorry about last summer and about all that I've done to you! I'm just so glad you're here!" I exclaimed, running out of breath. Somewhat taken back, Bud said nothing, but just held me in his arms.

The four days of the Thanksgiving weekend passed much too quickly, and when it was time for Bud to leave to catch his Monday flight back to Texas, we still had many unanswered questions. What were we going to do now? What was our future going to be? What was God's will for our family? Somehow we had to find out what God wanted us to do; everything depended on it. But we were as yet unresolved; nothing was clear. Lord, please help us, I prayed, as I waved good-bye to Bud. He'll be coming back in three weeks for Christmas; please show both of us what we are supposed to do.

The Ark was bustling with activity on the night of the Christmas Carol Concert. The big tree in the living room was trimmed, packages were wrapped and piled beneath it, and in every window the traditional candles gleamed. "Oh, I hope Daddy gets here in time for the concert," Leigh worried as she finished dressing.

"Now hurry and get into your cotta," I answered. "Daddy said he'd try to be here in time, but he rented a car to drive from Boston, and it all depends on how bad the traffic is. You all look lovely!" The children were dressed and almost ready to go down to warm up, when we heard the sound of a car outside. "Here he is! He made it!" And there was just time for quick hugs before they were on their way.

Soon Bud and I were hurrying to our seats in the chapel, just minutes before the concert was scheduled to begin. The soft glow from the candelabras lining the central aisle, the traditional Chrismon tree, and the floor-to-ceiling white angels on the wall just behind the altar were a breathtaking setting as the strains of "O Come, All Ye Faithful" began, and we turned to look back down the aisle. First in procession came the candlebearers, then one of the older boys, carrying the large cross, and behind that the double row of children, their faces shining as they sang. Bud reached over and took my hand, and we both knew that God had given us our answer. We knew that we were called to be part of the life of the Community of Jesus, and I was so grateful that God had given us another chance, in spite of how badly I had handled the first one.

After that, things moved quickly. Bud went back to Lamesa to begin preparations to sell the business and the farm, and several months later we went back one last time to pack up our belongings for the final move to Orleans. Many of our things went into storage, and it would be several years before I unpacked them again.

For the most part, the months at the Ark passed happily. It was good to all be back together again, and once more Bud and I began to learn how to be honest with each other and to care for one another by speaking up and trying to help each other stay in Jesus. When we got into a fight, we could always call for help to work through it. We felt very safe and secure with our family in the Ark and were quite unprepared for the news that Betty had for us one day just before Easter.

"A couple is needed at Nineveh, and it is time for you and Bud to take some responsibility in the life here," she told us, smiling.

But that would mean a move! I didn't want to move from the Ark! "Oh, no," I protested. "Bud and I are just beginning to get our feet on the ground. We're not ready for anything like that! And who will help us when we get stuck in an argument? And what about the children?" The whole idea was very frightening.

Betty took me over to the kitchen window, and pointed to the back door of Nineveh. "How long do you think it would take to walk from there to here?"

"About a minute," I said sheepishly.

She nodded, laughing. "You can come over here anytime. And this is the next step for you both. You can't stay in the nest forever, and you can't stand still in your Christian walk. You have to keep moving forward. It's time you started caring for other people; that's what this place is all about."

Once we were in, I loved Nineveh. Shaded by big trees and set on a sloping green lawn, it looked like a big dollhouse, and I loved its cheery colors of blue and green. "Funny that it should be decorated just like our house in Texas," I told Bud. Maybe that was a sign that this was the house that we were supposed to buy, for I was sure that God intended us to own a house. This is definitely the one for me, I decided. Of course we would have to wait a while, as Bud and two other men in the Community were getting ready to start construction of greenhouses to raise orchids for the wholesale market, but when things were a little more established, I would have to have a house.

Everything seemed to be moving along well for Bud. He was happy and content, starting the new business; and once the decision to sell the farm had been made, he was able to give it up without a backward glance. I was not like that. As time passed and the memory of those hellish months of rebellion began to fade, so did my grateful heart.

It had been months since I had prayed the prayer that Father Lane had suggested, that God really show me who I was, and I had long since forgotten all about it. But God had not forgotten, and when the time was right, He started to answer that prayer. It all began with the new non-resident Community member who was living in for a year, much as I had at my time of need. I had noticed her right away, for she was very attractive–and freely outspoken. I had seen her at coffee hour and at the Wednesday night pot-luck dinners in the Fellowship Hall, and I had taken an immediate disliking to her. It came as quite a shock, therefore, when Barbara Manuel called and said, "Sunny, we think that you could be a real help to Gwen. She's going to be moving into Nineveh, and you'll need to spend a lot of time with her. The two of you are very much alike."

Very much alike? Barbara had to be kidding! There was no resemblance whatsoever, that I could see. Why, Gwen had explosions! If she didn't like something, she said so loudly and emphatically. I *never* did that, and I looked with disdain on so much overt emotion. If I objected to anything, I at least did it politely and quietly, and always in a ladylike manner. No, Gwen and I were most certainly *not* alike, and she was the last person that I wanted to have anything to do with.

From the moment that Gwen moved in, it was World War III. She flew off the handle very easily, and I would start to help her in a calm, loving Christian way. But that lasted about two minutes. In no time at all, I would be just as angry as Gwen, and we would be locked in a battle with no holds barred. Finally friends would arrive to try to untangle us.

"Now, Gwen," Betty or Barbara would say, "why are you so angry at Sunny?" And Gwen would go on and on, giving a detailed recitation of all the things that I had done to her that day, while I sat and fumed. How could she be saying all those terrible things about me? If she had just listened to me in the first place, I would never have lost my temper at all. It was definitely her fault, and anyone should be able to see that.

Betty and Barbara would then talk to Gwen about her anger and her hurt, and Gwen would cry and say that she was sorry, and then when she had left the room, they turned to me. "And now, Sunny, why are you so angry with Gwen?" But I was so furious and so right that I refused to discuss it honestly, and would lie and say that I saw I was wrong to react to her the way that I did, and I was sorry and would try to make sure that it didn't happen again. I would tell them anything, if I thought that it would satisfy them. And later on, I would avoid Gwen. If she was going to be that difficult, then I certainly didn't want to have anything to do with her. And, while I didn't say so in so many words to her, it was pretty obvious how I felt.

But Betty and Barbara had not been taken in, and later they confronted me: "You know, we're really disappointed in you. You're absolutely unmerciful in your attitude toward Gwen. She has come here to get help; she's a very needy girl, much like you were, when you first came. You've been around here much longer than she has; it's your responsibility to stay in Jesus, when the two of you have a disagreement." "But you don't know how difficult she is! She is impossible! The other night I said something that she said hurt her feelings, and she got her car keys and ran out of the house and drove off! Of course, she came back in a few minutes, but she just makes me furious! I don't see why I have to put up with that!"

"You have really forgotten, Sunny, what people have had to put up with from you. You've hardly been easy to live with, either, and yet people have persevered and loved you."

I stopped arguing then; what could be said to that? But I still knew that I was right. The thing that upset me most about Gwen was the way that she made me lose control when I got angry at her. I had always preferred dignified, silent anger; often I would not speak to Bud for a day or two. Only in extreme situations did I make a scene, but with Gwen around every situation was extreme; I couldn't seem to remain aloof and frostily detached. When Gwen yelled, I found myself yelling back. In fact, it was getting harder and harder to maintain any semblance of a righteous, spiritual demeanor when we were averaging about two big fights a day.

One crisp fall morning Camie Ford, Gwen and I drove the half hour into Hyannis for a day of shopping. With the busy Community schedule, this was a real treat, and I had looked forward to it all week. My enthusiasm had been slightly diminished when I found out that Gwen would be going along; but I decided to make the best of it–with a little luck I would be able to avoid her. The first stop was Main Street, and we piled out of the car at Dunbar's, a small, expensive dress shop with a nice selection of daytime wear. It was one of my favorite stores, and I liked the friendly clerks who always remembered you and called you by name. I was still browsing through the dress rack, when I heard a chorus of "ohs" and "ahs." Looking up to see what was drawing all the attention, I saw Gwen modeling a light green wool knit with long sleeves and a stand-up collar. "It's just the right color with your hair," Camie was saying. "It's perfect for you!"

"Oh, yes," the clerk agreed. "You look beautiful in it!"

I felt a surge of anger. Gwen couldn't get that dress! And before I knew what I was doing, I said so. "No, Gwen, you can't get that dress! It's almost exactly like one of mine!"

Everyone turned to look at me in astonishment, but I went on heedlessly. "I don't want you to get a dress like mine! You can't. I bought one in that style here last year."

The saleswoman frowned slightly, then interceded tactfully. "But, Mrs. Hale, I don't understand. We've never had a dress quite like this one, I'm sure. Perhaps you bought another of the same brand, but no two are ever identical. And they are quite different each new season."

"I have a dress almost exactly like that," I insisted stubbornly. "It's green, and it looks just like that."

"I don't remember seeing you in anything like this," Gwen said, "and it's exactly what I've been looking for, for my trip. I think I ought to get it."

"I said, you can't get it!" I hissed.

Again, the saleswoman intervened. "Oh, now I remember the dress you bought, Mrs. Hale. As a matter of fact, it was green, but didn't it have short sleeves and a big round collar? I mean, this one is quite different in style, and of course this is wool, and I believe yours was a spring-weight fabric. I really don't think that it would be a problem."

"Sunny," Camie was giving me a strange look, "I really think Gwen should get the dress. I'm sure when you get home, you'll find that there is a lot of difference."

Without a word, I stalked out of the store and sat in the car until everyone had finished their shopping. I turned my head away from Gwen, who came out clutching her shopping bag, with my green dress inside. When Camie and Gwen were back in the car, Camie turned around to the back seat. "I don't know what that was all about, but I think you ought to pray about it. I was very embarrassed; Sunny, you were behaving like you were in a cat fight!"

A cat! Had I really sounded like that? And suddenly I got a very clear picture of the way I looked in that store, arguing about that dress. What could the salesclerks have thought? I was a cat, a *jealous* cat! It had been obvious to everyone but me. What was worse, the people in the store knew that we were from the Community of Jesus, and I had been making a scene! I felt like throwing up. How could I ever go in that store again? How could I have acted that way? Camie said that she had been embarrassed by my behavior! My face flushed red with humiliation, and I wanted to die and disappear under the nearest rock.

The rest of the day seemed endless. Lunch was a blur, and I didn't buy a thing all afternoon. All I wanted to do was get home. Over and over in my mind, I kept seeing a technicolor rerun of my appalling behavior in the store. And it was not Gwen who had behaved badly; it was I! I was the one who was jealous; I was the problem. I had been jealous of Gwen from the very beginning–jealous of her pretty hair, her trim figure, but most of all, her spontaneous openness and honesty. She was as real as I was unable to be, and everyone enjoyed having her around. She got a lot of positive attention when *I* wanted to be center stage, and in my jealousy I had attacked her. Here I was, supposed to be helping her, and I had been nothing but mean and spiteful and vindictive. And I thought of the hateful, cutting remarks I had made, and how deliberately hurtful I had been to leave her out of things.

The car was very quiet as we drove out the Mid-Cape Highway toward Orleans. We were almost at Exit 12, and would be home in just a few more minutes. I had to get straight with the others. "I want to ask you both to forgive me for acting like such a jerk in the store today. It was my jealousy. And, Gwen, I've really been wrong. I've tried to hurt you, and I'm really sorry. Will you forgive me?"

"Sure!" she said, with an easy smile and a shrug. Gwen was not one to hold a grudge. And after that day, by the grace of God, we became friends.

Months later, on a beautiful Saturday afternoon, I stood in the kitchen unloading a bag of groceries. Now, let's see, I thought, as soon as I'm through here, I want to pay my bills, and then I need to put some clothes away in the attic, and then maybe I'll have time to get out in the yard and work a little bit before it's time to start dinner. The phone broke in on my plans. "Oh, dear, who can that be?" I wondered, annoyed at the interruption.

"Sunny, this is Mary. Where are you?"

"What do you mean, where am I? Obviously I'm at Nineveh, putting the groceries away."

"But why aren't you here? We waited and waited for you, but finally the little girls had to go ahead and serve tea, and Kathy was so disappointed that you hadn't come."

Kathy? Oh, yes, the tea party at Capernaum that the

little girls were having. "But, Mary," I protested. "Were the mothers supposed to be there?"

"You're the only one not here," she said, "and I hope you can hurry on over."

The only mother not there! The words echoed in my mind, as I rushed out to the car and drove over to Capernaum, though it was only five minutes away on foot. The little girls were having a tea party, and I was the only mother not there! How could I have forgotten? No, I couldn't even use forgetting as an excuse. I had known about the party, and had seen Kathy go out the back door, all dressed up in her Sunday best. Well, I just didn't know that the mothers were supposed to go, I told myself. That's it; it was just a misunderstanding, or of course I would have been there!

As I hurried into Capernaum's living room, it was all too evident that the tea party was almost over. Kathy came over and gave me a hug, but I could see that her eyes were red from crying. She carefully brought me a cup of tea and a napkin and passed me the plate of cookies. "Oh, Kathy, I'm so sorry that I didn't get here!" I told her.

But as I looked around the room at the other mothers and daughters, laughing together and having a good time, I wondered how everyone else had obviously known to come. I leaned toward Virginia Smith. "Did Sarah invite you to the tea party?" I asked her.

"She didn't have to," she smiled. "When I heard about it, I called up and asked if it would be all right for me to come. I wouldn't have missed it for the world!"

At her words, I felt terribly ashamed. That was the difference between the other mothers and me: they had *wanted* to come; I had only wanted to do my own thing that afternoon. It was as simple as that. It just hadn't been important to me. When Kathy had told me about the party, I had said, "Oh, yes, Kathy, that's nice. You can wear your blue dress." And I had gone on with my plans for the day, never giving it another thought. I had simply ignored the whole thing. Five years before, on that horrible day in the hospital in Lamesa, I had seen a tiny glimpse of my selfishness as a mother, but this cruel indifference was even worse.

The picture that was emerging was a very different mother than the *Ladies' Home Journal* image of myself that I had always believed. Even though Bud and I had had our ups and downs, I had always prided myself on being a good mother. Didn't I love to take the children shopping? And I certainly bought them lots of presents. But on the other hand, how often had I ever given anything of myself–anything that cost me something personally? I had simply used my children, in the same way that I had used everyone else in my life. As much as I wanted to hide from the truth, I couldn't escape this. And how could I possibly be a mother, as long as I wanted to remain a little girl myself?

As time continued to pass, Bud continued to grow and mature, but deep inside I knew that there was still something very wrong with me. We had been in the Community for years, and though outwardly I managed to more or less cope, I knew that there was still a hardness within me, a deadness that I hoped no one else knew about. But God knew about it, and He loved me too much to let me go on in that way.

One day I was talking with Helen Helms and David Manuel. "You know, I've lived in this Community for a long time now, and I should be different from the way I am. I know that God has shown me things about myself, but still I keep right on acting the same old way, over and over again. And another thing, I agree with what people are saying to me, and I tell myself that I know it's true, but the moment I turn around and walk off, I can't remember a thing they said. I hear something and then promptly forget it."

Helen and David smiled. "You've got to *fight* to remember what you've heard, Sunny," David said. "Your will is so strong to hold onto your exalted image of yourself that you choose to remain in unreality."

Helen nodded. "You choose to have a mental tape eraser, and use it as soon as possible, even while someone is trying to show you something. You conveniently forget the truth about yourself, before God can really convict your heart."

"But why do I do that? I thought I wanted to know the truth about myself. Why do I fight so hard not to believe it?"

"Because, Sunny," David exclaimed, "if you believe it–if you ever look in the mirror and let it sink in instead of turning quickly away–you are going to *have* to change! And when you really see yourself as Jesus sees you, it's going to be pretty devastating."

I knew that they were right. I could see it just in the weight thing. As long as I had denied that I had a problem with weight, then I could avoid gaining weight and stay just as I was. And now I was playing the same game spiritually. As long as I could believe that I was not quite that bad, then I could stay the way I was. And that was not the worst of it; not only did I tune people out, or quickly forget what they said to me, but I was so resistant to being wrong that I would often turn and attack the person who was trying to help me. I had done it to Bud and to Rick, when God had confronted me about my weight. And I was still doing it to people as recently as last week. When someone told me something about myself that I didn't want to hear, I had twisted their words and accused that person and really knifed them in the back. When crossed, I was as dangerous as a snake in the grass.

Well, I was *not* going to stay that way. Mother Cay had said that there are times when we need to pray for a holy hatred of our sin–and I knew that this was one of those times. Please, Lord, I want to turn off my mental tape eraser, and I want to see my selfishness and my jealousy and my vindictiveness as You see it, and I want to hate it enough to give it up. Most of all, Lord, please give me eyes to see how I have hurt people just by who I am, without You. Help me to be willing to go through the pain of seeing who I really am, so that I can stop inflicting pain on those around me. Help me to look into the mirror, and give me the grace to accept what is there.

One day, not too long after this, I was jolted to attention during the daily communion service in the chapel. When Hal Helms stood up to read the New Testament lesson from the book of James, I couldn't believe my ears!

"Therefore, get rid of all moral filth and the evil which is so prevalent, and humbly accept the word planted in you, which can save you. Do not merely listen to the word, and so *deceive yourselves.* Do what it says. Anyone who listens to the word but does not do what it says, is like a man who looks at his face in a mirror and after looking at himself, goes away and immediately forgets what he looks like. But the man who looks intently into the perfect law that gives freedom, and continues to do this, not forgetting what he has heard, but doing it–he will be blessed in what he does." (James 1:21-25, Int.)

The words sounded so familiar that my arms got

goosebumps. That was *exactly* what Helen and David and the others had been trying to tell me! All my life I've been deceiving myself into thinking that I'm somebody I'm not. I started it years ago, and I've continued ever since. And nobody was fooled–only me! The whole thing was a lie–I've built my life on a pack of lies! Oh, Lord, I am tired of the lies! Please keep showing me the truth, but don't forget about the grace to go along with it!

It was a rainy April Saturday, a perfect day to finish unpacking and putting things away in our beautiful new bedroom and sitting room at Antioch. What fun it was to get out treasures that had been packed away for a long time and arrange them on our very own bookcase. Lord, You've been so good to us! The rain made a cozy sound as it hit the skylights in the ceiling, and I looked with delight out the big bay window at the waves being tossed up on the beach, just yards away. Who would have thought back in West Texas that someday I would wake up every morning to a view like this? I thought about how angry I had been about selling the house in Texas, and about the way that I had accused God when it had become apparent that we were not going to be able to buy Nineveh–and now, in spite of all that I had done, He had given us this beautiful place to live. God was faithful, even when I had not been. And it really is true that when You ask us to give up anything, Lord, You intend to give back so much better!

I dusted off the children's pictures and set them on the shelf near the bed. What a difference the last few years have made in their lives! Leigh's senior picture is really nice; she's growing up and has changed so much in the past year, thanks largely to the help she's gotten from Jill and Betsy. This is a serious pose for Michael–

he looks like the college student with all of life's weighty decisions about to be made. What a relief that he can turn to the Lord for help, and hopefully not have to repeat all of my mistakes. And here's Kathy; she was in the second grade when we first came to the Community and now she'll be going into high school next year. . . . Where has the time gone? Oh, look at this old picture of me. Good grief! How could I ever have believed that it was attractive to look like a stick? How much happier I am now in a size 12 than I ever was in a 7 or 8!

I think I'll put our wedding picture right here. I can't believe that next year will be our twenty-fifth wedding anniversary. How easily that anniversary might never have happened! I thought about a conversation I had had with Helen, a few days before.

"You know, Helen," I had said, "I've finally begun to see that I've been insanely jealous of everyone and everything; and 'insanely' is not putting it too strongly. Most of all, I've been jealous of Bud–jealous of him in college, jealous of his love of farming, his business, his family, and his popularity. I'm jealous of *who he is*–the kind of person that people just naturally like. I see how I've hurt him over and over again, and been spiteful and domineering, a real prima donna. I honestly don't know why he ever put up with me for all these years."

Helen had thought for a moment, and then answered very simply, "I think the reason is, Sunny, that he loves you." Tears sprang to my eyes then, because, having finally come to see a bit of who I was, I *knew* that that was a miracle of God.

Well, enough daydreaming, or I'll never get through. I wonder if all these big books are going to fit on this shelf. I smiled at Bud's collection of books on orchids and horticulture. When he gets through reading them, he'll probably take them out to his office at the Ponderosa. The Ponderosa–a real Texas name for the orchid ranch, with its greenhouses and landscaping business. This was the busiest time of year there, and with such a variety of kinds and colors of orchids in bloom, it was a stunning sight. I smiled again. Come to think of it, that was about as close to farming as anyone can get on Cape Cod, and in many ways Bud seemed to like it even better. God had certainly given him the desire of his heart, in a way that no one could ever have guessed. And, of course, that had happened for me, too; my job in the Community office was certainly challenging, and I enjoyed every minute of it. It really is true that when you finally accept God's call, you find fulfillment.

What time is it getting to be? Maybe I can empty just one more box, before it's time to go and help Camie get lunch on the table. Now that's another miracle! Only God could have brought the Fords from Cleveland and the Hales all the way from Texas to live in the same house together on Cape Cod! And it was even more of a miracle for two women, who are inwardly so alike, to be able to live and work together. What a help it has been for Bud and me to live with Dan and Camie and have them be part of our lives–we've experienced so many of the same things. And now Camie and I have the opportunity to talk with other people who have similar needs and similar problems. Of course, one of the chief benefits of living together is that we are a great check on one another. It takes an anorexic to know one!

What's in this carton? It looks like old letters and papers. Here's a faded newspaper clipping of me in cap and gown. "Top ten graduates at Texas Tech." I shook my head; that had certainly turned out to be worth absolutely nothing. All that striving to be perfect, to be best, didn't prove a thing; all it accomplished was to lead me into total delusion about myself.

I opened one of the letters. Oh, this was interesting—it was from Dr. Taylor, the internist that we saw in Dallas in 1964. Funny that he was saying the same thing to me then that I've heard ever since I came here. And to think it has taken me almost twenty years to really believe it! If I had just listened to him then, I could have avoided years of trouble. But what's this in my note to the doctor? "Weight, 1959, 88 pounds." I could *never* have weighed 88 pounds! Maybe 100 or so, but surely never 88! Anyone 5 feet 4 inches who weighs 88 pounds is one sick cookie! But here it is in my own handwriting: 88 pounds!

I sat down on the bed, the letter trembling in my hand. I did weigh 88 pounds, and I don't even remember it! That was even more startling: how could I have completely blocked the whole thing out? How little I have really known myself, after all!

Once again, I was looking into God's mirror, and it was illumined by a clear shaft of light, and I saw everything in much sharper focus than I had ever seen it before. I saw the real Sunny looking back at me, and she was much sicker than I had ever admitted to myself or anyone else, and far worse than I had ever believed. And there was nothing that I could do to save myself, and nowhere to turn, but to Jesus.

Oh, Lord, I am so needy, yet You have accepted me. And I can accept myself as who I am, because of You. It's okay to give up my high opinion of myself. It's okay to face the truth and to let myself believe it, because You came for sinners like me. I'll never be perfect, but with the Lord's help and by His grace, I can live in Christ and not in myself. Thank You for healing me, when I didn't even know how desperately I needed it. You have always known the real me, Lord, and yet You loved me enough to die for me.

Because of Jesus, I can give up the big act. I don't have to be a phony. I don't have to pretend anymore or to try to impress anyone or to fool myself. By Your grace I can accept reality and live in it, and learn to just be. Thank God, I don't have to be thin anymore!

And please, Lord, help me to remember what You've done for me. I don't ever want to forget it.

And now, I wonder what's for lunch? I'm starving!

Epilogue

Who is an anorexic? The only way that we can answer that is to try to describe ourselves. We hope that the common threads running through both our lives have been helpful to others who want to understand more about this serious problem.

Looking back, neither one of us felt very good about who we were. We found ourselves constantly trying to prove our worth, over and over again, not only to our parents and peers, but most of all to ourselves. And no matter what we achieved, it was never enough, and we each had to set another goal and try harder. We became perfectionists–about our personal appearance, at school, about our homes, and finally we demanded that same perfection from the other members of our families. Often negative, never grateful for our lives as they were, we were satisfied with nothing less than total perfection. When that perfection proved unattainable in the present, then we started planning for the next thing that might bring satisfaction and fulfillment.

We covered our strong wills by appearing to be "good girls" who did what we were told, not because we wanted to be obedient, but because we wanted our parents' approval. This inordinate desire for approval bound us to our parents, and for many years prevented us from growing up emotionally. Ultimately we always wondered, "What would Mother think?" Our willfulness went hand in hand with control. We wanted what we wanted when we wanted it, and we set out to make sure that we could have it. It takes an incredibly willful and controlling person to be able not to eat, when in truth she is starvingly hungry. And though on the surface we might appear to listen to what people told us, inwardly we held to our strong opinions, because we knew we were right.

Dissatisfied with ourselves, we set out to remake our lives by remaking ourselves. And as we began to feel in control of our bodies through our weight, we experienced a wonderful sense of accomplishment and exhilaration. This "high" created a feeling of power and superiority because we had mastered the ever-prevailing struggle for weight control.

We were–and are–both very competitive people, and from an early age were very jealous of siblings in our families. There has been a constant inner comparison of self with others, constantly checking to be sure that we looked as good as or better than those around us. At last we felt that we were winning the competition, when we felt that we were thinnest of all.

We wanted to be princesses and live in unreality. We wanted someone to take care of us and love, worship, and adore us. Totally consumed with self, our thoughts were mainly preoccupied with food and weight, how we looked, and what people thought of us. There was no room in our lives for loving care or concern for others, only for ourselves.

New situations in life often seem threatening, and we eventually found ourselves unable to extend our facade to include one more thing. We were unable to adjust to new stages in life, such as college, marriage, etc., and were very angry when we could no longer control all our circumstances.

As the standards we had set for ourselves became more and more impossible to maintain, we discovered that we had a tiger by the tail. The beginning of the way out of our self-imposed prisons came when we each realized that our lives were, in fact, very much out of control and that we desperately needed help.